T0333323

Killjoy

Killjoy

*Taking on a macho media empire
and winning*

PICADOR

First published 2023 by Picador
an imprint of Pan Macmillan
The Smithson, 6 Briset Street, London ECIM 5NR
EU representative: Macmillan Publishers Ireland Ltd, 1st Floor,
The Liffey Trust Centre, 117–126 Sheriff Street Upper,
Dublin 1, DOI YC43
Associated companies throughout the world
www.panmacmillan.com

ISBN 978-1-5098-8561-9

1 3 5 7 9 8 6 4 2

A CIP catalogue record for this book is available from the British Library.

Typeset by Palimpsest Book Production Ltd, Falkirk, Stirlingshire
Printed and bound by CPI Group (UK) Ltd, Croydon, CR0 4YY

Visit **www.picador.com** to read more about all our books
and to buy them. You will also find features, author interviews and
news of any author events, and you can sign up for e-newsletters
so that you're always first to hear about our new releases.

For Angela

No More Page 3 was a grassroots campaign started by Lucy-Anne Holmes in August 2012.

It petitioned the editor of *The Sun* newspaper to stop printing photographs of topless women that had regularly appeared on the third page of the paper since 1970.

The movement ran for two and a half years and gained support from over 150 MPs, Scottish Parliament, the Welsh Assembly, more than thirty universities and colleges and a number of trade unions, charities and organisations. It sparked a national and international conversation about objectification and representation within the press.

The campaign was run by a team of volunteers of different ages and backgrounds who were scattered across the UK. They had no experience of campaigning, no money and little idea what they were doing, but they shared a goal of ending one of the most sexist institutions of our time: Page 3 of *The Sun* newspaper.

I was one of the confused and ill-equipped volunteers, and this is my story.

Author's Note

What follows is not a history of the No More Page 3 campaign, rather it is a memoir of my own personal experiences of the movement and the people I met along the way. In writing this, I relied upon my own memories and mined my personal journals, along with approximately fifteen billion emails, texts, social media messages and newspaper and magazine articles.

The events you will read about in these pages really did happen, flash mobs and maggots included, although they do not necessarily appear in the order in which they occurred.

Comments from supporters (and trolls) are taken from the No More Page 3 petition or social media sites. The conversations in this book are either a product of my memory or are reproduced exactly as they appeared in the campaign's private Facebook group.

Most of my No More Page 3 teammates read a draft of this book and helpfully reminded me of things I had forgotten, corrected mistakes and said things like, 'Oh my god, if you write that I will absolutely kill you – I mean it, I'm not kidding.'

With this in mind, I changed the names and identifying features of some individuals who appear in this book and, to further respect the privacy of those involved, there are some composite characters. Additionally, some people and events have been omitted because, if I included everyone and everything, this book would never, ever end.

Prologue

Boudicca was buried on Peckham Rye, according to a local legend. The woman sitting next to me on the park bench told me all about it. She forgets a lot these days, but she remembers Boudicca – Boadicea, as they used to call her – because her daughter played her in a historical re-enactment on a school playing field in 1965 or 1966, she can't remember which. The mothers banded together to make props. They made an impressive Iceni chariot out of an old wheelbarrow from the allotments but, in the final act, her daughter fell through the bottom of it, which had gone rotten because of the manure. Theresa had to be carried to the doctor's in her Celtic robes and her ankle was bandaged until Good Friday.

I was paying close attention to the story, focusing on the details I'd tell my mum later on the phone, when she suddenly trailed off and said, 'Have you been gardening?'

I looked down at the bamboo canes and bits of card sticking out of my bag and said, 'Oh, no, I've been at a protest actually. They're signs, badly made ones –' I laughed nervously – 'but better than nothing.'

'What's that all about then?'

I explained that I was part of a group campaigning against Page 3 – the topless photos of young women that appeared every weekday in *The Sun* newspaper. We'd staged a big protest in Parliament Square earlier that day. I pulled the petition out of my bag and showed her.

'Hang about,' she said, fishing her glasses out of her pocket. She took the petition from me and studied it. 'Have you got a pen?'

It took ages to find a biro, but finally one appeared at the bottom of my bag, along with the lipstick I'd been looking for since April. She signed her name with a shaky hand, and the pen hovered above the 'reason for signing' box. She paused, before writing: *We need more rebellious women.*

I knew she wasn't talking specifically about Page 3, or the women who are photographed for it; a woman removing her clothes can be an act of rebellion in itself. I understood that she was talking about the culture that fuels a media where men are powerful creators and women are passive objects. Where men are pictured in shirts and ties and football kits, suited and booted for their lives of leadership, while women are young, beautiful and usually undressed. Women are taught to be quiet and never bossy or pushy or loud. The culture taught us – Page 3 taught us – to be silent, to look pretty, to smile, to be agreeable, pliable. Not to cause problems, ask questions or raise our voices, but to be ready to receive compliments, insults and sex. It is the same culture that makes older women invisible and reduces them to ghosts, doomed to float around Methodist Centre jumble sales or potter in the garden until death's sweet release. 'Old ladies', like the woman sitting next to me, were not supposed to be rebellious or inquisitive or outspoken, but lavender-scented and warm, filled with thoughts of wool and grandchildren and the bric-a-brac stall.

She handed the petition back. 'You shouldn't always do as you're told. Everyone has an opinion on what's best for you, and most of them want something from you. Yes, we need more rebellious women.'

I sat there on the bench beside her and thought back to the protest that morning.

A huge crowd had assembled at Parliament Square, and the air crackled with excitement.

I'd spotted Lucy, Max and Evie and lots of the usual faces, but there were so many people I'd never seen before: students, families and other women gathered in little groups. The photographers and cameramen (and they were *all* men) attempted to order us into formation, with Big Ben as a powerful backdrop. Protestors waved their hand-made signs, some with conspicuous Corn Flakes or Shredded Wheat logos on the reverse. The marker-pen messages spelled out 'No More Page 3!' 'News Not Boobs!' 'Brains and hearts, not just body parts!' I found myself standing next to Evie and she squeezed my hand. She was trying to keep an eye on Milly, who was marching up and down at the front, head held high, shouting, 'Sign our petition!' The photographers didn't know what to make of this brilliantly sassy eight-year-old girl. Some of them wanted to capture her on film, others wanted her to pick up a colouring book and sit quietly out of the way.

Max led us in protest songs. She'd sing a line and we'd repeat it, sort of like being in church, but without the draughts and guilt. She'd brought her little dog along and it kept shitting all over the place. When it was our turn to sing a line, she'd quickly bend down to shovel it up, then continue, with a placard in one hand and a bag of dog crap in the other.

The march headed towards Southbank, and Evie and I sneaked into the Christmas market to buy mulled wine. Everything is better with mulled wine, even the patriarchy. We took photos with human statues, cool kids with skateboards, and fundraisers in the middle of a marathon.

Most people we spoke to signed the petition. Nobody gave us much hassle, except one middle-aged man, who sleazed on Max.

'If I sign it, I want something back,' he said. 'What will you give me in return?' He eyed her up and down in the hungry way my niece looks at Toblerones.

'Here you go,' she said, 'have this,' and handed him a bag of dog shit. He didn't realise for a while, and just stood there holding it. She strode off snorting with laughter, while he walked around helplessly, looking for a bin.

Back at Peckham Rye, I smiled at the woman on the bench next to me. 'I know quite a few rebellious women,' I said, and she leaned forward and patted my hand.

'Good,' she said, 'keep them close.'

PART ONE

Striking a Match

The Shoe Cupboard

When I was five or six, and just beginning to learn things about the world, I would kneel at the bottom of my bunk bed with my eyes shut really tight and pray to the God I learned about at school, aka the old man who lived for ever and judged us from the sky.

Dear God, please don't let anything happen to my family, and don't let me ever grow up.

What I meant was: please don't take away the people I love, and don't let me become a woman.

Becoming a woman seemed like the worst thing you could do.

'What's a period?' I asked one afternoon, after hearing the word on TV. My older brother burst out laughing and left the room. My mum became silent and heavy and still. My dad looked at her. She didn't say anything.

'Well,' he said, 'it's a thing that happens to women.'

'Oh *don't*,' she said.

'Well, are you going to bloody tell her then? She needs to know.'

My mum got up and left the room, and my dad picked up *The Sun* and aggressively flicked through the pages.

I guessed that, whatever a period was, it was another one of those shameful things that women whispered about in living rooms. They'd sit in armchairs with their shoes off, drinking tea, and suddenly their voices would disappear and you'd over-hear snatches of secret sentences about thirty-six-hour labours and The Change and Maureen's daughter, who had got herself pregnant again.

Women were always getting themselves pregnant.

Mothers at the school gates would talk about it. They always looked exhausted from all the cooking and cleaning and getting other people's parents out of the bath. You'd think they'd be kind and understanding of each other's burdens, but they didn't appear to have the energy.

If ever there was an unexpected knock at the door, my mum would send me rushing upstairs with armfuls of crap to dump on the beds. 'Are the bedroom doors shut?' she would whisper anxiously, before she let anybody in. Women, apparently, judged each other's houses. 'They always ask to use the toilet,' my mum said, 'so they can look around upstairs.'

Most of my friends' mothers didn't work. I learned that if a woman went out to work, it was because, somewhere along the line, a man had failed, or she had failed to get a man. Single women worked, but the only married women who went to work were the ones with jobless or absent husbands or, occa-sionally, women whose husbands didn't mind them doing a shift or two at the supermarket, to earn 'a bit of extra spending money' for the holidays. Those women were judged mercilessly, especially if they had children.

'I don't know why they have kids if they go out to work and never see them,' people would say behind their backs.

*

I learned to read with Peter and Jane books. I'd squish up close to my mum on the sofa and trail the words with my finger, pausing to look at the pictures. Peter was always off building a fort or doing something with a chisel, and Jane was always helping her mum in the kitchen:

'We can make some cakes for Peter and Daddy!'

'You are a good girl!'

Jane was always watching Peter do things. She would just stand there all clean and tidy in her yellow cardigan, watching Peter have fun. I thought she was an idiot. I desperately wanted her to drop the plates and let them smash on the floor. I wanted her to pour the tea (such a good girl!) and purposely miss the cups, spilling it in patterns all over the carpet. I wanted her to elbow Peter hard in the ribs every time he walked past.

At my primary school, the classroom play area was divided in two: toy tools and diggers for the boys and prams and an A La Carte Kitchen for the girls. Sometimes, during Games, Mrs Lincoln would gather us into a circle, pull a boy into the middle of the ring and make us sing 'The Farmer Wants a Wife'. The boy would pick the prettiest girl as his betrothed and pull her into the circle, and we'd move on to the next verse: 'The Wife Wants a Child'. We were practising our grown-up roles; learning the kind of jobs we'd do, the kind of desires we'd have. The girls played at tidying up and pouring tea and wanting babies.

But I learned that there were other things that girls must do in addition to pushing prams and making flapjacks. My mum's magazines were filled with diets that changed every week and problem pages devoted to cellulite, eye bags and wrinkles. My dad's newspaper was filled with Page 3 girls; bare-breasted teenagers with big hair and wide smiles, posing in pairs of lacy pants. The messages were clear, yet contradictory: women should have babies but stay slim; bake cakes, but not eat them; know how to look after everyone around them, but never let wisdom, age or tiredness show on their face. They should be beautiful and desirable and smiling, always.

In my last year of secondary school, the careers advisor scanned my list of predicted grades, a neat row of As and Bs, and asked me what I wanted to do.

I was so nervous I could barely say the words. 'I think I might want to go to university.'

I didn't know a single person who had ever been to university. My brilliant older sister wanted to go, but it hadn't happened. She'd got married, and married women didn't go to university – they had children and silently assessed each other's bathrooms.

The careers advisor nodded, which usually means yes. 'Well, you'll need to do A levels if you want to apply for university.'

I nodded as well.

'A levels will improve your job prospects and, you never know, you might decide you don't need to think about university after all. It can be very expensive, and lots of girls do degrees and then get married and have children and wish they had saved their money.'

I knew he was saying that university wasn't for a girl like me. He had decided the course my life should take before I'd even walked in the room.

'Of course, the most important thing is to get work

experience,' he said. 'There's a new shoe shop opening at Retail World and they're looking for staff.'

I felt every bit of hope leave my body. He misinterpreted my expression.

'Don't worry, there are stockroom positions if you think you'd struggle with the till.'

He issued the same guidance to my friend Marie, who wanted to study history in Manchester. Our professional careers advice was basically: wait in a shoe cupboard until a man turns up to impregnate you.

I went home and wrote in my diary:

I am never having children. I am never getting married.
I am going to university.

I thought this kind of retaliation was the only way I could break free of what was expected of me, but I didn't have the confidence to write the words in ink.

I wrote in pencil, in case I needed to erase it all later.

Fish Out of Water

When I moved to London, my mum packed me a week's worth of sandwiches, a woman from Rotherham Council sent me a rape alarm (with a spare battery, in case I wore the first one out) and my grandmother, Nessa, gave me a madeira cake and a map of the Underground from 1972 with the Jubilee Line missing.

'That was the last time I went to London,' she said. 'But I'm not missing anything. They haven't got anything we haven't got.'

It was the month before my twenty-ninth birthday and I was about to start a postgraduate degree at the Courtauld Institute of Art, a college of the University of London.

'You'll not be the only one coming from a council house,' my dad said.

'She will,' my mum replied. 'I've seen pictures on the internet.'

It had taken me a long time to get to university. I left school and did my A levels, despite the careers advisor's scepticism. I earned enough money to get by, working in a pub, in a travel agent's, as a mystery passenger on South Yorkshire buses.

I saved up, I got into debt. I did my undergraduate degree when I was twenty-five, a BA in Art History at the local former polytechnic.

'It seems a funny thing to study,' my dad said, and he was right. It was a strange choice, since the only art I'd seen growing up were the paintings my mum borrowed from the library. She'd struggle home on the bus with an oil painting of a ship, wrapped in a bin bag, and it'd go on the living-room wall for a few weeks until it was time to return it and swap it for another one. I'd go to someone's house after school and see the same painting on their wall that we'd just returned and they'd just borrowed. Those same ships, drifting through the estates of Rotherham. But paintings, whether at Rotherham Library or the National Gallery, interested me; they were portals into other people's worlds and I liked mining them for clues. I thought that art might teach me about life and how to live it.

My mum didn't understand my degree choice either, but she was happy that I'd studied at the local ex-poly, because there were no posh people there. When she met a girl on my course with an affected accent, she said, 'She can pretend all she likes, but everybody knows she's from Maltby. Her mother works at Kwik Save.' She panicked when my tutor suggested I apply for a scholarship to study in London, worried that I'd feel out of place, homesick and lonely. London was unknown, and that was the danger. No one knew which alleyways to avoid, which buses to take, or whose mothers worked at Kwik Save.

It wasn't lost on me that by the age of twenty-eight my mum had given birth to three kids and my dad had sailed twice around the world with the Navy. By twenty-eight, Nessa had survived the Blitz.

But my age didn't matter. I was their baby, their single, unmarried and unprotected daughter, stepping into a city that didn't know me or care about me. There was no map for what I was doing because no one had ever had a chance to draw it for me.

My dad's parting advice was: 'Don't talk to anyone, don't draw attention to yourself and don't go out when it's dark.'

I kissed him on the shoulder (he was much taller than me) and said, 'Oh Dad, not even a hedgehog could stick to all those rules.'

'Phone me when you get there,' he said.

And then I was on my own.

The Courtauld was the kind of place where you could imagine masked balls being held; it was grand and imposing with elaborate sweeping staircases. Every time I stepped through the double doors into the foyer with its marble floor and classical statues, I felt like Julia Roberts in that snooty dress shop in *Pretty Woman*, but without her hair, teeth or height. The other students were so tall and healthy-looking. Their hair was bouncy and thick, their cheeks so ruddy you could almost smell the horses on them. They were well spoken and bilingual with names so long and sophisticated you had to have a little rest in the middle of saying them.

'Octavia Cholmondeley-Bentham-Bly – hang on a minute, I'll just have a sit down – Cholmondeley-Bentham-Arlington-Blyth? But you go by the name of Bumpy?'

They were intimidatingly clever, and I quickly realised that having a degree from a former poly carried all the gravitas of a needlework proficiency badge from the Brownies.

It was every bit as bad as my mum had predicted.

I lived in a flat in Dulwich with two 'young professionals' I had met on the internet. Rebecca had the much better upstairs bedroom, and Kevin lived in the wardrobe.

The wardrobe was a tiny room next to mine, about the size of the chinchilla enclosure at Pets at Home, with a dividing wall made of plywood, or papier mâché, or straw.

'The landlord uses this as his walk-in closet,' the property manager told us when showing us round, 'but if you really need to split the rent three ways, you could probably fit a small bed in here, at a push.' And it really was a push; it was such a tight squeeze the door wouldn't open more than ten inches without hitting the divan. At the end of each day, Kevin had to shuffle in sideways and launch himself like a salmon at the bed, which shook the dividing wall as if a wartime trolleybus was rattling past. My nightly soundtrack consisted of salmon launching, the syrupy tones of Kevin's girlfriend, Louise, talking in a cutesy baby voice and selected hits of Elton John. I've never seen *The Lion King*, but I know 'The Circle of Life' word for word, because Louise sang along whenever he played it, which was roughly every other hour in the brief interludes between *The Simpsons* blaring from his laptop and Louise shrieking 'stwop tickling meee!' Worst of all were the times when my room echoed with slapping sounds and noises like office furniture being dragged about. I don't want to imagine what was happening next door in the wardrobe, but it sounded like a pair of Ikea bookcases were being dismantled by seals.

Dulwich was a culture shock after Rotherham. It was the kind of place where you couldn't buy a normal loaf – all the bread had caramelised onions or cobnuts in it. The local shop sold dehydrated Mediterranean figs, but not baked beans. There were gastropubs galore, a gallery full of Reubens and Rembrandts and a home interiors shop, well stocked with a variety of repurposed lamps and organic pillow sprays. This was fine if you spent your days in a lavender mist, hydrating figs, but really crap if you just wanted a jar of Nescafé and some Weetabix.

My mum phoned every other day and Nessa sent birthday cards, get-well-soon cards, holiday postcards. She even sent a card on Pancake Day. She wrote like she talked, in block capitals with no full stops.

> *REMEMBER YOU'RE EVERY BIT AS GOOD AS*
> *THEM I HOPE YOU HAVE PANCAKES I CAN'T*
> *EAT THEM THEY GIVE ME INDIGESTION DID*
> *YOU SEE SHEFFIELD WAS ON THE NEWS*
> *YESTERDAY GOING FOR A WALK NOW SOON*
> *YOU'LL BE HOME AGAIN XXX*

The MA ended, but I didn't go home; I'd won a scholarship to stay on for a PhD. I was getting a little more settled in London. Instead of having children of my own, I got paid to look after other people's, which funded trips to the pub and a new coat in winter. And I had my boyfriend Will to go to the pub with. We met at the Courtauld. He was studying art under Stalin and I was studying art under Hitler, which meant that nobody wanted to talk to us at parties, so we ended up talking to each other. He was posh, but he didn't seem to mind that I was common, and I didn't hold it against him that he went to public school or pretended to like opera.

I started to feel a little more at home in Dulwich and a little less at home in Rotherham. My dad said I'd been away too long and had picked up fancy London ways. After all, I had an Oyster card, I spent Saturdays at the British Museum and I knew about pancetta.

'It's not good enough for our Joanne any more,' he would say, if I refused fish fingers and chips. 'She's doing a PhD, you know.'

The truth was, I hated the PhD. I dreaded the supervisions and the conferences and networking events. Whenever I was packed into a room filled with academics, I found myself offering around glasses of wine and canapés, like a waitress. I couldn't escape the feeling that I should be serving the people around me. I always felt like an interloper who had crawled in through the cat flap while no one was looking.

I became terrified of speaking. I'd noticed when I moved to London that people sometimes repeated back to me what I said. This happened especially with words like 'bath' and sentences like 'shall we go to the pub?'

'Aye lass, let's guh t'pub,' Charlie, a Home Counties PhD Arsehole would say, laughing. 'Av thisen a pint o' bitter.' At first, I thought it was done in good humour and I laughed along with him, but after a year it wore thin.

'What's tha conference paper on – pies an' whippets?'

I would smile but my eyes would say, 'I hope you fall down a manhole and drown in a sewer.'

I had always loathed public speaking, worried that I'd say the wrong thing, but now I was also anxious about how different my voice was from everybody else's. No one else had an accent like mine. I avoided speaking at any symposium, seminar or, worst of all, roundtable discussion. I managed to inflict myself with every virus, migraine or emergency scenario I could conjure that could get me out of these situations. Other PhD students had online profiles listing every paper, publication, review, speech. Mine said: 'Jo's area of interest is the artwork created by refugees from Nazism in Britain c.1933–1945' and then . . . nothing. Publications: empty. Conferences: empty. Links to my LinkedIn: empty. That's exactly how I felt. Empty.

But then, in September 2012, a conference arrived that I couldn't get out of. I had used up my bank of excuses. My tutor kept mentioning important people who would be there, a professor who had written a 'seminal' book, a research fellow who lectured in America. The stakes were high, and I couldn't afford to mess up.

Will set up his ironing board like a lectern and I practised for hours, rounding off the Rotherham accent, smoothing out the Yorkshire vowels. He sat in an armchair facing away from me, because he knew eye contact would throw me off, and every now and then he'd say, 'That was really good – can you just say it normally?' Or, 'A bit louder maybe, for the people lurking by the exit.'

Natasha, one of the Dulwich mums I babysat for, lent me

a book about managing fear. The day before the conference, I read a bit of it in the bath, careful not to get the pages wet or crack the spine. It was 50 per cent photos of laughing Nepalese children, 40 per cent quotes about flying (in a font completely at odds with the airy-fairy spiritual vibe) and 10 per cent blank pages. At dinnertime, I accidentally singed the edge of it when I turned on the wrong gas ring in the kitchen. I panicked and knocked it into the sink with a ladle, amazed that I'd managed to soak the book in oily water *and* set it on fire.

I laid my conference clothes carefully over the back of a chair and went to bed early. I got up the next morning before Rebecca and Kevin, and walked to the station, to begin the ninety-mile journey to the conference centre.

Why Am I Running?

At 8 a.m. sharp, the conference attendees were ushered into a beige room with a long table at one end, bedecked with tinned-salmon sandwiches, an urn of strong tea, a plate of ginger nuts and four pots of Bisto-coloured coffee. The atmosphere was similar to that of a funeral wake held in the function room of a cricket club, but with name badges and a printed schedule of the day's events.

I stood behind a large potted plant and looked around the room.

The women, chatting in groups of three and four, wore skirt suits and separates in black or navy polycotton. The look was conservative, enlivened with the jazzy twist of a bright chiffon scarf or a fun brooch. It was what I imagined the flight attendants would wear if Jehovah's Witnesses had their own airline.

The men wore linen and had very loud voices. They all appeared to be called Julian.

In the conference room, I sat as close to the doors as possible. The first speaker was a foot shorter than the microphone and she struggled to adjust it.

'Sorry, but we can't hear you, I'm afraid!' one of the Julians shouted. He reclined in his seat with his legs crossed, looking not a bit sorry or afraid.

Flustered, she pressed something and her slides disappeared off the large screen behind her. When she found her place and started speaking again, another Julian shouted, 'Still can't hear you!'

The woman sitting across the aisle from me kept pushing her glasses further up her nose, coughing, then taking them off and cleaning the lenses with a handkerchief. I noticed her name badge, checked the programme and saw she was up next, just before me. I was on in forty-six minutes. The Julians would still be energised from all the tinned salmon and ginger nuts. They'd have questions and, worse still, comments. I felt faint. It was too hot and one of the lights above my head was flickering. It suddenly felt like there was no room to breathe, as if the walls were contracting and closing in. The woman across the aisle coughed again, one of the Julians complained about the feedback from the microphone and I remembered a breathing exercise from the fear book I set on fire. Apparently, if you're really bricking it before giving a speech or having a root canal, you should go somewhere quiet, ideally outside in the fresh air, take one long inhale and then breathe out quickly three times, like you're giving birth on *Call the Midwife*. All the while, you say in your head what you're doing: *I'm taking a long, deep breath, I'm pausing, I'm pulsing it out – one, two, three.*

I slowly stood up, picked up my bag and walked towards the door. I didn't turn around, I just carried on walking, slowly, purposefully, like a zen master, until I was in the car park. I took a long breath in.

I'm taking a long breath in, I said to myself. *I'm pausing, and now I'm pulsing it out – one, two, three.*

I tried it a second time.

I'm taking a long breath in, I'm pausing . . . and now I'm walking out of the car park, turning left and now I'm running. Shit, I'm running, WHY AM I RUNNING?

I had no control over my legs. I was like a woman possessed. I careered down the high street as if I'd just stolen something from Boots. My laminated name badge on the lanyard around my neck kept swinging up and hitting me in the face.

People stared.

I looked insane.

I ran all the way to the station, tearing down the platform as if my trousers were on fire and jumped on the train just before it pulled out.

Shiiiiiit, I thought. *What have I done?*

Catastrophic scenarios flashed through my mind. The conference organiser would announce my name and realise I wasn't there. My tutor would find out. What if I got chucked off the PhD and lost my scholarship? I wouldn't be able to pay my rent. I'd end up living in a bin like that pissed-off monster on *Sesame Street*, popping up every now and then to shout at passers-by before disappearing back into my nest of garbage.

I took a deep breath and phoned Will to tell him what had happened. It sounded like he was opening mail or shuffling papers and he seemed distracted and annoyed.

'We practised it,' he said. 'We went over the talk again and again. You can't just run away from things all the time.'

'I didn't mean to.'

Why Am I Running?

'It looks *really* bad. You're next in line to speak and you just run home.'

'I just couldn't do it,' I said. 'I just really couldn't do it.'

I hung up, held my head in my hands and felt dreadful for a while, until the scenery started to change and hills dwarfed the train carriage and the sun streamed through the windows. I bought a gin and tonic from the buffet bar, and relief suddenly washed over me.

Yes, my boyfriend, my tutor and the other PhD students might think I'd behaved poorly and childishly, but at least I wouldn't have to sit through the post-conference dinner with a group of Holocaust academics at Bella Italia. I had a table to myself on the train, I had gin, and for a brief magical moment, I was free.

In the days that followed, I took my dad's advice. I didn't talk to anyone, I didn't draw attention to myself and I didn't go out after dark. I stayed small, quiet and indoors, like a house-trained rabbit. I emailed my tutor and the conference organiser, apologising for my absence and blaming my sudden phantom sickness on the tinned salmon sandwiches. I called the families I worked for, feigning a throat infection. I phoned my mum. 'Pack in the PhD and come home,' she said. I heard my dad in the background shout, 'Keep at it!'

I needed to distract myself from my feelings of worthlessness, so I spent a lot of time eating crisps and watching *Downton Abbey* on my laptop. I'd wait until Kevin and Rebecca had gone out before scuttling to the kitchen or the bathroom, avoiding all chance of seeing anyone. I managed three days before I ran out of Hula Hoops, Corn Flakes, KitKats and wine, and realised I'd have to venture outside.

The sun burned through my bedroom window and I could hear the clanging and banging of builders working at the house on the corner of the street. I dreaded walking past them in all weathers, but none so much as full sun, when they'd take their shirts off and lurch about like that frantic, frothing dog in *To Kill a Mockingbird*.

Half of Dulwich appeared to be constructing a glass-cube kitchen extension with bifold doors at exactly the same time, so there were builders everywhere. Some days they shouted or made jeering sounds. Once a builder said that I looked like a dog – that all the women around here were dogs. I was learning that it was most dangerous to look really bad or really nice, and usually aimed for something in the middle. It was my wish to always look bland enough to become invisible and to slip beneath the radar, but that didn't always work, because my expression mattered too. I noticed that if I looked too happy, they would say something to bring me down and if I looked too sad they would shout that it wouldn't kill me to smile, would it? If I put my head down and walked quickly, they would sense my discomfort and try to embarrass me by shouting crass comments about my body. I hated all of it.

I brushed my teeth and combed my hair and even though it was unseasonably warm, I zipped my coat right up to the top.

I made it to the shop without comment, but on the way back, a scaffolder at Goose Green told me to cheer up. I was struggling across the road with a bumper box of Persil, milk and a multipack of toilet rolls and had just nearly been run over by the P13 to Streatham, so I didn't take it well. As I turned onto Underhill Road, another builder looked at me and whistled, like a cartoon sailor. People always talk about being whistled at like a dog, but I've never actually seen anybody whistle at a dog. Dogs are usually treated with more respect, especially the ones in Dulwich that trot about in miniature wax jackets and have names like Orpheus or Tybalt.

I got back to the flat, double-locked the door, and slumped at the kitchen table. It shouldn't have bothered me. It was nothing really, but I just stared at the wall and wished I could disappear.

The Papier-Mâché Turtle

I couldn't afford to have any more time off work so, the following morning, I reluctantly shuffled to Natasha's house to see what tasks she had set me that day. In addition to making dinner and assisting with homework, she wanted me to unblock the upstairs sink with baking soda and to help Livia make a papier-mâché turtle for the school assembly. School assemblies in Dulwich were like full-scale productions at the Civic Theatre in Rotherham, but with good costumes and acting. Enough newspapers had been piled on Natasha's kitchen table to make a turtle of dinosaur proportions. Livia was laid on her stomach watching the telly, ignoring me, and I looked at the stack of papers and groaned.

I hadn't bought *The Guardian* since they featured a midweek supper recipe with fennel pollen in it. Most nights, I couldn't be bothered to go to the chip shop, let alone crawl around the neighbour's garden, harvesting pollen. And the pollen was the tip of the iceberg (or, for *Guardian* readers, the tip of the endive) – the recipe also included preserved lemons and a spice with a name like a sinus infection. All to make a tiny frittata that looked like a bath sponge decorated with pencil shavings and grass. But I was still in a bad mood because of the builders and I didn't want to make the turtle, and *The Guardian* was right there, so I picked it up and flicked through the pages.

And that's when I saw it.

A picture of a woman wearing a T-shirt with 'No More Page Three' printed across the front, in a 'Frankie Says Relax'-style font. She was standing on a busy high street, her hair swept across her face, the sleeves of the shirt rolled up, little woven bracelets on her wrist. She was just standing there, taking up space as if the street belonged to her, as if she didn't want to be invisible, as if nothing would induce her to cross the road to avoid being woofed at by builders with their shirts off. Looking at her, I thought, *I bet she doesn't avoid talking to people, drawing attention to herself or going out after dark.* Looking at her, I thought, *I bet she does whatever she wants.*

I scanned through the article. I learned that the woman in the picture was an actor and writer named Lucy-Anne Holmes, and she had launched the No More Page 3 campaign after buying a copy of *The Sun* during the Olympics. Although Victoria Pendleton and Jessica Ennis had just won gold for Great Britain, the topless photo of the Page 3 model was still the biggest image of a woman in the entire paper. The editor of *The Sun*, Dominic Mohan, had defended the topless photos, claiming that Page 3 represented 'youth and freshness' and was an 'innocuous British institution'. But Lucy-Anne Holmes disagreed, insisting that the pictures were there purely for men to look at, to objectify; the women's bodies theirs to lech over and then throw away. The pictures said this is what women should be, this is what women's bodies are for. In comparison to the size and dominance of Page 3, Jessica Ennis and Victoria Pendleton's achievements were just footnotes.

I thought about the builders publicly reviewing my body like a B&B on Tripadvisor and the effort I put in each day to try to become invisible; to not look too pretty or too slovenly, but to be perfectly unremarkable. I thought about the Julians holding court at the conference, interrupting the female speakers, saying, 'I don't have a question, more of a comment really,' and then talking and talking and talking. I thought about the careers advisor, suggesting that my most important job was that of wife and mother. I thought about all the times I had been grabbed or groped in pubs and clubs or at work, and all the times I had been told to be quiet. And I thought some more about Page 3.

Youth and Freshness

Page 3 was launched in November 1970, a decade before I was born. The nude photograph of model Stephanie Rahn was printed on the third page of *The Sun*, causing both controversy and an upsurge in sales, which convinced Rupert Murdoch to make it a regular feature. It was a profitable decision; by the end of 1971, sales of his newspaper had doubled.

Others followed suit: the *Daily Star*, *The People*, the *Mirror*, the *Sunday Sport* and the *News of the World* all started publishing their own topless pictures on Page 3. By the time I was born, it was a firmly established tabloid feature. I had never known a world without it.

Growing up, I saw Page 3 everywhere: in the house, on the bus, at the chip shop, in the dentist's waiting room. My sister remembers the Page 3 calendar pinned to the wall in the doctor's surgery. It was in the butcher's as well; the women hanging behind the counter with the hunks of meat.

My dad was a *Sun* reader. He worked nights, driving lorries up and down the country, and each morning yesterday's paper would appear on the dining table. My mum would try to keep Page 3 away from me, but my dad would sometimes ask me to draw clothes on the model, for a laugh. It caused rows between my parents and I would freeze with my felt-tip in the air, unsure whether to draw a jumper or quietly back away from the paper. The messages were mixed. My mum was red-faced and upset, and my dad thought it was all hilarious.

My friend Michelle used to play at Page 3 when she was seven or eight. She'd take off her clothes and strike a pose like the one she'd seen in the paper, while her cousin pretended to take photos. Her dad had pictures of Samantha Fox pinned up in the garage where he kept his motorbike. Michelle worshipped her dad, and she too became obsessed with Samantha Fox, her bedroom becoming a shrine to her idol. My walls were covered with Kylie, Tiffany and Belinda Carlisle, but Michelle's were plastered with Samantha's face. She wasn't allowed topless photos on the wall, so her mum snipped away at the Page 3 pictures with a pair of kitchen scissors, severing at the neck. Michelle's bedroom was wallpapered with disembodied heads, and I have often wondered if her dad kept the decapitated bodies for himself. I can't imagine him letting a pile of Samantha Fox's tits go to waste.

'I'm going to be a Page 3 girl,' she used to say, all the time. There were no pictures of her, or her mother, or any women other than topless models on the walls of her dad's garage. Michelle learned, without even leaving her house, that to be valued, women have to be sexually attractive, undressed and available. There were few job prospects for girls in Rotherham in the eighties, and Page 3 must have seemed a thrilling way to be seen and appreciated; a way to escape the life that was prescribed for her.

Youth and Freshness

'Don't you just wish something would happen,' she used to say. 'As soon as I'm sixteen, I'm getting out of here. I'll go to London and I'll be rich, and I'll come back to visit and you won't even recognise me.'

It was when I started secondary school that I began to rip Page 3 out of the paper, chuck it in the bin and pour cat food on top.

'Bleeding hell,' my dad would say, 'I wanted to read the article on the back of that.'

Page 3, which used to confuse me, had started to embarrass me.

Boys would bring *The Sun* to geography or German and try and humiliate the girls with the pictures. Sometimes, the models would wear school uniforms with shirts unbuttoned to the waist, school ties hanging loosely between their bare breasts. Before the law changed in 2003, the models were as young as sixteen. The *Daily Star* sometimes counted down the days until models came of age. They photographed the girls clothed at fifteen, and topless on their sixteenth birthdays. I remember being called to the head of year's office to explain an absence and seeing *The Sun* open at Page 3 on his desk. There were piles of papers heaped on top, but I could still see the model's face smiling up at me, and my skin crawled to think of my teacher looking at pictures of undressed teenage girls in his office.

In year 7, there was a game where boys would corner a girl, put their hands on her leg and slowly move them up under her skirt, asking repeatedly, 'Are you nervous?' If she said yes she was called a frigid bitch. If she said no she was sexually assaulted in public by a gang of boys. After school, we'd walk home, and a man in a car would slow beside us, wind down his window and shout obscenities or offer us a lift.

With the mid-nineties came lad culture, and the coolest girls were ladettes. They would swear like sailors and drink the boys under the table, all the while being 'up for it'. This was sold to us as empowerment, a way to level-up with the boys. If we were more offensive than them, then we couldn't be offended by their behaviour.

During the height of this cultural moment, I often looked like I had walked straight out of a *Daily Mail* photo exposé on Booze Britain. My friends and I would spend three hours getting ready to go out on a Friday or Saturday night. There was a dress code: our skirts had to be tight enough so that no one could pull them up and bandeau tops were off limits because they could be pulled down. Side zips were preferable to back zips, because this made it harder for men to undo your dress while you stood in a queue. We would go out with a fiver in our pockets and never spend a penny of it. The bouncers would wave us in, we'd go to the bar and someone would buy us drinks, and we'd down anything we could until we felt drunk enough to dance. We thought we were the winners, we came out on top. We got in everywhere for free! Blokes were paying for our drinks! We were quids in!

We never questioned why men wanted us drunk, never wondered why we were never asked for ID, even though we were clearly underage.

We were sixteen, the same age as many of the models on Page 3.

Youth and Freshness

'They're the ones coming out on top,' my dad would say, as he reached to get the paper back out of the bin, shaking off the chunks of Sheba. 'They're the ones making money, the men are paying for it. The girls are the winners.'

And yet something told me it wasn't that simple.

Hello, Revolutionary!

I signed the No More Page 3 petition online. It was easy to do: I just filled in my details, ticked a little box and my name appeared on the list of signees. Then, almost immediately, I received a deluge of emails about saving whales and libraries, and I realised I really shouldn't have ticked that little box. I love whales and libraries, but by the time I'd finished with all the petitions and newsletter subscriptions, my bath had gone cold and I had to run another.

Before bed, I logged on to the campaign's website and ordered a No More Page Three T-shirt. I knew I'd never wear it outside, but I thought I might sleep in it. I liked the idea of airing my opinions quietly, under my duvet, in the dark.

A week later, a parcel arrived addressed to me in swirly handwriting. The sender had written 'Hello, Revolutionary!' on the packaging, with a little sketch of a woman smiling and waving. I ripped it open and tried on the T-shirt immediately. Looking in the mirror, I felt empowered and fat at the same time. Then I felt guilty for worrying about my fat bits when I'm sure feminists aren't supposed to give a crap about their weight. True revolutionaries don't obsess about flab. You never saw Trotsky buying Spanx.

Hello, Revolutionary!

I checked the No More Page 3 Facebook page and saw that Lucy-Anne Holmes had added a post about an event tomorrow. It was to be the campaign's first ever protest, and she wanted supporters to join her at Wapping station before heading over to News International HQ. I felt a spark of interest and then quickly swatted it away like a bothersome moth. I wasn't the kind of person who attended protests. I'd had a bad week and wanted to stay in and watch *Downton Abbey* in my pyjamas. I had even washed my dressing gown with 'spring breeze' fabric softener to make it extra fluffy and comforting. I didn't want to smash any systems, I just wanted to recline on my bed and watch Maggie Smith in a magnificent hat say bitchy things to her servants.

And that is how I would have spent the weekend and, possibly, the following three years if it hadn't been for the pigeon.

I'd fallen asleep, but was suddenly woken by an alarming noise coming from the fireplace. It sounded like a large chicken breast had been thrown from the top of a multi-storey car park and had landed with a wet slap on the roof of a Ford Fiesta.

I jumped up and made a horrified yelping sound.

A dead pigeon had hurtled down the chimney and scattered maggots across the rug at the foot of the bed. It was like a visitation from Father Christmas, but with worms instead of presents.

I became very quiet and very still. I didn't run around screaming for at least four minutes. I just thought, *Ah, yes. I'm quite depressed. I'm failing my PhD and ran away from a Very Important Conference, so I might lose my scholarship. I've gone into my overdraft to replace Natasha's fear book because I set her copy on*

*fire, I'm too fat to be a revolutionary and there are maggots under
my bed. Huh.*

I phoned our property manager, Brandon, who had a grating
voice and wore trousers two sizes too small. He said he'd cut
to the chase and be straight with me: it'd take some time to
get the chimney blocked off, possibly weeks, possibly months
realistically speaking, because the job would require scaffolding.
He advised me to dispose of the pigeon and to cover up the
fireplace with a bin bag or a sheet of heavy-duty cardboard,
then the waitress came to take his order so he wished me luck
and hung up. I looked at the scene of devastation on my rug.
A maggot wriggled. I ran to the booze cupboard.

I mixed gloopy raspberry liqueur with the leftover vodka
from Christmas and made a French martini, which tasted like
fizzy nail varnish remover because the pineapple juice at the
back of the fridge had gone off. I caught my reflection in the
mirror and cry-laughed for a moment. The No More Page 3
social media accounts were filled with images of supporters
doing cool things in their T-shirts, like scaling Ben Nevis, playing
the saxophone, running marathons and holding new babies,
often all at the same time. I thought maybe I should take a
picture and post it to the Facebook page: 'Here I am in my
tee, hoovering maggots off my bed, looking like absolute shit
in a pair of trousers I've had since 1998, drinking a curdled
martini. Hello, Revolutionary!'

After the pigeon had reached its final resting place in the
bottom of a Tesco bag for life, I had three showers then sat in
the kitchen, staring at the wall. I no longer wanted to spend
the weekend in my room. I wanted to be as far away from the

fireplace as possible. I thought about the No More Page 3 protest, and logged back on to Facebook to read the post again. The spark of interest was still there.

Maybe I should go to the protest, I thought, *just for a bit, to see what it's like.*

I opened the scorched fear book at a random page, hoping for encouragement.

'Everything you want is on the other side of fear,' it said, in a sensible Argos-catalogue-style font. It annoyed me and I threw it on the floor, but it did get me thinking . . .

I'd rather sit on my own in a room that might be flooded afresh with maggots at any moment than do anything out of my comfort zone. And my comfort zone isn't even comfortable. It's a zone nobody would want to live in, populated by routine and working and drinking and boredom and clothes I bought fifteen years ago that I no longer like that are covered in red wine and biro stains.

So, I decided to go.

I'd never been to a protest before, but I'd seen plenty in Trafalgar Square, on telly and on holiday in France, so I had an idea of what to expect. There'd be huge crowds of people waving signs and shouting things. No More Page 3 had thousands of followers on Facebook, and hundreds had liked the post about the protest, so I was sure loads of people would turn up. I would go for ten minutes, stand somewhere out of the way drinking coffee, and feel good about leaving the house and doing something out of my uncomfortable comfort zone.

I'm in! I wrote on the Facebook page, before I could change my mind.

Protest

At 10 a.m. the next morning, I put on the unflattering No More Page Three T-shirt, covered it with a jumper, fastened my coat and left the house. I got to the gate and realised I was wearing my slippers so I went back in, put a scarf on, ate some flapjack and went outside in my slippers again. On the third attempt, I made it past the gate in shoes.

I walked across Peckham Rye, trying to get my head together, and stopped at the newsagent's to buy a bottle of water. The shopkeeper's daughter – probably seven or eight – ran out of the back room followed by a little Pekingese. Her father shouted at her from behind the counter, telling her not to let the dog in the shop. Ignoring the awkward shouts and woofs, I turned to look at the magazines and it hit me smack in the face. The wall of women: glamour models in bikinis on the covers of lads' mags, six-foot supermodels striking edgy poses on fashion magazines, celebrities with their flaws circled on gossip rags and porn stars censored with luminous stickers on the top shelf. And, in front of it all, a row of tabloid newspapers with covers showing wardrobe malfunctions, nip slips and soap stars bending over on the beach. The *Sport* didn't even bother with a cover story; the front page was just a giant upskirt photo of a television presenter's undercarriage. I couldn't even tell which presenter it was, they didn't bother showing her face. Seeing all these images together was overwhelming, unnerving. Creepy.

It made me think about the girl with the Pekingese, and how she must see this wall of women every day. What would she learn about her value in the world from these images? I paid for the water and set off with renewed determination.

As I made my way up the escalator at Wapping station, I prepared myself for the crowds, but as I shuffled towards the ticket barrier it was eerily silent. I scanned my Oyster card and looked around, bewildered.

There was a member of staff sweeping the floor near a tube map and a woman standing on her own near the entrance. I thought I must have misread the Facebook post and got the wrong time or place, but then the woman turned around and I saw she was wearing a No More Page Three T-shirt with the slogan proudly on view, unlike mine, which was hidden beneath a hoodie and a jacket and a big, thick scarf.

'Are you here for the protest?' she asked.

'Yes,' I replied, and a voice in my head screamed, *Why didn't you say no, you stupid cow – you could have turned around and gone home!*

'Well,' the woman said, 'looks like it's just the two of us!'

I felt my spirit leave my body.

'I'm Max, by the way.'

'I'm Jo.'

An awkward silence followed. I nervously pulled the zip on

my hoodie up and down just for something to do with my hands, but then Max shot me a look, so I stopped. She wasn't fidgeting, she was just standing there, tall and regal in her T-shirt, looking utterly composed.

I thought that she was probably the kind of person who would send back a dish in a restaurant if she wasn't happy with it, and would know exactly how to say no to the checkout staff at WHSmith who try to upsell you a bottle of water and a giant bar of Whole Nut every time you buy a newspaper.

I looked at my watch. If no one else turned up within the next three minutes, I was making my excuses and going home.

Two minutes and thirty-four seconds later, Max said, 'I think that's Lucy-Anne Holmes.'

A woman was running across the street, weaving in and out of pedestrians. She darted in front of an oncoming taxi, shouting 'Oh my GOD!' and ran at us with outstretched arms. It was like being greeted by a toddler or a fox terrier or the TransPennine Express.

'You here for the protest? Thank you thank you THANK YOU for turning up!' She put an arm around Max and me and pulled us in for a quick hug. 'I had nightmares that it'd be just me! I'm a bit nervous. OK, breathe, Lucy!'

We introduced ourselves, and Lucy showed us the signs she'd made at her kitchen table last night.

'They're not very professional,' she said. 'They look like a three-year-old has made them, but, oh well . . . Shall we get a coffee?'

We stopped by a cafe and bought large Americanos, and then strolled towards Thomas More Square. I was so nervous my voice shook a little as I made conversation.

'So, is this the first protest you've arranged?'

'Yeah,' Lucy said, 'and it's the first protest I've actually *been* to. Well, I went to the rally against the Iraq War years ago with my friends, but that's all. I'm just going to be honest here and say I have absolutely no idea what I'm doing.'

'Imposter syndrome,' Max said.

'Maybe,' Lucy said. 'But this is all new to me. I've never campaigned about anything before. I was *the* most unlikely person to start a petition. I don't do confrontation; if someone walks into me on the street I apologise. Everybody who knows me was so surprised. Especially my parents. They went on holiday to Spain and came home and I'd started this campaign about boobs in the paper, and they were like, "What *happened* to you while we were away?"'

I laughed and started to relax. 'What did happen to you?'

'Oh, it was just a lightbulb moment, really.' Lucy took the lid off her coffee and blew into the cup to cool it down. 'My brother always said *The Sun* is the best paper for sport, so I bought a copy for the Olympics coverage. And I was reading about these incredible athletes and it was so inspiring, and then I turned the page and there it was. A huge photo of a topless twenty-two-year-old woman, which just dwarfed all the images of the female Olympians, and it felt like a slap in the face. I couldn't stop thinking about it. And then I remembered an expression I'd heard my entire life in response to these pictures: "Look at the tits on that!" And I'll tell you what got me – I'd never noticed the word "that". Like she's not even a person, just a thing. And I was talking about this in a radio interview the other day and the presenter said, "We have to apologise for the language" and I was like, "You shouldn't be outraged by the word *tits* you should be outraged by the word *that*".'

'You hear it all the time on Twitter,' Max said, in her loud, clear voice. 'I'd smash that, I'd bang that.' The man who had just walked past us turned back to stare.

'Exactly,' Lucy said. 'It's stuff I'd heard so many times before, but hadn't really thought about until that lightbulb moment. And then I thought, if I'm bothered by this, maybe other people are too. So, I set up the petition and my teenage nieces helped me to make Twitter and Facebook accounts – I'm absolutely shit with computers. Then this lovely woman named Evie got in touch and offered to make T-shirts and, yeah, suddenly there were journalists and reporters wanting to talk to me about it. Actually, it was a journalist who encouraged me to arrange this protest – she said why not just go for it, what are you waiting for? So, I posted on Facebook "does anybody want to protest with me?" and –' she looked from Max to me and back again – 'yeah, here we are!'

We had arrived at News International HQ. A security guard eyed us up and down and then disappeared inside the building. A woman approached us, with a huge camera strung around her neck. She was a press photographer who had heard about the protest on Facebook and had come to take pictures. She laughed when she realised there were only three of us, but insisted she could edit the images so no one would know about the poor turnout.

'I'll take a few test shots,' she said, messing around with the zoom lens.

She snapped away, then squinted at the image she had just

taken on the screen. 'I'll just crop it creatively,' she said, frowning. 'OK, let's have you walking towards us holding the signs. Take off your coats so we can clearly see the T-shirts.'

Lucy and Max put down their bags and started faffing about with cardigans and scarves. I stood there for a minute as the realisation sank in that I too would have to be in the pictures.

Trying to photograph me is like trying to shampoo a cat. It's farcical and unpleasant for everyone *and* I'm difficult to catch. I stared at the photographer and memories began to surface of having my photo taken at school. The bloke behind the camera would bark orders that I simply couldn't follow, while the rest of the class lined up waiting for their turn. 'Sit naturally on that wooden box. Point your knees this way, turn your shoulders that way. Let's have a smile – where's your teeth, Grandma? Turn a bit to the left, no to *my* left. OK. Relax. Don't worry about the camera. Just be yourself. No, that's not working. No, really just relax. YOU'RE NOT RELAXING.'

Max and Lucy looked at me expectantly, and I realised there was no way I could excuse myself without looking like a massive idiot. If I made a fuss it'd only draw more attention to my plight, so I'd have to just be in the pictures, get it over with and then go home and never leave the flat ever again.

We lined up, chilly in our thin T-shirts, and Crop-It-Creatively snapped away. My hair blew in front of my eyes and my nostrils kept flaring. I looked at Lucy and Max and we laughed nervously.

'You're supposed to be angry,' Crop-It-Creatively shouted. 'Angry! You can't be laughing your head off on every photo. Look furious!' She shouted directions and we tried to adopt serious expressions. She needed more movement – we were standing about like scarecrows! She asked us to carry the placards and walk towards her, looking fierce. I felt self-conscious and forgot how to walk. 'Go!' she shouted, and I trip-trapped towards her like a spooked horse.

Then a voice shouted 'Lucy!' and we turned to see a woman striding towards us, waving and smiling. Lucy cheered and ran over to her.

'This is Priya,' she said, 'we met in the pub yesterday!'

'Hiya,' Priya said. 'This is Adam, my friend from work.'

We turned to see a tall man wearing film-director glasses, standing a short distance away, shuffling uncomfortably from foot to foot. 'He didn't want to come,' Priya whispered, 'he's doing it as a favour. I guilt-tripped him into it.'

Crop-It-Creatively immediately put a stop to the chat and lined us all up again. She started snapping close-ups and the poor bloke looked like he'd rather be anywhere else on earth. Lucy thought we should be more vocal so we chanted 'News not boobs!', which accidentally morphed into 'Boobs not news!', confusing our message slightly. She passed us clipboards with petitions attached and handed out pens, as if we were on a geography field trip. There weren't many people walking through Wapping at that time on a Saturday, but Lucy approached every person she saw, saying, 'Excuse me, would you like to sign our petition?' I hid behind the tall bloke, bracing myself for angry replies, but most people were happy to talk and almost everyone signed the petition.

'I can't believe Page 3 still exists in this day and age.' At least five people said a version of that. Two blokes refused to sign, saying, 'It's just a bit of fun, it's not harming anyone.' Another man said he was against press censorship.

'Me too,' Lucy said. 'We don't want to ban anything, we just want the editor to voluntarily end Page 3; to recognise that the feature was launched in a very different era, and we've come a long way since the seventies in terms of equality. We don't want to make it illegal for topless or naked photos to be in the paper, because it's all about context. It's not really about nudity at all. If we saw people of all genders, ages, ethnicities and body types naked in the paper every day then that would be a different thing entirely. I think that would be great actually! But Page 3 isn't about celebrating the naked body, otherwise we'd see nude pictures of eighty-year-old blokes sitting cross-legged under a tree.'

The man ended up signing the petition, probably just so he could get away from us as quickly as possible.

We talked to a few more people on the street, then Lucy looked at her watch and shouted, 'Shit, I've got to catch a train from London Bridge in twenty-five minutes. It's my niece's birthday and I really can't be late.' She ran around gathering her things together and then paused in front of us.

'I'm so sorry to run off like this,' she said, hugging us all in turn. 'But thank you so much for coming. I so appreciate it. And it was actually fun, wasn't it, even though it was really fucking weird?'

'It was the most fun I've had in ages,' Max said.

'Hope to see you all again sometime.' Lucy blew kisses and set off jogging down the street. Max and the bloke left in opposite directions – he practically sprinted away – and I ambled towards London Bridge with Priya as Lucy ran ahead of us. We watched her disappear into the station.

'Well,' I said, 'maybe I'll see you again at another protest.'

'I hope so, Jo.' I noticed that Priya often said people's names at the end of a sentence. It made you feel important, listened to.

She boarded a train heading north, and I caught one going south. I got off two stops early and smiled as I walked home.

I felt different. I felt six feet tall. Or at the very least, five feet six.

Either way, bigger than I was yesterday.

Scarecrows

On Boxing Day, I usually wake up with a sore throat and a sense of dread, brought on by social fatigue, prosecco breakfasts and the realisation that soon the decorations will have to go back in the loft and I'll have to travel home on three rail-replacement buses with a hangover.

The morning after the protest, I felt the very same way.

I checked the No More Page 3 Facebook page to see if Lucy had posted anything, and instantly regretted my decision. Crop-It-Creatively had uploaded the photos from the protest. I looked at them and made a noise like a long-haired tabby bringing up a hairball. We were standing rigidly in line, looking furiously constipated with eyes watery from the cold. Lucy's hair was wild, like a 1980s troll doll, while mine was plastered to my face like an ironed wig. Priya looked nervous and chilly, as if she'd just sat her GCSEs in a draughty sports hall, and Max looked like she had been barred from a pub for fighting in the toilets. The only normal-looking person was the man in film-director glasses, who towered above us in an embarrassed, apologetic way.

A few blokes left scathing comments beneath the pictures,

calling us ugly and jealous, and saying how rubbish we'd look on Page 3. They had a point, it really would have been the most surreal Page 3 ever: a row of crazed women holding cereal boxes covered in pen, who look like they might kill you with scissors. A bold editorial move.

I put my head in my hands. I couldn't believe what a mess I'd made of the past week; I'd run away from the conference, binned a dead pigeon and gone to a deserted protest. And now there were photos of me all over social media, looking like a walrus in a wig.

I moped for a while until Will came over. We'd barely spoken since the phone call on the train and I was still annoyed with him, but I really needed help blocking off the fireplace. I'd taped bin liners over the opening, but it looked awful and made alarming rustling sounds in the wind. I'd had a nightmare about the poor pigeon that died, and woke up convinced that the rustling sound was the flapping of the dead bird's wings as it tried to escape.

I told Will about the protest while we fixed big sheets of corrugated cardboard over the chimney breast. He was struggling to find the end of the Sellotape, so it took him a while to grasp what I was saying.

'You went to a protest?'

'Yeah.'

'About Page 3?'

'Yeah.'

He looked at me as if I'd just said: 'I joined the circus yesterday – I had to somersault backwards through a ring of fire and land upside down on a prancing horse.'

'You don't go to protests.'

'I do now,' I said, which made it sound like I was planning to go to another one, which was categorically untrue.

He was quiet for a while, and then said, 'Well, Page 3 *is* really bizarre. And pretty creepy. But I'd never buy *The Sun* in a million years, and you don't buy it, so . . .'

'Yeah, but I see Page 3 all the time,' I said. 'On buses, at the chip shop, in cafes, at the library. I see it everywhere, even though I never buy it. You can't escape it.'

He paused, as if thinking how to respond, then said, 'Do you want a cup of tea?'

Will is the kind of English person that American tourists fantasise about. He's well spoken, nicely dressed, unfailingly polite and always making tea. He's mad about animals in a stereotypically British way. Strolling through a park, he's often ten steps behind, having found a sickly hedgehog or a nestling fallen out of a tree. We've spent hours at animal hospitals and rescue centres, cradling injured birds wrapped in blankets. He cares about people too, but they exhaust him. Upon seeing a decorative plate in a shop window, bearing the slogan 'friends need no invitation', he was so horrified he stopped in his tracks. 'Who made that plate?' he whispered. '*Who made it?*'

His worst fear is someone turning up unannounced. His second-worst fear is making a fuss. A protest would be his idea of hell.

We drank the tea, and then my mum phoned.

'Come home for a bit,' she said. 'You can pick up your birthday things. It'll be nice to see you and you can have a little break from the maggots.'

It's a sentence you never want to hear from your loved ones.

It wasn't the future I'd envisaged for myself in childhood. That I'd be in my thirties and going home to my parents' house to have a little break from the maggots.

Home was everything that London wasn't. There was no pretension, no intellectualising, no rushing and no bread with cobnuts in it. The only thing that ever changed at my parents' house was the colour of the walls which, due to their obsession with decorating, became a slightly brighter shade of magnolia every three months.

My mum was putting the winter curtains up when I walked in the house; the thicker, heavier ones the colour of autumn leaves. She got down off the dining chair, hugged me for a long time and said, 'Your presents are on the table.'

My mum always bought everybody's presents, knowing she could never rely on my dad to remember dates, cards or gifts. Only once did she refuse to do this, leaving my dad to buy my birthday present. He gave me a pair of men's slippers, both left feet, one a size 9 and the other an 11. They were cigar-smoking warthogs wrapped in gift paper with 'Happy Silver Wedding Anniversary' printed all over it.

My parents were stuck in the roles that were handed down to them. While my dad was out driving lorries on his night shifts, my mum stayed at home and did absolutely everything else. Whenever he wasn't at work, you'd find my dad on the settee, in his underpants, being outraged by things.

'Have you seen this?' he'd say, as you were on your way

to the kitchen, and you'd have to pause in the doorway and listen as he read out a newspaper headline about tax evasion, a Westminster scandal or things that give you diabetes. His favourite stories were about political correctness or health and safety 'gone mad'. During these lengthy recitals, my mum and I would glance at each other with desperation. Sometimes she would yawn, sometimes she would pretend to shoot herself in the head. We had learned over the years not to argue or offer an opinion, or to even walk away, otherwise he'd get angry and the atmosphere in the room would sour for hours. All you could do was stand there, silently held hostage until he'd finished. Then you could make a cup of tea.

I put the kettle on before I told them about the No More Page 3 protest.

My mum said, 'Oh Joanne, you don't want to anger *The Sun*. They're not the kind of people you mess around with, they could make your life an absolute misery.'

My dad said, 'A protest? Well that's not going to do anything, is it? I bet they're quaking in their boots at *The Sun*.' He took a sip of tea. 'Besides, the Page 3 girls are making good money out of it.'

I said he was entitled to his opinion, and then spent twenty minutes outlining why his opinion was wrong and why he wasn't entitled to it. It led to a spectacular argument, more heated than necessary because I'd forgotten to put the lasagne in the oven and we were both really hungry.

★

We went to visit Nessa afterwards. She wasn't like the grand-mothers in stories or on TV. She was argumentative, fierce, capable and strong. She stuck up for herself, she fitted her own carpets, she laughed until she doubled over in her chair. My grandad, Nessa's husband, died long before I was born, and she never remarried. She travelled to Switzerland, the Hebrides, Italy, Spain. She ate exactly what she wanted at the times that suited her. She stood with her feet planted firmly on the ground, knowing her worth. If a person or place offended her, their name would be written in a small notebook and crossed out.

'I've put a line through it,' she'd say after a disappointing jacket potato in the Debenhams cafe. The act of crossing out Debenhams meant that she'd never go there again. They had lost her for ever. Nessa drank whisky in her tea and passed rainy days with grisly thrillers and films where animals and children always seemed to die at the end.

We constantly ran around after her, saying, 'Let me carry that,' 'Are you cold?' 'Can I get that for you?' and she brushed us all aside. She showed me that you can do everything for yourself, that you have all you need, that you don't have to ask permission. That your life is yours, and no one else's.

I told her about the protest while she pottered about in the kitchen. 'Well,' she said, 'you always stood up to people when you were little. If you saw anybody doing anything that you thought was wrong, you'd march up there and tell them. Nobody would mess with you when you put your mind to something.'

I had never thought of myself in that way before and I wondered if that was who I was before I learned to be nice and not to answer back. I wondered if I had been slowly diluting myself my entire life.

Nessa left the room and returned holding a tin of Quality Street and a birthday cake, an iced one from Marks & Spencer with flowers on it.

'No candles?' my dad said. 'I bet they're not allowed any more, are they? Health and safety gone mad.'

I leapt up and hugged Nessa and offered the chocolates around. When I got to my mum, she hesitated, and then purposely picked out the flavour she knew nobody else would want. She always did that. If I asked if she wanted a cup of tea, she'd say, 'Are you having one?' If I asked what she wanted for dinner, she'd say, 'What do you fancy?', as if years of putting everyone else first left her unable to say, or even decipher, what she herself wanted.

I loved her so much it made my bones ache, and I wished she'd put herself first, if only with the Quality Street.

'You're not having the rubbish one,' I said, and I replaced the toffee penny in her hand with the purple hazelnut caramel.

Resolutions

I was going to get the train straight back to London, but Will suggested we meet somewhere halfway and stay overnight to celebrate my birthday. My dad was blessed with a photographic memory of the A–Z road map of Britain and had delivered fruit and veg to most of the nation's supermarkets, so he sat on the settee with *Top Gear* on mute and listed every town located between Rotherham and Dulwich, noting which local Tescos have difficult unloading bays. I didn't really want to spend my birthday in Peterborough or Leicester, so he suggested Stamford, which had both a Waitrose off the A606 *and* a Sainsbury's in a retail park just out of town.

We stayed overnight in the sort of pub you'd go to for locally sourced rare-breed sausages rather than a pint of Stella and a bag of normal crisps. We ambled through the Georgian town, but it started bucketing it down as we were halfway through Burghley Park, so we had to run to a nearby tree and hide beneath it. I ferreted about in my bag and grabbed the book I'd bought from a gift shop; a beautiful, pocket-sized book of English verse with a delicate, Victorianesque cover. It opened at Keats, and I read the line, 'Season of mists and mellow fruitfulness.'

'Why don't you read it in your own voice?' Will asked. I was doing an affected John Gielgud impersonation, the voice I always adopted when reading poetry.

'Alright then, "season of mists and mellow fruitfulness".'

'Now you're making it more Rotherham on purpose.'

'I'm not.'

'Yeah you are. You sound like you're off *Coronation Street*.'

'*Coronation Street*'s set in Lancashire, not Yorkshire,' I said, but he had a point. I realised I could only read poetry in a voice that sounded like I was taking the piss out it, as if I didn't feel worthy to read such splendid sentences with my accent. I kept trying to read it in my own voice, but I just couldn't.

'We've been standing here a really long time, haven't we,' Will said, looking desperately at the rain, as I read the opening line for the fiftieth time.

In a box under the bed at my parents' house, I still had my school report from 1995. My English teacher, Mr Springfield, had written: 'Joanne's written work is excellent, but I've never heard her speak.' I'd sat in his class for four years and had never opened my mouth. Things hadn't changed that much. My PhD tutor was always saying, 'You need to contribute more in seminars – ask more questions, share your opinions.' But I never did.

I thought about what Nessa had told me about resolutions. She said the best time to set them wasn't New Year's Day, but on your birthday. It makes more sense, because it's the start of a fresh new year of your life. As we walked back to the pretentious pub in the rain, I ran a mental inventory of major things I'd like to change, but none of them felt right and I kept coming back to the stupid poem. This will be my resolution, I thought. To say things in my own voice, regardless of how stupid I think it sounds. To say what I think and what I feel, instead of staying silent because I'm afraid of being wrong or sounding weird or making others uncomfortable, disappointed or angry.

When we got back to the room, Will took a shower and I tried the poem one more time.

'Season of mists and mellow fruitfulness.'

It still sounded awful, but I carried on reading right through to the end anyway.

The following weekend, Assad came to stay with me in Dulwich. We'd been best friends since we met at sixth-form college in Rotherham. It was the late nineties, I was doing my A levels and Assad was studying business and computing. We didn't have classes together, but I saw him in the common room and canteen, or walking around the corridors. He was immaculately dressed, always talking loudly with a big group of friends, never studying quietly in the library. I thought he didn't like me at first, because he always seemed to frown in my direction, but I later discovered that it wasn't personal; he was waiting for his new glasses to be delivered and had to squint to see where he was going. Once we did start talking to each other, we never stopped. He was the most fun, kind and generous person I'd ever met. We had many differences, but so much in common. He was a Muslim boy whose parents had come to Britain from Pakistan in the fifties, I was a white girl with a Church of England education whose relatives had lived within a ten-mile radius for generation after generation. Yet our families were similar in many ways: our parents had worked exhaustively to keep a roof over our heads, our dads brought home the wages while our mums did everything at home. Our parents also had similar values regarding family, community, sharing, and the uselessness of the local council. They often said the same things, but in different languages. Each Christmas Eve, my mum would fill the table with food and force Assad to eat just one more mini pizza and just a few more bits of quiche. At Eid, Assad would turn up at the house with homemade curries for my mum and dad. He was always there, helping me out, getting me out of hot water and tricky situations.

'Mate, you owe me for this,' he'd say, laughing, after doing me yet another big favour.

The weekend of his visit, we'd planned to see the Tower of London, walk around Southbank and maybe watch a film at the BFI. Will was coming with us, and we were discussing plans over breakfast at my flat.

I was making coffee when I picked up my phone and saw a Facebook post about another No More Page 3 protest happening that afternoon. As time passed, the previous protest had morphed into something quite different in my mind. It was like a trip to the dentist; eye-wateringly uncomfortable at the time, but afterwards you felt better and were glad you'd been.

I realised I wanted to go, so I tried to look confident and laid my revised plans on the table, with the croissants.

'Will you come with me to a protest?' I asked nicely. Assad puffed out his cheeks and exhaled loudly, in an 'I've got a lot on' sort of way. He was holding his croissant in the air like a boomerang. Will just said, clearly and immediately, 'No.'

'Please,' I said.

'Can't be arsed,' Assad replied.

I looked at them and thought, *You think this isn't about you, but it is. Page 3 isn't doing you any favours either.* Neither of them were comfortable with lad culture. Neither of them wanted to down pints and have fights and 'man up'. They were both sensitive, intelligent, emotionally mature people. I looked at them and thought, *This toxic culture damages you as much as it damages me.*

I thought of my dad, and how he would assess the manliness of other blokes. 'Look at his hands,' he would say, if he saw a man in a shirt and tie, 'he's never done a day's work in his life.' Men should have rough, tough hands, cracked and wrecked from hard labour. Moisturisers, conditioners and lotions were for women. 'I've just done my skincare routine,' my dad would say in a high-pitched voice if my mum forced him to put hydrocortisone cream on a patch of eczema. He washed his hair with washing-up liquid if the shampoo smelled too floral.

I used to babysit for an eight-year-old boy who would only wash his hands with his 'special' soap, which was shaped like a grenade. He would only clean himself if his toiletries looked like weapons of mass destruction that could annihilate a village. That's not a relaxing bath time. You've really got to question the culture when girls get Herbal Essences and boys get anthrax.

'Come with me,' I said again to Assad and Will. 'Please!'

They shook their heads. This continued for forty-five minutes, until I wore them down and they reluctantly agreed to come.

'OK,' Will said, 'OK. But I'm not saying or doing anything.'

Two hours later we were standing in a deserted Thomas More Square.

'You must have got the wrong day,' Will said gleefully. 'Oh well, let's head off!'

A McDonald's bag skittered across the square, like tumble-weed.

'No, I haven't got the wrong day. It said this afternoon. People must be running late, that's all.' Where was Lucy? Where was Max? I'd expected the two of them to be there, and maybe Priya too. Were three people too many to hope for? I sat on the wall and waited, but no one came.

'OK.' I stood up and grabbed my bag. 'Let's go.'

'Excuse me, sorry to bother you, but are you here for the protest?'

Two women were power-walking towards us, dragging wheelie suitcases.

'I'm Emma, from the Bristol Student's Union – this is Lou. We're making a radio piece about No More Page 3, but there doesn't seem to be anyone here – have we got the wrong day?'

They looked wildly confused. The protest consisted of me, a bloke standing behind me, puffing his cheeks out, wearing a T-shirt with 'I Love Biscuits' printed on it, and a posh blond boy, lurking on the edge of the pavement, nervously checking his watch.

'Do you mind if I interview you? I was supposed to speak to Lucy, but she's not here.'

My hands felt hot. I swallowed. My heart fluttered.

'Well, we were just going,' I said, looking at Assad and Will. 'Please, it'll only take a minute.'

How could I say no? I was the only who had turned up. It was only a week since I set my birthday resolution to speak more, to say what I think, in my own voice. I briefly wished that I'd never set those intentions. I wished instead that I'd promised to listen to *Woman's Hour* every day, or to visit the library more often.

'Yeah, OK,' I said, watching in horror as a microphone emerged from a wheelie suitcase.

They asked me about my experiences of Page 3, and I nervously told them about the pub I used to work in, that had the *Daily Star* and *The Sun* on the bar and Page 3 posters on the wall in the men's toilets. How the regulars would loudly rate the women behind the bar out of ten and would try to grab us as we collected glasses and cleaned ashtrays.

Then they asked what I thought the worst thing about Page 3 was, and I thought for a moment and replied, 'News in Briefs.'

News in Briefs was a caption, in the style of a speech bubble, that was supposed to express the Page 3 model's thoughts. In the early 2000s under the editorship of Rebekah Brooks, News in Briefs furnished the models with social and political statements that supported the paper's views. The models were seen to make comments on immigration, benefit cheats and the Iraq War. When Dominic Mohan took over in 2009, News in Briefs became a parody, and the models were instead seen to be making intellectual statements about the Hadron Collider, the free market or French literature.

'It's supposed to be funny,' I said, 'the joke being that working-class women with big breasts are too stupid to ever think about such things.'

I felt exhausted when it was over. I stood up to leave, but the woman with the microphone turned to Assad and Will and asked if she could interview them too. Will politely declined and backed away until he was at a safe distance; the sort of space you'd put between yourself and a sparking Catherine wheel or a spitting camel. Assad surprised me by saying yes, and I sat back down on the wall next to him as he delivered an ad-hoc feminist manifesto in a thick Yorkshire accent.

'I feel really uncomfortable when I see someone looking at Page 3,' he said. 'I think it's just really awkward and unnecessary and when men look at it in public places – on the bus or the train – it's just really disrespectful. Like, I've got loads of amazing female friends and family members – like Jo, she's my best friend, and Page 3 . . . well, it's just shit really, innit?'

That night, I messaged Lucy on Facebook to tell her I'd done the interview. I felt I should let her know that I'd spoken about the campaign, just in case I'd done or said anything wrong.

Oh, bless you, she replied. *I'm so sorry I wasn't there, I was at an event thing which overran. I'm slightly frazzled at the moment. There's a lot going on.*

She told me there was another protest planned for 17 November, just two weeks away, in honour of the fortieth anniversary of Page 3. It was being organised by three groups: OBJECT, Turn Your Back on Page 3 and No More Page 3, and large crowds were expected. Supporters were encouraged to wear campaign T-shirts or plain ones with their own messages scrawled across the front in marker pen. Alternatively, they could come dressed as typically British things, as a nod to editor Dominic Mohan's statement at the Leveson Inquiry that Page 3 is a 'British institution'.

'I think you should go as a tin of beans,' Assad said later that night. 'There's nothing more British than baked beans.'

'It's such a pity you won't be here,' I said. 'You could've gone as a Yorkshire pudding.'

'Yeah, shame, but I'm washing my hair that day,' he said, stroking his bald head.

British Institutions

I decided against fancy dress. It felt too risky. I just couldn't chance being the only person to turn up to a deserted protest dressed as a tin of beans. Instead, I baked biscuits that I thought I could hand around to hungry protesters; little gingerbread men wearing campaign T-shirts made of icing. They were packed in an old Quality Street tin in my bag and I walked very carefully and slowly, like a bridesmaid drifting down an aisle, so as not to break off their heads.

I was so amazed by the crowd assembled outside News International that my mouth actually fell open. It was a proper protest, like you'd see on TV. People waved banners and placards. People wore berets. I was in shock.

In the centre was a group of women who appeared to be leading the event. A woman with curly hair was shouting into a megaphone next to some people holding a giant birthday card covered in pictures cut out of newspapers. One side held all the photos of women taken from every tabloid paper for six weeks; the other side showed all the photos of men from the same newspapers. Across the top, it said 'spot the difference'. The women were naked, topless, or wearing underwear or bikinis. All so young. All with the same body type. Almost all of them were white. The men were footballers, cricketers, rugby players, politicians. They were wearing sports kits and suits, and none of them were bending over a chair, raising their eyebrows in a surprised manner and pouting. Not one of those blokes was suggestively licking an ice cream. None of them were stripped to the waist, covered in baby oil and laughing at a beach ball.

I scanned faces, but I couldn't see Lucy, Priya or Max, but somewhere towards the back of the crowd was a woman dressed as a cup of tea. She was the only person in fancy dress. I felt for that woman. I wanted to tell her it was a good costume, really original and very well done – was it papier mâché? But she was busy shouting and pointing, so I just felt relieved I wasn't dressed as a tin of beans and started handing out the gingerbread. Two people asked me if the gingerbread men were vegan, then somebody asked if they contained refined sugar. Ten minutes later, a woman asked if they were gluten-free. She also half-jokingly corrected me and said, 'Gingerbread *people*.' Part of me, quite a large part, wanted to throw the tin up in the air and make a noise like a wild boar. I didn't though, I just smiled and got on with it, like a flight attendant handing out pretzels in a pocket of turbulence.

Then a camera crew approached and asked if they could film me signing the birthday card. Everyone was scrawling messages around the pictures, saying why there should be no more Page 3.

'I can't,' I told them. 'I can't think of anything to write with the camera there. It's making me nervous.' They filmed me anyway, standing awkwardly and rigidly with the pen held aloft like a wand. I wrote 'women', then Lucy turned up, dressed in 1970s flares and platforms with a badge that said, '*The Sun*: stuck in the '70s' and the people with cameras swooped in on her instead. I put the pen down and shuffled away, without ever finishing the sentence. My contribution to the birthday card was 'women'.

Soon after, the woman with the megaphone decided the time was right to present the card to News International, and a sea of people pushed towards the entrance. The security guards had locked the doors and some of the protesters tried to break them open. I stood on the pavement, hugging my clipboard to my chest, watching from a distance. Their anger unsettled me. I prided myself on hardly ever losing my temper. If something really angered me, I simply swallowed it like unpleasant cough syrup. Whenever the builders shouted at me, I swallowed it. Whenever my dad offended me, I swallowed it. Whenever Charlie the Home Counties PhD Arsehole made fun of my accent, I just swallowed it. I let it all burn inside and never allowed a flicker of it to show on my face.

My mum rarely got really angry – she usually went straight from pissed off to disappointed, and apart from Tyra Banks shouting at a contestant on *America's Next Top Model*, I didn't even see angry women on TV. Female soap characters were sometimes called 'feisty' in the *TV Times*, and in the storylines men often had 'psycho' ex-girlfriends, but pure, burning-hot female rage? I hardly ever saw it.

I was standing on the kerb when the police turned up. They'd received complaints from News International and had come to investigate. Since I was dawdling by the road, I was the first person the officers approached when they got out of the car. They looked at the group of women shouting in front of the doors, then they looked back at me.

'We're protesting against Page 3,' I said.

'I can see that,' one of the officers replied.

'It's a peaceful protest,' I said, and they whispered quiet words to one another.

Police make me nervous. I was brought up to believe that they would never protect me from anything.

'There's no point ringing them,' my mum always said, 'because they'll never turn up.'

They did turn up, however, the one time I reported a sexual assault, but the officer took down my statement with his back to me, unable to take his eyes away from the TV across the room. He advised me to wear a fake wedding ring to avoid attracting unwanted attention from men. I felt stupid for telling them, as if I was wasting their time, and when it happened again, I didn't bother picking up the phone.

The officers stopped whispering and turned to face me. One of them said, 'We don't have *The Sun* in the police station actually. We used to have it years ago, but we don't now. Page 3 is offensive to the female officers.'

This was not what I was expecting.

'Well, in that case, would you like to sign the petition?' I asked.

One of them replied that they weren't allowed to express political views while working, but the other said that technically, they were supposed to be on their break, so why not?

He took the pen from me and wrote 'women deserve respect from the media'.

As the officers left and attempted to break up the crowd by the door, Lucy ran towards me and said, 'Can we just take a minute to process the fact that News International called the police, and they turned up and SIGNED the petition?'

I packed up my things and slowly walked towards the station. The tube was busy, and I stood at the end of the carriage, by the door. I stepped back to let a woman get off at London Bridge and, as she squeezed past, she said, 'Thanks. I agree with you, by the way.'

I stared at her, confused. No one ever talks on the tube.

She pointed at my T-shirt and I realised I hadn't buttoned up my coat.

'No More Page Three,' she said, and then the doors closed and she was gone.

Goodwill to All Mansplainers

In 2008, Rebecca Solnit wrote the essay 'Men Explain Things to Me: Facts Didn't Get in Their Way'. In 2010, *The New York Times* named 'mansplainer' one of their words of the year. But it wasn't until 2012 that I discovered the term for myself. I'd gone online to check a reference for my thesis, but had ended up googling Carrie Fisher, buying new bath towels and watching a video of a man in a dinosaur costume falling down a flight of stairs. This led to Facebook and a dark half-hour of hating my friends, before I landed on the No More Page 3 page. Supporters regularly posted messages on the wall, sharing their reasons for signing the petition. They talked about how Page 3 made them feel about their own bodies. Some women wrote that they felt inadequate, that they'd never measure up to the standard set by Page 3. Others didn't mind the pictures themselves, but didn't think they should be printed in a newspaper alongside endless photos of fully clothed men. Lots of people mentioned how they hated seeing Page 3 in their schools, workplaces and homes; in cafes, libraries, hospitals. There were so many reasons, so many differing opinions. And yet, there were so many men on hand to explain why all of these perspectives were wrong. Some were trolls, who replied to the women's posts saying, *Of course you want no more page 3, look at you. You're jealous.* It was repeated over and over: *You're just jealous 'cos your tits are shit.* Other men weren't overtly abusive, they just clearly wanted to educate the women who had posted on the page, and carefully outlined to them why everything they believed was wrong. They typed these long replies with bullet points and everything.

Nuclear levels of mansplaining, one woman wrote, and that was my introduction to the word.

I thought about how much of my life was taken up with men explaining things to me, and I was angry at myself for letting it happen.

I pictured the mums of the kids I looked after, running around searching for PE kits, making packed lunches and doctor's appointments, while the dads always just seemed to lean against the fridge drinking coffee, telling me things. Even Livia's dad was annoying, and he was the nicest of all the Dulwich dads. He once spent half an hour explaining Picasso to me, even though he knew I was doing a PhD in Art History. I did what I usually did in those situations: just waited patiently for him to stop talking. So much time spent waiting patiently. I observed how he was with Natasha and was constantly annoyed by how much praise he required for doing the things she usually did without a fanfare. 'I've got the laundry out of the dryer,' he'd say, waiting for thanks even though he'd just dumped it all in a pile in the spare room, without even thinking about ironing or folding or putting it away. 'I've made Liv a sandwich!' he'd shout upstairs, while Natasha was running around getting ready for work, arranging everything for the school trip and simultaneously talking to his mother on the phone.

The Julians from the conference drifted back into my mind, with their twenty-minute-long 'comments', their posture – that way they had of leaning back in their seat, one leg casually crossed over the other, taking up so much space that the person next to them barely had room to breathe.

I poured a glass of wine and forced myself to think of other things.

It was the weekend of our Christmas party. Rebecca organised one each year at the flat, and invited neighbours, work colleagues and people she'd gone to university with. She had recently bought a vintage black and white dress, the kind of thing Jean Shrimpton might have worn, so she decided we should make it a 1960s-themed party, to give her an excuse to wear it. Assad balanced on a ladder, hanging gaudy foil decorations, and I phoned my mum to ask how she used to do her hair and make-up when she was a teenager. She said she'd use half a bottle of hairspray and lots of mascara on Thursday morning and then it'd be perfectly smudged and fashionably messy by Friday night. I didn't have thirty-six hours to spare, so I just spent seventeen minutes upside down with a comb. I backcombed my hair so much the comb broke, and some of its teeth got lost in the candyfloss of it all, but the effect was quite pleasing.

'Everybody looks like they're in fancy dress,' Rebecca's

boyfriend Tom said, 'but Jo actually looks like she's from the sixties.' This kind of thing has been said before, when I was a Victorian urchin and a land girl on school trips. I can pass for a working-class person from any era. It's a gift.

Rebecca and Tom hadn't been together long, and were still a bit clumsy, awkward and embarrassed around each other. If Rebecca looked at Tom for any length of time, he would flush bright red. They'd just got back from visiting his mother in Scotland, which was a big deal for both of them. I was trying to make conversation to make Tom feel comfortable, so I asked about his mother's house, and he told me that she owned a horse with one eye that lived in a paddock at the bottom of the garden.

'Did you ride the one-eyed horse?' I asked Rebecca, and she started coughing and Tom turned purple, so I dropped the subject.

People started turning up around seven. Assad ran around making drinks. He must have squeezed five hundred limes. He kept complaining that his hands were stinging, but nobody really listened because the margaritas were so good. I was talking to my friend Maggie about No More Page 3, when Tom interrupted to introduce me to his mate from university, a mousey-haired man who was studying volcanology. I said hello, and carried on talking, but he leaned in and said, 'Sorry, did you say you're campaigning against Page 3?'

'Yes,' I said, smiling, and turning back to Maggie.

He took a step closer, until his elbow was touching mine. 'Surely you can see that to ban Page 3 would be to censor—'

'Well, we're not asking for a ban,' I said, 'just for the editor to reconsider a decision made in the seventies to use photos of topless women to sell papers.'

'Let me tell you the problem with this kind of censorship.'

I felt a dull throb in my head. My PhD was about the art of émigrés from Nazi Germany, who'd had their work burned, seized, stolen, pilloried. I'd written my undergraduate dissertation on degenerate art, my MA thesis on iconoclasm. I'd spent years studying book burnings, art theft, cultural destruction and propaganda. Everything I'd studied was about the complexities of censoring, banning and destroying images. He was studying volcanoes.

He talked for such a long time that Maggie sauntered away and trotted upstairs with a handful of peanuts, but I was rooted to the spot. He was so patronising the effect was almost hypnotic. He stood with one arm crossed casually against his chest, lazily gesticulating with the other. He made a grand sweeping motion and his hand rested over the mince pies. He picked one up and took a bite, and I felt another pulse of fury in my forehead. They were *my* mince pies. I didn't make them, because I couldn't be arsed, but I bought them from Tesco and arranged them nicely on the little glass plate from the charity shop. I watched him wang on about press freedom between bites. He went on and on. Little crumbs of pastry tumbled down his chin and I thought, *No. Not today. I've had a week filled to the very brim with turd. Natasha made me clean the slime off her bathroom tiles with a folding travel toothbrush. I had to sit through two secular nativity plays, queue for four and a half hours at A&E with a seven-year-old who fell off a scooter, read a five-hundred-page book about Kristallnacht and I've got blisters from these shoes. I deserve this party. You are not ruining mulled wine and Dusty Springfield for me. Not in this kitchen, mate.*

But just as I was getting really worked up, Assad spirited me away upstairs, quite literally. He'd just escaped lime duty and was holding a margarita in each hand. He passed one to me and I drank half of it by the time I reached the landing. I asked if I could have extra salt around the rim, because I'd licked it all off. All I wanted was more tequila, a lot of salt and all the mince pies. And that song by The Ronettes from *Dirty Dancing*.

It was so much better upstairs, I don't know why people were hanging about in the kitchen, where it was too warm and smelled of Stilton. The Christmas tree was upstairs, and the fairy lights! People were dancing and Rebecca's line manager was caressing her own back, pretending to be getting off with somebody under the mistletoe. Assad had recreated all the best cocktails from Nigella's Christmas book and I laughed until my cheeks flushed with Cointreau and happiness. Will danced sarcastically to Darlene Love and spilled beer all over himself. *This is the best party ever*, I thought, eating some salt.

But then the door opened and Mr Censorship strolled in, and within four minutes he was at it again. I can't remember how the conversation got going that time, because I'd inhaled a tray of margaritas, but I'm 30–65 per cent sure I didn't start it.

'I agree censorship's a problem,' I said. 'Think about what's suppressed from the tabloids. Women's sport, for example, receives barely any coverage. Most of women's achievements are absent. The whole of womankind is represented by Page 3, Theresa May's shoes and people off *Hollyoaks* bending over in Marbella. Everything else that women do or say is suppressed.'

'That's not the same thing,' he said. 'You can't want to ban a feature—'

'I mean, we're not asking for a ban.'

'Well, the issue with a ban—'

'We don't want a ban.'

'If you'll let me finish, the problem with a ban—'

'We're not asking for anything to be banned – we don't want a ban – we just want the editor to recognise that—'

'—is where you draw the line. That's the issue with censorship of this kind. I doubt you'll be successful – they'll never remove Page 3—'

Suddenly, something just clicked in my head and I lost it, like that scene in *Withnail and I* when Paul McGann chucks a bag of shopping at a bull. My face felt hot. My hands made involuntary fists. I shouted so loud that my voice quivered with rage.

'That's it, get out!'

'What?' Mr Censorship's mouth made a little O.

'Go on.' I pointed, unnecessarily, to the door. 'Get out!'

He still stood there, speechless.

'I have enough of this shit in the outside world without having it in my living room. You heard me, *get out.*'

The music was still playing, but no one was dancing. People stared and whispered. Will tried to intervene, Assad burst out laughing and tried to hide it with a cough. Mr Censorship glared at me, then grabbed his coat and pranced down the stairs in a huff, probably pocketing my mince pies on his way out.

Goodwill to All Mansplainers

I could feel everyone's eyes on me.

'What?' I picked up another margarita.

'You just turned into a character off *EastEnders*,' Assad replied.

PART TWO

HQ

New Year, New You

It was the first week of January, and the supermarket aisles were filled with workout DVDs, giant inflatable balls and yoga mats. The only leftover relic of the season of goodwill was a bargain bin filled with cinnamon-scented candles and shop-soiled Christmas crackers. I scuttled down the magazine aisle and was assaulted with endless 'New Year, New You' diet plans. I hadn't even taken down the tinsel and they wanted me in Spandex, hating myself. I groaned and shuffled to the till. The cashier looked at my face and said, 'Things aren't that bad, are they?' His badge said, 'Kenneth – here to help!'

I trudged back to the flat with my shopping bags, past rows of skeletal Christmas trees dumped on pavements. Most of the needles had dropped off and they looked patchy and pathetic, like cats shaved for hysterectomies. The air was thick with the scent of pine, garbage and damp and the whole of Dulwich smelled like the inside of a National Express coach.

The atmosphere was equally depressing in the flat, since Rebecca still simmered with resentment after I'd turfed her boyfriend's mate out of the Christmas party. I'd apologised, but we both knew I didn't really mean it. The rage had been bubbling up inside me for ages and Mr Censorship just pushed and pushed until I couldn't hold it in any longer.

I was safely holed up in my room writing a card to Nessa, thanking her for the owl calendar she'd sent, when my phone pinged with an email alert. I didn't check my inbox right away, because I presumed it was the imprisoned Ghanaian prince again, who regularly asked me for fifteen thousand US dollars to fund his escape. I ate a couple of custard creams, fixed a stamp on the envelope and then picked up my phone.

From: Lucy-Anne Holmes
To: Jo Cheetham
6 January 2013

Hello!
No More Page 3 Lucy here.

I am writing because I want to share with you where I am at and see if there's a solution that you might be able to help me with.

Basically . . . I'm kinda like fucked.

I started No More Page 3 in the summer and went ballistic with it. And then just before Christmas I sort of hit a wall, and realised I'd totally burnt myself out with it all.

Anyway, I've had a bit of a rest and a bit of time out. And I don't know what to do now.

I feel as though I have pretty much thrown all my resources in terms of money, energy and inspiration at it. I'm spent.

BUT . . . and there is a but . . . I love No More Page 3, I believe we'll get there, I love the platform that exists, I love the creativity it's prompted and the stories that have been shared.

I don't want to say 'laters' but at the same time I know that my burntout-ness isn't helping it at all.

There are a couple of options that I'd like to put to you, and see what you think:

1) I just say 'I'm done' and No More Page 3 is no more.
2) I reach out to a group/team and we could man and woman it together.

This email relates to point 2.

Would you be up for that?

I put down the phone and the custard cream. I had tingles, goose bumps, that shivery feeling of excitement that happens in dreams, when the seasons change or when boarding an aeroplane, unless it's Ryanair.

Will came over, so I didn't reply right away.

'I just got an email from Lucy-Anne Holmes,' I told him.

'Who?'

'Lucy, from No More Page 3. She's asked if I'd like to join the campaign team.'

'Will you get paid?' he asked.

'No, of course not, there's no money. The campaign doesn't make any money.'

'But shouldn't you be focusing on your PhD?'

I looked at him and nodded. 'Yeah. I should.'

Hi Lucy, I typed, later that night. My hand hovered over the keypad. I let all the potential excuses run through my head. There were so many to choose from; having barely any free time, having so much work to do, having a phobia of public speaking and being photographed, not knowing what Twitter is. I thought about all the things I *should* do. But that feeling of shivery excitement was still there.

Yes, I wrote, *I'd love to join the team.*

And then I clicked 'send'.

A Cheese Sandwich for George Michael

In my early twenties, when I worked as a travel agent, I was regularly sent across the country to training sessions and sales seminars. I liked the free lunches and the branded stationery we got to take home, but I hated the introductions that kicked off every event. 'Tell us your name, where you've come from and a fascinating fact about yourself!'

It was painful. The first two questions were easy enough, but a fascinating fact? I was envious of the people with scars from childhood accidents who had an obvious story to tell. The ones with interesting hobbies – beekeeping, gymnastics, doll making – had it easy. The rest of us wracked our brains in desperation to think of anything remarkable that had ever happened in our lives.

One time a woman stood up and said, 'I'm Kayleigh from the Coventry office and I once made a cheese sandwich for George Michael.' It was perfect. Everybody immediately knew that she was interesting without being showy; she hadn't been a backstage VIP at a concert or sat next to him on a transatlantic flight, she'd merely made him a sandwich. We all wanted to hear the story immediately.

Years later, on a freezing January morning in 2013, I found myself stuck in the cycle of introductions all over again, but this time with feminists on the internet instead of travel agents in a seminar room in Cardiff.

Lucy made a private Facebook group called No More Page 3 HQ, and invited in the people she had asked to help. I clicked 'join' and was the only one in the group for a while, like the loser who turns up early for a housewarming party. This gave me time to reflect upon the rubbishness of my Facebook profile. There was nothing 'feministy' on there; no links to blogs about the tampon tax, no fundraising attempts for Women's Aid, no *Guardian* articles about the pay gap. I was drunk in 70 per cent of my photos, and in fancy dress in at least half of them. I googled 'famous feminists' and saw Gloria Steinem, bell hooks and Mary Wolstonecraft. None of them were drinking Cuba libres dressed as a giant pineapple. I thought that the others in the group would judge me by my profile. All the posts, the photos and my friends' comments would be used to build an idea of who I was. My profile was my fascinating fact, my cheese sandwich for George Michael, and it was limp and disappointing.

Notifications pinged as people joined the group, and I stopped obsessing over my own shortcomings and put my full attention on discovering theirs instead.

Max, the confident, assertive and slightly frightening woman I met at the first protest, had joined the group. Her profile was filled with all the feministy things that mine lacked – there actually was a link to a *Guardian* article about the pay gap – but there were also pictures of her looking glamorous in the kind of restaurants that I wouldn't dare walk past, let alone hold a fork inside. Her clothes looked expensive, her dog looked sparkly-eyed and blow-dried. I marvelled that she was even more intimidating online than she was in person. Her profile said, *I'm powerful and sophisticated and, yes, I know about beurre blanc, but I'm also informed about the current reproductive rights of women in Brazil.*

My stalking was interrupted by another ping, and a woman named Kate appeared in the group. Her profile was all Manchester, marathons and music festivals with a sideline in NHS funding pitfalls. She looked a bit older than me, maybe early forties, and if I hadn't read in the 'about' section that she was a nurse, I would have guessed a Zumba instructor. She was all swishy blonde hair and day-glo Lycra with a wide smile, the kind that goes down instead of up at the corners.

Evie and Jess appeared at the same time. Ping! Ping!

Evie had a mass of tumbling corkscrew curls and looked thoroughly Victorian. Even in jeans, she looked like Lizzie Siddal or Alice Liddell or those girls who faked the fairy photos. In most of her pictures, she was laughing her head off in a pub and it just seemed all wrong, like when Joan of Arc wandered into a shopping-mall aerobics class in *Bill & Ted's Excellent Adventure*. She would have looked more at home on a clover-covered riverbank, staring wistfully at passing clouds.

Jess looked like the kind of person I'd be intimidated by at the hairdresser's. It was immediately apparent that she was cool. She wore the kind of clothes that most people would look an absolute dickhead in, but she carried it off effortlessly. There was a ludicrously beautiful child in the pictures, and a man with a five o'clock shadow who appeared to have been styled by *GQ* magazine.

That's as far as I got before Lucy typed her first post.

Lucy: Welcome everyone! Pull up a chair. Drink? Olive?

Lucy: I am sitting down to write this with such a big smile on my face.

Thank you all so, so much for responding to an email I felt very vulnerable about sending with so much energy and loveliness and excitement.

Lucy: This is a big warm hello to you, Kate, to you, Jess, to you, Evie, to you, Max and to you, Jo. Shall we start by introducing ourselves?

I waited for someone else to go first.

Kate: Shall I go first? I'm Kate. I'm 42, from Manchester. Divorced with two teenage kids: Chloe, 15 and Jay, 13. I'm a nurse. Overworked and underpaid! I started getting involved with NMP3 last Septemberish and have done a few petition signings in Manchester and a couple of radio interviews. I'm happy to do speaky things – I have no media training or anything though, I'm just gobby.

A Cheese Sandwich for George Michael

Jess: Hi Team! I'm Jess, 27, originally from Newcastle but have just moved to Shropshire with my husband Matt and 3-year-old daughter Ruby. I do web stuff and helped Lucy to build the website, which is how I got involved. I was so happy when you emailed me Lucy. Thank you for letting me be a part of this, I'm so excited to get started!

Evie is typing . . .

Evie: Hi everyone, it's so nice to meet you all. I'm Evie, 31. I am a designer and currently sell the campaign tees which I love, I get a warm feeling every time an order comes in and another revolutionary is born! I have two girls, Milly, 8 and Sofie, 4. We live in Kentish Town and my husband runs a pub here – we can use the function room for meetings if we ever get to be in the same place at the same time.

Max: That would be perfect – meetings always go better with a gin and tonic IMHO. I'm Max, 46, and I live in London with my pampered dog. I'm good on social media – happy to cover Twitter etc. I'm super busy at work though (finance, big firm), so we'd have to have some kind of rota?

I googled IMHO, then I quickly typed my own introduction before I could overthink it.

Killjoy

Me: Hello everyone (I'm waving at my screen).
I'm Jo, I'm 32 and I'm a student and a
babysitter, though people tell me not to say that
– I'm supposed to say, 'I'm conducting research
for my PhD and I'm a part-time childminder'
because it sounds more grown-up and
impressive. I'm so excited to get started with
this! I don't know what Twitter is, but I promise
I'll try my best not to mess it up.

Lucy went last, and her introduction was the longest.

Lucy: Hi everyone! I'm so happy you're all here.
I know I've met some of you before, but I'll
introduce myself anyway. So, I'm Lucy, 36, a
writer/actor. I started the campaign last year,
after I inadvertently discovered feminism . . .

Lucy: What happened is, I'd found myself single
at 35 and I didn't want to jump into another
relationship, I felt I had to work out what was
going on with me and men first. The sex I'd
had when I was last single in my late 20s had
generally happened when I was off my tits and
I never knew where I stood. I found myself
thinking, 'I'm in my mid-thirties and I don't feel
I've even skimmed the top of how amazing sex
can be.' One night I was looking at porn online
and turned it off and felt really manky. Then I

typed 'beautiful sex' into a search engine and got this porn video – 'Daddy loves to hatefuck daughter' and an article – 'How to Get Beautiful Women to Have Sex With You', and all the time this advert was popping up saying 'shag a slapper!' And I just thought THIS IS ALL WRONG! WHAT HAVE WE DONE TO SEX?

Lucy: Anyway, this led me on a bit of a journey. I wanted to have beautiful sex, but I was riddled with insecurities about my body and totally unable to express my needs to men. I started to unpick all this and discover why this was the case, and found myself unearthing a lot of deep-rooted stuff that I'd absorbed just by being a woman in our society.

Lucy: This was the backdrop to my headspace when I realised that the Page 3 image was bigger than the photo of Jessica Ennis during the Olympics. I wrote to the editor of *The Sun* and found myself waking in the night thinking about Page 3 . . .

Lucy: I suppose at the root of all this is the fact that I think women are phenomenally powerful, and I would love becoming a woman to be the amazing thing it should be rather than the fraught, insecure, self-loathing experience it is for so many.

I am blown away by your enthusiasm and
energy. And seriously excited.

So, how about I stop talking and we get started?

Lucy had created a 'how to' manual packed with everything she had learned: advice, tips, passwords, instructions. We talked through the aims of the campaign: to provide a platform for discussions about Page 3 and sexism, to support other groups doing similar work, to focus on the positive, to act with integrity and kindness and to block any trolls who told us to eff off and kill ourselves. Lucy said she was happy for people who disagreed to voice their opinions, because that inspired debate and debate is good – but to draw the line if anyone was insulting or abusive. The campaign was supportive of glamour models and sex workers and was focused purely towards objectification and misogyny in the press. Lucy said we'd have to constantly monitor social media to ensure that conversations remained respectful and non-discriminatory.

Lucy: So, let's start with a social media rota.
We can take it in turns to cover Twitter and
Facebook. The login details are in the email I
sent you all, but I've temporarily changed the
password. It's now pooinabox

Lucy: It's a long story, and I'm not proud.

Jealous Bitches

I was standing by the broccoli in Sainsbury's, deleting pictures of tits on my phone. Trolls had covered the campaign's Facebook page with topless photos and porno screenshots. I deleted an image of a naked woman on her knees with her hands tied behind her back and one of a topless model covered in baby oil pulling the side of her bikini bottoms down. As quickly as I could delete one, another would spring up.

'Excuse me, could I just squeeze past? I just need to grab some pak choi.'

As the woman leaned in, I saw her glance at my phone. She shot me a shocked, disgusted look, then marched off towards the carrots.

It was my first day on social media. I thought I was prepared. I'd read Lucy's notes and I'd watched what the others had posted and how they'd dealt with the trolls. There'd been a ton of them since HQ had been formed, attracted by all the sudden activity on the campaign's social media pages. The trolls left comments as well as pictures. A supporter had written on our Facebook page:

Killjoy

I'm sick of guys thinking that it's normal and OK to view me and my friends as sex objects – there to be ogled at, whistled at, gestured to, called names, harassed, slapped, grabbed and generally intimidated. There are lots of guys who need to find a renewed respect for women – and this can't happen when the country's most popular newspaper clearly shows that it has no respect for women.

The comments beneath this read:

Shut the fuck up and get your tits out bitch.

I can't think of any other use for women apart from looking at their boobs. You are jealous cos no one wants to look at yours.

Have you seen how dog ugly these women are – jealous bitches lol.

Feminist killjoys should never be allowed to ruin things!

I hit delete and logged into HQ. Kate was online. I was so relieved, I let out a long breath I hadn't realised I'd been holding in.

Kate: You OK Jo?

Me: Yeah, fine. Just so many trolls out today.

Jealous Bitches

Kate: There were loads yesterday as well. Sad bastards with nothing better to do. I took some screenshots because I thought it would be interesting to monitor the page. This was my fave:

'Only flat chested tit envious boiler suit wearing dykes would object to page 3.'

Me: Have you got a boiler suit?

Kate: Five in different colours and a sequinned one for the weekend.

Me: I'm still getting used to it all. I'm at the supermarket. I've been walking around holding some crumpets for twenty minutes, deleting tits. I can't remember what I came in for.

Kate: Mmm crumpets. Well I'm on my break, I can take over for ten minutes if you like? Give you chance to get through the till without any more boobs getting in the way?

I gratefully accepted and vaguely floated around the aisles holding the crumpets, avoiding the pak choi woman. I found myself staring at teabags for ages without blinking. I felt disoriented, like I was coming round after gas and air at the dentist.

I found it so interesting that the trolls were trying to use women's bodies as weapons against women. It was a power thing. Those men were saying, 'We own this space. We have authority over women's bodies. We are the ones in control.' It was our appearance they tried to use against us. We were the wrong size and shape, we were too old and fat and short, our faces were wrong, our hair was wrong, our breasts were always wrong.

> Me: It's just so telling isn't it, that the most hurtful thing these men think they can say to women is that we're ugly. They don't criticise specific things we say or do, just what we look like.

> Kate: And the annoying thing is that it sticks. It does hurt even though I don't want it to. And then I catch myself thinking they don't know what I actually look like. I'm tall and toned, I work out, I look after myself, I'm pretty. I scrub up really well. And then I realise that I'm basically saying how much I want to fit in to these beauty standards that we're speaking out against.

> Kate: It's all a massive headfuck basically.

When I got back to the flat, I started tidying the kitchen and found a pleasing rhythm to the afternoon. I set my laptop on the table and began washing the dishes. I worked out that I could wash a mug and a plate, take three steps to the table, delete a troll's threat or retweet a supporter's comment, then take three steps back to the sink and wash another couple of things. It became a perfectly timed routine.

I stepped back to the laptop. *Wish these women would campaign as hard to stop FGM!* a man tweeted.

Lucy said this happened a lot and she always responded by directing them to the work of Nimco Ali and Leyla Hussein, whose organisation, Daughters of Eve, worked to protect girls and young women who were at risk from female genital mutilation. We admired and supported their incredible work, and Nimco sometimes wore a No More Page Three T-shirt when speaking on panels or at festivals.

I was just about to draft a response when Max posted in HQ.

Max: I see you've met Michael Waldon, Jo!

Me: Is this the bloke going on about FGM on Twitter?

Max: Yes. He's a former deputy editor of *The Sun*. You're lucky he hasn't mentioned badgers. Or wheatgerm.

Me: What?

Max: Read this.

She sent a link to a *Huffington Post* opinion piece that he'd written about No More Page 3. It said, in block capitals, that NO ONE CARES about our stumbling campaign despite 'the hysteria and shrill over-the-top support'.

Killjoy

How nice of him, I thought, *to drag words like 'shrill' and 'hysteria' from the depths of the Victorian Gentleman's Dictionary of Women's Afflictions. If a woman had written an article like that, men on the internet would have lined up to say, 'time of the month, darling?'*

He went on to list all the attributes that he imagined No More Page 3 campaigners would share; we were middle class, whining, self-serving, wheatgerm-eating and humourless, with 'no real idea' of the lives of *The Sun*'s working-class readership. These working-class people didn't worry about Page 3; they worried about 'their kids' health, the rent, putting food on the table, work, their relationship, benefits scroungers, immigration, the telly, and a drink at the weekend'.

I didn't know whether this had been Michael Waldon's experience growing up, or if this was simply the way he imagined working-class people live. None of it reflected my experiences of working-class culture; the pride, the community, the creativity, the camaraderie, the richness and ingenuity that fuelled our lives. At home, our garden was lined with messy rows of cabbages, beds of strawberries, swedes, gooseberry bushes. I could go to school in the morning, and by the time I was home for tea, my dad would have made a piece of furniture out of an old wooden crate, and my mum would have painted and upholstered it. They made everything: sofas, patios, bread, clothes, toys, beer, Christmas presents. My dad was interested in astronomy and built a telescope so powerful that a man from the local observatory telephoned to ask if the committee could come and see it. I would spend hours and hours at the local library. My older sister would read me

Wuthering Heights from the bottom bunk as I snuggled under blankets in the top.

'Read that again,' I'd say, and I'd hear, 'Oh, Cathy! Oh, my life! How can I bear it?' Her bedside lamp casting just enough light for me to make shadows dance across the wall with my hands. We shared everything. There was no 'them and us' mentality. Sometimes, so many neighbours and kids would turn up at the house that my mum would grab a screwdriver and take the living-room door off its hinges, balancing it on a pair of stools to create a makeshift buffet table. The word scrounger didn't exist. Everyone we knew had suffered from the closure of the pits and the steelworks, and everyone was on benefits at one time or another.

The people I grew up around didn't use words like 'inter-sectionality', but we saw its definition on the streets around us. We saw bus drivers drive past Black students waiting at bus stops without stopping. We saw Muslim girls have headscarves pulled off on their way to school. The Polish women I knew were underpaid in factories on zero-hour contracts. My friend Keri's family were travellers, and she was followed around every shop she went in by security guards who expected her to steal something. My mum's best friend Dianne was in a wheelchair, and people spoke to her as if she was stupid. Dianne and my mum had so much fun together that they would double over laughing and people would stare at them, horrified, as if fifty-year-old women in wheelchairs ought to be quiet martyrs, unseen and unheard. Every now and then someone would call her brave for laughing. 'You're so brave.' But she wasn't laughing because she was brave, she was laughing because she and my mum were both absolutely hilarious and they knew that life was hard and painful and really, really funny.

Sexism didn't evaporate in the face of other inequalities – it was amplified – and Page 3 didn't go unnoticed when bigger burdens were carried. It just added to the weight.

I thought about all of this for a while, and then I went back to Michael Waldon's article.

I forced myself to read to the end, at which point he unfavourably compared No More Page 3 to a petition against a badger cull – a petition that most of us had signed – and provided a list of alternative topics that we could turn our attention to instead of Page 3: 'Why aren't those petition signatories putting their energy into campaigning against, say, female genital mutilation? White slavery? Sexual stereotyping in the workplace? Forced marriages? Under-age sex and pregnancy?'

Me: *White* slavery???????

Max: I KNOW

Max: Did you see him on *Newsnight*? He was talking about Page 3 with Harriet Harman. Kept interrupting and talking over her. It was SRSLY embarrassing.

Lucy: It's strange, isn't it? He no longer works for *The Sun*, but he's the only person from their camp who's actually acknowledged that we exist. It's like he's the self-appointed spokesperson for Page 3.

Jess: That article makes me so angry. Where's he got this shit from – that we're all bored middle-class busybodies?

Max: I'm pretty middle class TBH, but even I don't eat wheatgerm.

Evie: I'm just so sick of men telling us what we should be focusing our attention on.

Kate: Then you'll like these two comments I deleted the other day:

'Why not try change the world in a productive way? Go cure cancer or something.'

'There are way more important fish to fry than Page 3 . . . Get off your self-righteous horse and try helping the poor or child soldiers!'

Max: Alright, let's prioritise . . . Page 3 first, then cancer, then child soldiers? Or the other way round?

Kate: Don't forget white slavery!

Jess: Guys, we're gonna need a spreadsheet

I browsed *The Sun*'s website, to see how much attention they were focusing on the important issues that we were being told to prioritise.

I used the search bar to find articles about domestic violence. There were 869 results, in contrast to 18,726 for the word 'sexy'. I carried on searching. *The Sun*'s 120 news stories about female genital mutilation were buried beneath the 6,742 articles about 'boobs'. I found nine times more articles written about bikinis than sexual abuse.

The UK's biggest-selling newspaper clearly wasn't focusing on the big issues affecting women's lives. They were focusing on the breasts of teenage girls. And that was the problem.

Glamorous Fashionistas

I got to know my teammates by the style and rhythm of their messages.

Max got straight to the point without dancing around it. She loved acronyms. Boring blogs were dismissed as TL;DR. Things needed doing ASAP. She'd BRB as FYI she was just about to get on the DLR. That kind of thing. I had to constantly have a search window open to google what all the letters meant.

Kate said words like bugger, bastard, tosspot. She made words up and got names wrong. If Max mentioned a famous feminist she was unfamiliar with, instead of quietly googling them, she'd say, 'Betty Friedan? Never heard of her. Oh, hang about, actually wasn't she on *Coronation Street*?'

Jess called us babe individually or guys collectively – two words I couldn't bring myself to say. She said shit a lot, as in 'what's this shit?' Or 'don't even try *that* shit.' She often described the ways her emotions were physically inconveniencing her; 'Guys stop it – I've just nearly pissed myself laughing. I'm serious – my pelvic floor isn't what it was,' or 'I've just cried and snotted all over my clean T-shirt. I'll have to wash it again now.'

Evie was more measured, always trying to mediate and keep the cart on wheels. She'd offer an opinion and say, 'But that's just what I think – I could be wrong, and it's up to everyone, obviously.' Evie always made sure that everyone felt heard. If you posted a message that no one replied to, she would like it and type a response. She never left anyone hanging.

Lucy was exactly the same online as in person: open-hearted, optimistic, enthusiastic, always giving virtual hugs ('let's have a LONG hug, like a twenty-second one that gets really awkward towards the end').

Soon after bringing the team together, Lucy told us she was going to Germany to spend a week at a silent meditation retreat in the woods. I could see the appeal, sort of. Being quiet in the woods sounded lovely, but being quiet in the woods with loads of other people who were also being quiet in the woods sounded unsettling and weird. But each to their own. She'd be offline all week, but would try to walk somewhere to get mobile reception whenever possible, just to check that nothing major had happened.

'But really, nothing much should happen while I'm away,' Lucy said.

'We'll be *fine*,' we replied.

All we had to do was carry on manning social media, replying to messages, deleting death threats and porn and posting out T-shirts. Easy.

Lucy left on 10 February, the first fine day since Christmas, and I dragged my desk into a patch of light by the window to feel the warmth of the sun on my face. There was a holiday atmosphere in HQ, as if the headmistress was away and we were loafing around with our feet up on the desks, making paper aeroplanes. Kate stood in as supply teacher. I don't know if Lucy put her in charge or if she just naturally took the reins because she was the most organised person in the group. In fact, Kate was the most organised person I'd ever met, probably because as a single parent and full-time nurse, she had to expertly manage her time and plan everything meticulously. She was the one you'd want on your team at a work training exercise; she'd be up at the whiteboard in a flash, drawing mind maps and Venn diagrams and putting little dots next to bullet points.

Kate had named that Sunday 'Tweet Murdoch Day'. Since the editor of *The Sun*, Dominic Mohan, had ignored us completely, we thought we would change tactic and instead contact the CEO of News International, Rupert Murdoch. We encouraged supporters to tweet Murdoch, saying why Page 3 should go. They sent heartfelt messages and funny ones. One woman wrote: *Boobs are only newsworthy if they rob a bank.* A man tweeted: *I don't trust any newspapers that have Page 3 for the same reason I wouldn't trust News at Ten if Trevor McDonald had his dick out.*

We chatted about the tweets in HQ, but also drifted on to other topics, like Jess's husband. She'd posted a picture of him helping her at a No More Page 3 petition signing, along with a series of photos of him renovating the house – knocking down walls and tiling the roof. A handsome man fighting objectification of women who was good up a ladder? There was much swooning. He didn't really do it for me, to be honest – he was really good-looking, but with the air of a footballer who'd sustained a knee injury and gone on to host a TV talent show. Not my kind of thing, but I could see the appeal. Evie was a fan.

Evie: He's got a touch of Beckham about him. You're a lucky woman!

Jess: I know! And he's an amazing cook too

Evie: How long have you been together?

Jess: Since we were 19. We met in a club and really hit it off, then we moved in together and had Ruby and yeah that was it really

Me: She is a ludicrously angelic-looking child.

Jess: She's not so angelic in real life, believe me. She's hard work. It's easier now though – I had a tough time when she was younger. I wasn't really prepared for how hard it was going to be.

Kate suddenly appeared in caps lock.

Kate: WOW WOW WOW!!!!!!!!! Sorry to interrupt but you've got to check these tweets out!!!!!!

Glamorous Fashionistas

@Kazipooh: @rupertmurdoch #nomorepage3
Seriously, we are all so over page 3 – it is so
last century!

@rupertmurdoch: @Kazipooh page three so
last century! You maybe right, don't know
but considering. Perhaps halfway house with
glamorous fashionistas.

Me: Murdoch has replied?

Kate: Yes!!! To a supporter who's just tweeted
him!!!!

Evie: Wow, he's considering it! He's actually
considering scrapping Page 3!

Jess: Yeah, but what's this glamorous
fashionista shit?

Jess: So he's proposing to put CLOTHED
women on Page 3 but the general tone and
message won't change? Women are just there
to be looked at

Me: And what does he mean by a halfway
house? Like pants and . . . a cardigan?

Jess: Maybe it's the mid-point between treating
women as objects and treating them as actual
people

Killjoy

Max: Crazy out-of-the-box suggestion here – but how about removing Page 3 and filling the page with . . . some actual fucking NEWS?

Evie: But it could be a step in the right direction? We'll have to wait and see. We don't really know what he means yet.

Me: And on the bright side, at least he's acknowledging us now. I wonder if it will get in the papers tomorrow?

Whirlwinds

I opened one eye. It was still dark. It was also freezing. Rebecca and Kevin liked to keep the heating bills low and the radiators off, which made getting out of bed in February a thing that you had to psychologically prepare for, like filing a tax return or shopping for garden furniture at B&Q on a bank holiday Monday. I bravely reached an arm out from under the duvet and grasped around in the darkness for my phone. When I pressed the button to illuminate the screen, I immediately noticed two things: it was 8.15 a.m. and I had 176 Facebook notifications. I logged on to HQ.

> Kate: Gahhh another 3 interview requests – anyone around?
>
> Kate: They want a press release – do we have a press release? I know nob all about press releases???
>
> Kate: A DM from a journalist in Paris . . . Anyone speak French?

Killjoy

Kate: Shit the bed! Another one from America.
Oh my god MEXICO!!!

I leapt out of bed. Interview requests? France? Mexico? I never imagined that Murdoch's tweet was such big news.

Me: I'm here! What on earth is going on?

Kate: It's bloody mad! I've got to start work in a minute. Max has got a meeting in Amsterdam this afternoon – she'll be boarding the plane now. Evie's doing the school run and Jess is taking Ruby to nursery. I've messaged Lucy but god knows when she'll see it. And I doubt she can really do live radio phone-ins from a silent woodland retreat in Bavaria???

Me: LIVE RADIO PHONE-INS?

Kate: Yeah! I've made a list – just pick the ones you can do.

Me: Oh God I'd be rubbish on the radio – shall I have a go at the press release?

Kate: I think Max is drafting something on the plane. And she's writing a piece for *New Statesman* or whatever it's called.

Kate: Don't worry about sounding daft on the radio, you'll be fine. Just go for it! I'm speaking

to a journalist in Dublin on my break, and I'll
check in when I can throughout the day.

Jess: I'm back guys! I'm just going through the
list. I'm going on 5 Live later and I'm waiting
to hear back from a couple of local stations.
Jo, could you do some of the other BBC Radio
ones?

I had a sudden flashback to an afternoon in the eighties, when I was off school with a sore throat. I was lying on my stomach on the carpet, sipping Lucozade, while my mum perched on the edge of the sofa, watching a Tina Turner concert on TV. As the camera panned across the stage to the backing singers, she said, 'Look how much fun they're having! That would be the best job, being a backing singer. You get all the adventure and none of the attention.'

That's what I wanted my role to be in the campaign. I wanted to be Lucy's backing singer. For her to have the attention, to be in the photographs and do the interviews, while I shuffled about in the background, looking busy.

But Lucy was omming and downward-dogging in a patch of German woodland, and we were all suddenly thrust into the spotlight without her.

I jangled with nerves as I scanned the list of radio interview requests. I chose BBC Wales and BBC Somerset, because I didn't know anyone who currently lived in Wales or Somerset.

The first phone-in was the worst. The presenter attempted to get a debate going between me and the glamour model on the other line. It was ridiculous, because our argument wasn't with the models at all, but with the editors – the men who decided to use half-naked teenagers to sell newspapers. He tried to pitch woman against woman to get an argument going, to suggest it was a women's issue about whether women should pose topless and how other women feel about it. Women, women, women. Meanwhile, the men responsible for creating Page 3 and capitalising on it for forty years were brilliantly absent, as if none of it had anything to do with them at all.

The presenter said Page 3 seemed harmless and was really quite tame in comparison to the stuff you see on the internet. I wish I'd asked him what stuff he'd seen on the internet. He quoted the former Page 3 photographer, Beverley Goodway, who said that the sexiest thing about Page 3 was the look in the model's eyes. I almost laughed down the phone. Whenever people mention Beverley Goodway, they say three things: the crap about the eyes, that he was a 'legend' and that he treated the models with respect. People always say the same about Benny Hill; he treated the women in bikinis so nicely after he chased them around the park, as if these men deserved praise for treating their colleagues like human beings. Well done! You managed to treat a woman like an actual person!

I wondered if Beverley Goodway only pursued such a macho career because his name was Beverley. I bet that went down well at school.

The interview ended when I said something about Page 3 being a relic of the Jimmy Savile era and the presenter panicked, implied I was talking rubbish, and backtracked massively until the whole thing was over. There was probably a big red Savile button at the BBC that interviewers pressed to eject themselves into space if anyone mentioned *Jim'll Fix It*.

I quickly made a cup of tea and phoned my mum.

'The cat's stuck up the cherry tree,' she said. 'I'm up a ladder.'

'I'll let you go then,' I said, before talking incessantly and not letting her go.

'Joanne, you *haven't* been on the radio,' she said when I told her. 'Nobody in our family's ever been on the radio.'

'I've got to do another interview in a bit.'

'Well, don't give them your address.'

'Mum, I'm not going to just say my address on the radio.'

'Come on, that's it, have some tuna. He's on the bottom branch now. You're clever, aren't you clever!'

'Mum, I'll let you go.'

'Give them a fake name,' she said. 'Hope it goes well.'

HQ was a whirlwind of activity, and it was almost impossible to keep up with what was going on. Max had been in touch from the back seat of a taxi, updating us on the press release. Evie had spoken to a reporter on the way back from school. Kate would soon be on her lunch break, taking the call from Dublin in the staff car park behind the hospital. It was like being in the middle of the *Wizard of Oz* tornado, with all the normality of life swept up and spinning all over the place, but without the comforting presence of a Yorkshire terrier.

I listened to Jess's interview and instantly loved the sound of her voice, which was soft and raspy with a slight Geordie lilt, as if the lovechild of Cheryl Cole and Mariella Frostrup was doing the voiceover for a cartoon rabbit. The presenter followed the same formula as my phone-in, and pitted Jess against a glamour model. She refused to get into any arguments.

'What will you do,' the presenter asked, 'if you don't succeed?'

'We won't stop until it's gone,' she replied, and I cheered, alone in my room.

I caught the very end of Kate's interview and only heard her speak for a minute, but she managed to say 'pants' at least three times. 'A woman just standing there in her *pants*.' She put such emphasis on the word, in her strong, confident Mancunian accent.

Evie's interview was different. Instead of trying to get her to argue with a model, the presenter offered up David Banks, a former assistant editor of *The Sun*. He admitted he never took the paper home, because his wife hated Page 3 and he didn't want his children to see it. The presenter also said it was *always the models' eyes* that grabbed his attention.

Me: Why doesn't *The Sun* listen to this feedback and replace the topless photos with close-up shots of a model's EYES? Perhaps the whole page could be filled with a massive picture of a woman peering seductively through a cat flap or a letterbox?

Max: They'd save so much money on metallic bikini bottoms and fake tan.

Jess: Evie you did so well!

Whirlwinds

Evie: Thanks, I think it could have gone better though. The presenter kept saying we want to ban Page 3, which annoyed me, because it turned into a discussion about press freedom instead of objectification. I'm so tired of explaining that we don't want a ban. I think I'll have it etched on my tombstone:

Here lies the mortal remains of Evelyn Hill, who died of boredom on Radio 4.

'She did not want a ban.'

My second radio phone-in was better. Lots of callers said they agreed with the campaign and I didn't mention Savile, so the producer was nice to me at the end. Afterwards, I answered a series of questions via email for an American reporter, and spoke to a pair of French journalists, who wanted to interview me face to face.

Me: The French journalists have offered to come to our office for the interview. They think we have an office!!!

Evie: Did you see the DM earlier from a woman who asked if we were looking for interns 'even if just to help with paperwork and making tea?'

Jess: They think we have paperwork! We must sound much more professional than we are

Me: She's welcome to come to my flat and make tea.

Jess: Imagine if all these reporters and radio producers knew that we were doing all this from our living rooms, skint, knackered, with absolutely no idea what we're doing. I haven't even brushed my hair today.

Evie: I haven't brushed my teeth yet.

It was quiet for a few minutes and then Jess posted again.

Jess: Guys I've just been on the phone with a producer – I'm going on *BBC Breakfast* in the morning!

Me: You're going on telly?

Jess: YES! I'm terrified! And did you see the message from ITV? They want someone to contact them about going on the news tonight! Evie, Jo, could one of you do it? You're the only ones currently in London.

Evie: I don't think I can get childcare – can you do it Jo?

I jumped up from my chair as if it there was a spider on it and flapped in a circle around the kitchen. Appearing on TV was one of the things I never wanted to do, ever in my life. It was up there with visiting an abattoir and attending a school reunion. In fact, I would have rather toured a meat processing factory with Mrs Broadman, my former PE teacher, than appear on an ITV news segment. I ran to the bathroom to put on some mascara, just in case. Would there be a make-up person? What about my hair? I was growing out a fringe and was struggling through the 'Mark Owen from Take That' stage, where it hung in limp curtains around my face. I careered down the hall to my bedroom and frantically emptied my wardrobe onto my bed. What do you wear on the news? I didn't own a trouser suit or a shift dress or a blouse. Could I wear jeans? Could you go on the news in jeans?

Jess is typing . . .

Jess: Shit. The TV interviews are cancelled

Jess: They have bigger news

Jess: The pope has just resigned.

Me: WHAT?????

Jess: It's breaking news – the pope has resigned

Jess: Other stories will be put on a back burner, that's what the woman from the BBC said.

I googled 'pope resigns' but nothing came up.

Me: I can't find any headlines about it?

Jess: It hasn't gone live yet

Kate: The sodding pope!!! stealing our thunder!!!

I collapsed face-down on the pile of clothes on my bed. Of all the outcomes I could imagine, I never would have dreamt that Pope Benedict XVI would be the person to get me out of appearing on ITV news.

Kate: So many messages from journalists all cancelling interviews

Max: I wrote the article, but they said they don't need it any more. All that work wasted FFS.

Evie: But we've all done so well today. I'm proud of us!

Jess: Me too. We were thrown into this with no time to prepare. I can't quite believe today was real.

Lucy is typing . . .

Lucy: Oh my life, I've just got phone reception and have been catching up on everything!!!

Me: Lucy!

Evie: Hi!

Whirlwinds

Lucy: Isn't it mad that I'm in Germany? You couldn't write it! How am I supposed to quieten my mind when all this is going on?! And how hilarious and bizarre about the pope!

Kate: In my head I'm going, 'screw you pope'. Is that wrong?

Lucy: I liked that comment, then immediately unliked it again. I went to a convent school.

Lucy: How are you all doing?

Kate: A bit knackered.

Lucy: I bet! But it's so inspiring to see how you've been handling everything and supporting each other. It's weird for me being here, but I can see you've got everything beautifully womaned.

Kate: We make a bloody good team, don't we?

Despite the fact that we lived in different homes in different parts of the country, in city flats and crumbling country cottages, and in terraced houses with trampolines in the back gardens, we all woke up to similar situations on the morning after our media whirlwind. Dishes were piled up in kitchen sinks, piles of laundry formed small peaks on carpets that needed vacuuming. There was no milk in the fridge, or bread for toast. We all had headaches of varying degrees. And yet we were so excited to see stories about the campaign popping up all over the internet. On the BBC News website, the top stories were: 1. the pope resigning; 2. warnings about snow; 3. concerns over urban foxes; 4. No More Page 3, and 5. Charlie Sheen.

> Max: There we are! Sandwiched between urban foxes and Charlie Sheen.

> Kate: A position I never thought I'd find myself in to be honest.

> Evie: Makes a change from badgers though, doesn't it?

Will had come over that morning, and he had an awkward conversation with Kevin in the living room while I ran around in rubber gloves, cleaning manically. The French journalists, surprised to hear that we didn't have an office, were coming to the flat to interview me and I didn't want them to see the used teabags sitting on the draining board, or the weird brown stains that dripped down the wall behind the pedal bin. I didn't bother asking Will and Kevin to help, because I knew they'd whine so much it would make my headache worse, so I just gave them strict instructions not to come anywhere near the kitchen while the interview was taking place.

'I mean it,' I said. 'They'll be here in a minute. Don't go

past the hall, don't listen to what I'm saying. Maybe play some music? But not *The Lion King* soundtrack, or better still, just talk. But don't make your voices too loud. Just be normal. And don't put *The Simpsons* on. Just relax.'

They looked at me and blinked slowly.

'Well, talk then,' I said. 'BE NORMAL!'

At nine on the dot, two exquisitely turned-out French women arrived on my doorstep and I invited them up to the sparkling kitchen. I offered them a drink and they asked for milky tea, which was a surprise, as they looked like they should be drinking champagne or Perrier or something else classy and bubbly. I didn't offer them a biscuit because I only had Penguin bars, and I just couldn't imagine a French woman in such a lovely blouse eating a Penguin.

The interview was fine; they nodded at almost everything I said and only frowned once or twice, which was probably due to my confusing Rotherham accent. They were very supportive of the campaign and had already signed the petition. They kept saying they just couldn't believe that Page 3 was 'a thing'.

I was pleased with how it had gone but, just as they got up to leave, I noticed one of the women staring at something over my shoulder, and I realised I'd left a pair of pants drying on the radiator. They must have been through the wash five hundred times and the elastic had given up a long time ago. They politely looked away and left the room, and I closed the door behind them and burned with shame.

Later that afternoon, after Will had gone home, I went to collect Livia from school. For the first time ever, she asked *me* to slow down. I had so much adrenaline. When I got to her house, I wished I hadn't rushed; Natasha had left a note, asking me to make pancakes for tea. Not the type I had as a kid with sugar and a squeeze of Jif lemon; Livia had hers with sliced avocado and smoked salmon. It was a disaster. Every pancake ended up looking like an old lace doily: thin, slightly grey and full of holes. It brought back memories of the deep unhappiness at home every Shrove Tuesday, when my mum faced this exact stress. 'For every one that works out, I have to throw five away,' she'd say, wiping sweat angrily from her forehead. I was so tired and demoralised by the time Natasha came home that I almost burst into tears. She looked at me pityingly in that way she often did, as if I was a guinea pig abandoned by its mother, and picked up a bit of pancake from the edge of Livia's plate. She ate it, as if in solidarity. This would have pushed me over the edge if she hadn't pulled a face and coughed after swallowing it.

I trudged back to the flat and caught up on all the missed messages in HQ. The mood had changed and everyone was tired and angry. Murdoch had tweeted again:

> @rupertmurdoch: So page 3 tweet is breaking
> news . . . Typical OTT reaction by the UK PC crew.
> Just considering as we do every page daily Buy it
> and see . . .

> Jess: The women who wrote to us saying they
> had Page 3 mentioned to them while they were
> being raped or sexually assaulted – are they
> being OTT then?

Whirlwinds

Kate: I have a nose bleed. He has literally made my nose bleed.

Max: Did you see Michael Waldon on the news? He thinks Murdoch had no intention of getting rid of Page 3. And he talked about badgers and FGM again – two things you so rarely hear mentioned together in a sentence.

Jess: Murdoch is just fucking with us. He's doing it all for publicity.

Me: I'm so, so tired.

Lucy: My lovelies, I've gone for a walk to get mobile reception and to catch up on everything. I know you're angry and frustrated and knackered and rightly so, but you're doing an amazing job and I'm so proud of you all.

Lucy: I've been thinking back to how exhausted I felt when I emailed you all a couple of weeks ago about starting a team. The replies you sent were so beautiful and now we have this glorious, powerful, fun, supportive, inspiring space we've created. Anyway, my eyes are wet and I just wanted to say thank you.

Lucy: But please take care of yourselves. Social media is addictive and draining and your

wellbeing is the most important thing. Take
breaks. Step away if it gets too much.

Max: Yeah, it's been a bit much TBH.

Max: But this is hands-down one of the most
exciting things I've ever done.

Kate: I love you all, even without the influence of
wine (on my second glass)

Jess: I love you guys! (still on my first glass)

Evie: Sending a HQ group hug

It was a full-on love-in.

I had friends I'd known for fifteen years and I'd never told them I love them. I come from a family who think that sitting next to one another on a settee is overly sentimental. And yet I was starting to feel like Lucy, Max, Kate, Evie and Jess were more than just people I talked to on the internet. They were beginning to feel like friends.

Roots

There was a moment one evening, around 7.30 or 8, when most of us were online at the same time. Work was done for the day, toddlers were in bed, older kids were up in their rooms, pretending to do homework. Lucy was still away, so we were all covering social media in our turns, but Twitter and Facebook were quiet. There were no emails to respond to or calls to make, and even the trolls were silent for a while.

Kate: Now we've got a minute can I talk to you all for a sec?

Evie: Of course, we're here.

Max: Go for it!

Kate: I've been feeling a bit confused and conflicted lately about my body and Page 3 and where I stand with it all.

Kate: I'll try to keep it short and to the point, but

I don't really do short and to the point so I might wang on a bit

Kate: So when I was a teenager, I was really aware of what my body was supposed to look like. I got really clear messages. I knew that being sexy was important. I knew that the way my breasts looked was important. My dad used to put Page 3 pictures of Linda Lusardi on the wall at home and my mum really bloody hated it. I think it made her feel really bad about herself. She had a boob job after they divorced. And then later on I had one as well.

Kate: At the time it felt like the only option. I'd had two kids and I started to feel really bad about my breasts. I bloody loved them when I was breastfeeding, but my kids fed for a LOOOONNNNGGG time and bled the poor buggers dry. I wore constant scaffolding bras full of gel and I always kept my bra on during sex. I felt so bad about myself that I cashed in a policy I had maturing and spent it all on the boob job. I suppose I had learned that to be sexy you had to have the right kind of breasts and I'd hung a lot of my identity on being sexy.

Kate: I used to do pole dancing classes. I got so good I even started teaching them myself.

Kate: I feel conflicted about it all now. Part

of me feels a bit hypocritical – like what self-respecting feminist would have fake tits? Like I'm part of the problem. I feel like I'm supposed to say, 'This is what I did before I had this big feminist awakening and now I regret it', but I don't. And I've been worried about what you'd think of me if I told you.

Jess: Babe, we love you! We'd never judge you or think badly of you

Evie: Oh darling, you received the same message we all received – that women have to be sexy, that our bodies have to look a certain way to be acceptable. We are given such clear examples every day of how we should look. You were just sticking to the rules.

Max: And besides, it's totally up to you what you do with your own body. It's nobody else's fucking business.

Jess: I had Botox. My hairdresser talked me into it. I don't know how I feel about it. I think I'm still messed up about my body, like if I skip a meal, I'm pleased with myself.

Jess: You know as a teenager I used to look at Page 3 and make myself sick. I would literally hold it and look at it whilst making myself throw up. People always think it's fashion magazines that girls use for 'thinspiration' or whatever, but I never saw *Vogue* or *Cosmopolitan*, all I saw was *The Sun* every day. Page 3 was the only place I ever saw a naked female body and I thought, 'that's what I'm supposed to look like'. And yeah, they all had massive boobs, but they were also thin with tiny waists and then sometimes they'd print the models' 'vital statistics' so they literally gave me a formula – exact measurements of what shape my body should be. I hate those words 'vital statistics'. Like the size of a woman's body is the most important thing – the most VITAL thing.

Max: I was always called a tomboy at school – I wore boys' clothes and all my friends were boys. I just rejected anything that I considered feminine. I sort of looked down on it, but at the same time I knew I could never live up to what was expected of me as a girl. The local pub had strippers perform every Friday lunchtime FFS – and Benny Hill was on telly chasing after models in bikinis and Page 3 was everywhere. It was NOT a great time to be a teenage girl.

Max: But as I got older, a big part of me wanted to be accepted. Wanted men to like me. And

Roots

when I was seventeen this guy approached me in town and said he worked for *The Sun* and offered me £50 to take topless photos. I don't know if he really worked for *The Sun* or not, but he gave me his card and I took it home and just sat looking at it for ages. And I couldn't stop thinking, *he thinks I'm good enough*. He must think I'm pretty. He must think I'm sexy. It's like he could tell how insecure I was and he knew exactly what to say.

Kate: Did you do it? Did he take the photos?

Max: I thought about it. I nearly phoned him so many times, but I didn't in the end. I was too scared.

Me: A friend of mine had a similar thing happen to her. She was approached by a photographer when she was out shopping. She was only 16. He told her she was beautiful and made her feel good about herself and he kept following her around and phoning her at home. In the end, she agreed to pose for topless pictures and they were published in this seedy little porn magazine. She's been worried for nearly 20 years that they'll surface somewhere. She's never told her husband about it.

Killjoy

Kate: The more people I talk to the more I realise just how many of us have a story about how Page 3 has negatively impacted our lives in some way

Evie: For me it was when I was breastfeeding Milly. We'd be out somewhere, and so many places wouldn't let me feed her. I remember one day sitting in this cafe and I was getting disapproving looks for trying to feed her, and they had *The Sun* right there on the counter. People could have a coffee and stare at Page 3 without anyone judging them, because they were looking at these idealised, sexualised breasts, but I was judged for feeding my daughter. It made me so angry.

Jess: Oh god the same happened to me

Jess: It's interesting how we all grew up seeing Page 3 and topless calendars and shit everywhere, but there are still these moments that just stand out where it suddenly hit us like HANG ON this is just not OK.

Me: I can remember a moment like that so clearly. I was 16 and trying to find my first proper job, and I went to the Job Centre and there were all these ads for 'dancers at a gentlemen's club' and 'female bar staff who must be comfortable with nudity' and 'ladies who love to chat, who are confident, outgoing and unphased by adult conversations'.

Me: There were also a couple of cleaning jobs and a role at a nursing home and that was it. They were the jobs for women: you could clean, you could care or you could take your clothes off.

Max: God that's grim

Me: It really was, because girls like me weren't taught that we had a wide variety of options.

There were barely any jobs and everybody was desperate for money. And newspapers showed us half-naked teenagers and said: 'This is what girls like you can do.' The Job Centre showed us adverts that said: 'These are jobs for girls like you.'

Me: The message was: your body is the most profitable thing you have, but you have to sell it in order to survive.

What I didn't say in HQ is that we were the lucky ones, those of us who believed our bodies were ours to sell. Plenty of girls in Rotherham had no ownership of their bodies at all. More than 1,500 girls were abused and raped by gangs of men in my hometown and newspapers called it a sex scandal, then a grooming scandal, then a race scandal. People talked of shock and outrage, of monstrous abuse kept under wraps by the authorities, but none of it was a secret. Not only had the victims repeatedly told the police, but everybody saw what was happening. Walk past a taxi rank and you'd see very young girls sitting in cars with men older than their fathers. Adult men would pick up their 'girlfriends' at the school gates at three in the afternoon, in front of teachers, parents, passers-by. In the bus station, security guards would wrap their arms around twelve- or thirteen-year-olds, picking them up, pulling them onto their laps, in front of everyone, on CCTV. It was in plain sight. You saw men of colour with white girls. You saw white men with white girls. Of course, the victims weren't all white, it was just the white girls who were seen.

The authorities did nothing, because the girls were the 'wrong kind' of victims; poor, working class, often from broken homes. Many of them had also committed the crime of crossing the racial divide. People in my town were racist, but no one spoke about race. We weren't taught about racism at school, or misogyny, or consent, or abuse. Everything we knew came from what we saw around us.

Newspapers counted down the days until a child turned sixteen and could be photographed naked. Cover stories showed upskirt pictures, or topless images of women on holiday, taken with zoom lenses by men hiding in bushes. Child rape victims were described in articles as 'Lolitas'.

This was the mainstream culture, the tape that played in the background as the abuse in Rotherham, and so many other towns, happened over and over again.

Was this culture directly responsible? Probably not. But combine that culture with extreme poverty, vulnerable children, a corrupt police force, criminal gangs, segregation between communities and boiling racial tensions – and you have a perfect climate for the grooming and abuse of girls on a mass scale.

The English Defence League held protests in the town centre after the news became public. I'd trawl through Facebook photos of white men with bared teeth and steel-toed boots kicking each other and smashing bottles on the pavement, and I'd think, *Are you really pretending you're doing this to protect girls from violent men?* While people argued about the ethnicity of the perpetrators, the victims – girls who had been ignored and overlooked for so long – were ignored and overlooked all over again.

'You still see it,' a friend who lives in Rotherham told me recently. 'Walk through town on any weeknight and you still see it – young girls hanging round taxi ranks, takeaways, the bus station. It's still going on. People pretend to care, but they don't.'

I didn't say all this in HQ, because I was only just beginning to examine my own feelings and experiences, realising how damaging cultural beliefs could be, how deep the roots could go, and how important the media is in how we see ourselves and each other.

Guarantees

The supportive friendships we had built in HQ carried us through the following weeks. After the excitement of the media interest died down, we faced an onslaught of garbage. Crap was thrown at us from every angle for the next two weeks.

First came Valentine's Day, an occasion that, thanks to my absolute inability to stomach sentimentality, extravagant displays of affection or heart-shaped balloons, I always find wincingly awful, but 2013's was especially unpleasant thanks to *The Sun*'s coverage of Reeva Steenkamp's murder.

I saw the front page as I was walking Livia to school. It showed a full-size photograph of a woman posing in swimwear, suggestively pulling down the front of her bikini top. The headline read:

**3 SHOTS. SCREAMS. SILENCE. 3 MORE SHOTS.
BLADE RUNNER PISTORIUS 'MURDERS LOVER'**

I felt a pain in my head when I saw it, and hurried past the shop with Livia, chattering away about the upcoming Roman-themed assembly. Normally, this kind of conversation would have induced anxiety about potential Colosseum papier-mâché projects, but not that day. I couldn't get that headline out of my mind.

The Sun had purposely sourced a 'sexy' photograph of a murdered woman, a victim of domestic violence, to sell news-papers. Just like Page 3, she was there to titillate, to excite, to arouse, except, unlike the models on Page 3, she was dead. The headline didn't even name her.

I learned Reeva's name in HQ.

Max: #hernamewasreeva is trending on Twitter. People are very, very angry. One woman has set up a petition calling for an apology

Jess: I feel physically sick. I can't believe they've done this.

Kate: There's no Page 3 today

Me: I suppose they didn't need it. Reeva Steenkamp replaced it for free.

Jess: Is Reeva a glamorous fashionista then? Is this how they plan to replace Page 3?

Kate: Have you seen all the messages in our inbox? Look at this:

'since a bikini picture of a domestic violence murder victim is deemed a suitable replacement

for Page 3 today, shall we suggest to Dominic
Mohan that he makes a regular feature out of
the two women killed through domestic violence
by their current or ex-partners every week in the
UK? It will save him money on photographers
and models and we could give it a catchy name
like . . . Readers' Wives' Corpses perhaps?'

Max: Someone just DM'd: 'I can't believe they've
gone for the *look at the tits on this dead woman*
angle.'

Evie: And Michael Waldon has tweeted, saying
the storm over the Reeva reporting is totally fake
and the complaints are from the usual suspects
who never read the paper anyway. He said *The
Sun* was justified in using that photo because
the victim was a model. 'If it was Michael
Phelps, he'd be in his swim gear.'

Me: If Michael Phelps had just been brutally
murdered by his partner, *The Sun* would not
print a photo of him oiled up on a beach,
seductively pulling down his swimming trunks,
and refer to him as his girlfriend's 'lover'. They
would never, ever do that.

Max: Did you see Marina Hyde's article in *The
Guardian*? She used to work for *The Sun* and

describes a specific editorial meeting, where
a man from the circulation department gave a
presentation on how to maximise sales. Hang
on, let me get the quote.

'If you put a picture of Caprice on page 1 – and
any old stock one was fine as long as she had
very little on – you could guarantee a 30,000
uplift in sales. Nell McAndrew would get you
20,000. Geri Halliwell would do 10,000. They had
maths for it and everything.'

Jess: I'm sorry guys but this is just really
affecting me. I'm so angry and so sad. Nothing's
going to change, is it? Nothing is going to ever
fucking change. Women, dead or alive, are just
a collection of body parts to them. Not even
worthy of a name.

There was increasing evidence, from sources including the UN, that the sexualisation of women in the media had a broader impact on societal attitudes towards women and girls. Just three months earlier, in November 2012, the End Violence Against Women Coalition, Eaves, Equality Now and OBJECT presented evidence to the Leveson Inquiry, showing how the reporting of violence against women and girls was frequently glamorised and eroticised by the press. Terrifyingly, Alison Saunders, Chief Crown Prosecutor for London, insisted that the treatment of women in the media has an impact on the justice system and jurors' attitudes.

But editors weren't listening, and it felt like the situation was getting worse and worse.

Page 3 was absent from *The Sun* again a few days after the Reeva headline. Rumours circulated that Page 3 would be removed from the paper one day a week, to monitor the effect on sales. Trolls bombarded us with threats and furious messages and we all hopped on and off social media, covering for each other when it got too much. The mood in HQ oscillated between despair, rage, anxiety and unexpected laughter.

Me: Page 3's absent again

Me: Replaced with photos of a woman in a bikini on a beach. This is the headline:

RUSSIAN MODEL BASKS IN THE SUN AS SHE CUPS HER BUM AND SIZZLES

Evie: Basking? Sizzling? Is she a lizard?

Lucy: Or a sausage?

Jess: If this is how they plan to replace Page 3 I hate it.

Jess: I really fucking hate it.

Guarantees

Kate: Hang on, CUPS HER BUM?

Me: I didn't even know it was possible to cup
your bum?

Kate: Well I suppose it depends on the size of
your arse. And hands.

Jess: I've just spat my tea out

Jess: I love you guys

Jess: Just when I've reached the depths of
despair you pull out 'cups her bum' and now
I've lost it

But the mood oscillated quickly back to anxiety when we
discovered, later that day, that a rival petition had been set up,
asking *The Sun* to keep Page 3.

Max: The Page 3 models set it up. Here's a link:

Keep Page 3!

The Page 3 girls are arguing against the petition on
the internet, asking for the ban of topless models
within *The Sun* newspaper.

A lot of people think it's demoralizing for women,
whereas it is actually our chosen career path. There
are many people that stand to lose jobs if Page 3 is

discontinued. We do not believe this is demoralizing for us or for women. It is our choice to take this path in life. *The Sun*'s Page 3 has been the turning point in many of our careers.

We bring a smile to millions of people's faces every day. We boost morale among the troops. Not forgetting we raise A LOT of money for charity together as Page 3 girls of *The Sun* newspaper.

Evie: Why is it a woman's job to take her clothes off to make men smile?

Me: And why does *The Sun* think that women have to be topless to raise money for charity? Can't people of any gender fundraise, whilst wearing a coat or a cardigan?

Max: Coatigans are a thing now apparently. They're all over the Boden catalogue FFS.

Evie: We don't want a ban!!!

Kate: The job thing though. I've thought about this loads. Oh god this is so bloody hard. I don't want to put women out of a job.

Max: But *The Sun* will put them out of a job soon anyway. They all disappear as soon as they get 'too old' – probably when they hit 25 or thereabouts. Besides, *The Sun* has shitloads of money. They could even keep Page 3 as a brand. Create a separate top-shelf magazine filled with soft porn with no news to get in the way

Jess: They'd never do that. Remember David Sullivan – the owner of the *Daily Star* – saying he'd calculated there was more money to be made by putting porn into newspapers than via porn mags?

Lucy: I am totally with you all, but it's only fair the models have their say. We've got our petition, we've got to respect theirs.

Max: But SRSLY have you seen the supporters' reasons for signing their petition? I mean, look at this:

I signed because:

'I like page 3 and this is not a Muslim country.'

'At the end of the day all these anti-Page 3 protests are just women moaning because they're reminded that they gained weight with age.'

Killjoy

'The only people who probably have a problem
with page 3 are the people who protest against us
having the English flag outside our houses! They're
also probably a mess, don't take care of their
appearance and don't get any attention off males.'

'I say if some 22-year-old bimbo from essex doesn't
have enough intelligence to get a normal job let
her get her rack out, its your taxes that go up when
they all sign on'

'Wanking material.'

Me: Wow, how supportive these Page 3 fans are
of the models.

Kate: Wanking material. That says it all really,
doesn't it?

Lucy: Someone has just tweeted that the cover
of tomorrow's *Daily Star* will say 'Page 3 girl
guaranteed every day'.

Lucy: They're clearly hoping to lure readers away
from *The Sun*

Jess: Are you kidding me? They're offering a
GUARANTEE

Guarantees

Me: Like you'd get for a new toaster or a posh
mattress?

I was so tired I felt hollow inside. On my way to pick up Livia,
I was so distracted that I forgot to walk the long way around,
and didn't realise I was about to walk past the builders until it
was too late. One of them, from his position on the scaffolding
high above my head, stared down. I could feel him watching
me. As I looked up, he smirked, ran his eyes down my body
and opened his mouth to say something.

'Don't,' I said.

I saw his expression change. 'What the fuck's wrong with
you?' he shouted.

'Don't,' I said again. That was all I said.

I carried on walking as he shouted after me, 'Like I'm going
to waste my breath on you, you fucking ugly bitch.'

A few months ago, I would have gone home, sat alone in
my room, closed the curtains and cried. But now I had HQ.

Evie: Find out the name of the construction firm
and I'll report him

Evie: Not having anyone talk like that to our Jo.

Max: I was just typing the same thing – tell us
what the company is – if you want to. But if that
would cause any stress then you don't have to
obvs

Killjoy

Kate: I was on a run earlier and a man randomly shouted 'tits' at me, so I just shouted 'BOLLOCKS, COCK, ARSE' as if it was a word-association game

Jess: A man in a car the other day slowed down beside me, wound his window down and just looked at me nodding and said 'heyyyyy, wanna come for a ride?' Like I was going to throw myself at the car screaming, 'Oh god, YES, let me get in!'

Instead of crying, I hugged a pillow to my chest and laughed and felt seen and understood and safe.

Sunfragettes

'Do you think they'd prefer cheese ploughman's or tuna mayonnaise?' my mum asked, as she pinned the sash to my ruffled Edwardian blouse. My hat kept falling off whenever I moved my head.

'Hold still, I'm going to move this hat pin.'

'I think cheese ploughman's is better,' I said, keeping my head perfectly still and talking out of the side of my mouth like a ventriloquist. 'I'm not sure if any of them are vegetarian.'

I was sitting on a dining chair in my parent's living room, dressed as a suffragette. My brother, who has an artistic flair and a steady hand, had been roped in to making a No More Page 3 sash, my mum had found an old lacy blouse at a jumble sale, and Nessa had attended to my millinery requirements.

'You need a suffragette hat?' she'd said, without asking why. 'Let me have a look in the wardrobe in the back bedroom.' And she'd reappeared with a perfect Edwardian concoction trimmed with silk ribbon. My family had got used to me talking about the campaign, and my mum had started to enjoy hearing stories about what my teammates and I were up to.

In HQ, we'd spent weeks discussing Murdoch's tweets, answering journalists' questions and responding to sexist reporting. What did we think about Murdoch's idea of glamorous fashionistas? How did we feel about the Reeva Steenkamp coverage? Could we respond to the Keep Page 3 petition? It was all other people doing things, and us reacting to it. We thought that maybe it was time to take action ourselves.

'They're never going to just drop Page 3 out of the goodness of their hearts,' Kate said. 'It's all about money. We need to hit 'em where it hurts.'

We made a list of all the companies who paid to advertise in *The Sun*, in the hope of convincing them to stop paying vast amounts of money for promotional pieces while Page 3 was still present in the paper. Lucy had contacted a number of advertisers the previous year before HQ was formed, and most companies were completely disinterested. But as we scanned the list of advertisers, we paused at Co-op.

The present-day Co-op supermarket was born of the co-operative movement, founded by the Rochdale Pioneers; a working-class group who aimed to initiate a fairer way of living for their community. They created a member-owned organisation to provide local people with quality, affordable food and goods during the austerity of the 1840s. Impressively, the Co-operative Women's Guild campaigned for the rights of working women, including the right to vote, maternity rights, financial support and access to contraception.

From their small shop in Rochdale, the organisation grew its membership and their model became a blueprint for co-operatives across the UK and the world. That original shop is now a museum dedicated to preserving the story of the Rochdale Pioneers.

> Kate: This is what the museum's website says: 'The cooperative movement stands not just for solidarity, but action for positive change.'

> Kate: It also says that the museum is a source of inspiration for people who want to be part of that positive change.

> Kate: We should arrange a protest. Outside that museum.

> Lucy: oh god I'm traumatised by protests.

> Lucy: I'll go along with the majority on this, but I'm scarred from the previous ones where no one turned up.

> Kate: I'm off work next Friday?

> Max: I'll have to be in the office, but I can cover Twitter and Facebook during breaks

> Evie: Sounds good but I'm pretty skint at the moment – let me check train prices

> Me: I'll come, as long as it doesn't cost too much

Evie: Ok the cheapest ticket to Rochdale is £85

Me: £85?!

Jess: Matt works Fridays so I'd have to work out childcare

Lucy: I'm broke too at the moment. I'm going to have to do some more waitressing.

Kate: We'll work something out. But it's bloody annoying that we can never afford to do anything.

After several hours, we came up with a plan: Kate would visit her mother in Ashbourne that weekend and could give us a lift from there. Lucy and Evie would get the (much cheaper) train to Derby and hop in the car and Kate would pick me up en route at a retail park near Rotherham. Jess would drive over from Shropshire, dropping Ruby off with Matt's sister on the way, and would meet us outside the museum.

Kate had suggested we dress as 'sunfragettes' – part suffragette, in acknowledgement of the role the cooperative movement played in supporting women's right to vote, and part No More Page 3, in reference to the ongoing fight for equality. Evie was in favour, which seemed appropriate because of her anachronistic face, and I am almost always up for fancy dress, but Jess didn't seem into it.

'I might just wear jeans and a campaign T-shirt,' she said.

I wasn't surprised. You never see people who look like Jess dressed as a panda or a Tudor or Father Christmas, and if on the rare occasion they do dress up, it's always something minimalist and ironic.

We set the date, contacted the museum and invited supporters to join us. It would be the first proper action we'd taken as a team.

I was nervous about meeting Kate, Evie and Jess. What if we didn't get on in person? And I was also nervous about the car journey. I'm an excellent passenger if travelling in the front with the seat pushed all the way back, with wide-open windows, on straight, newly tarmacked roads at a speed of approximately twenty-six miles per hour. But I had a feeling that none of those conditions would be met and I was increasingly nervous about the fate of the picnic my mum was insisting I take for the journey.

My dad reluctantly agreed to drop me off at the retail park where Kate was picking me up. I was keen to get going and stood by the door with my coat on, but he spent twenty-five minutes doing the *Daily Mail* crossword on the toilet, then he had to de-ice the windscreen and check the oil. Still, we somehow managed to arrive before the others, so I sat in the car outside Halfords in full Edwardian dress with twenty sandwiches on my knee.

When Kate finally arrived, I kissed my dad on the cheek and nervously, excitedly, hopped out of the car. He watched as I scampered towards a Volvo full of laughing suffragettes and then he started the engine and drove off with an alarmed look on his face. Kate jumped out of the car and we flapped towards each other like disturbed crows. She was taller than I thought she'd be; her legs finished somewhere around my waist and, as we hugged, I felt like a Sylvanian Families mouse being embraced by a Barbie doll. Lucy was in the front, struggling with her seatbelt, so I hugged her awkwardly through the open door and tried to be mature and act like a grown-up when I realised I'd have to sit in the back. I squeezed in, next to Evie, with her ringlets and perfect posture, and she smiled shyly.

'Sorry, is all this stuff in the way?' She gathered up a pile of scarves and coats, eyeing up my enormous carrier bag.

'I've got twenty cheese sandwiches in here,' I said. 'My mum made them, in case anyone was hungry. And there's crisps and bananas.' I peered inside the bag. 'And KitKats and a wheel of shortbread. And some apples. And a massive bar of Whole Nut.'

'Oh, bless her,' Lucy said from the front seat. 'I'm starving, can I have a sandwich?'

We set off towards the M1 and I clutched the back of Lucy's seat, thinking if I vomit in Kate's car then that's the end of this whole thing. I'd never be able to speak to any of them ever again. I tried to be normal and attempted a back-seat conversation, but the engine was noisy and drowned out what Evie was saying. Evie has a soft, low voice and she speaks quietly, so every now and then I completely misheard what she said. It felt rude to ask her to repeat herself, and I feared I wouldn't hear her the second time either, so I just accepted the confusion – like, did she just say something about a goat or was she talking about her coat? My suffragette hat only exacerbated the problem, flattening my hair over my ears and muffling all sound. The fight for women's rights must have been much more of a struggle than we can imagine, what with the clipperty-clopperty shoes, the long skirts that trip you up and the hats that render you deaf. 'You have a goat, Emmeline? Something about your coat? Ahh, you want the VOTE!'

I had turned grey by the time we arrived in Rochdale and was desperate to get out of the car, but instead of taking us to the Pioneers Museum, the GPS directed us to Lidl over and over again. We'd leave the car park and the GPS would recalibrate, take us down a cul-de-sac, around a roundabout and back to Lidl. We eventually gave up, parked the car on a side street and asked a bewildered man in an underpass for directions to the museum. We were nearly an hour late. Jess was waiting for us outside.

Of course, she wasn't in fancy dress; she was wearing skinny jeans, a cropped campaign T-shirt and a denim jacket with little fur cuffs. As I got closer, I thought she looked pale and drawn.

'I'm so sorry we're late,' Lucy said, 'have you been here ages?'

'A while,' she said, in her husky cartoon-rabbit voice. 'I want to hug you all, but I've got this horrible cold and I don't want to pass it on.' We attempted to hug anyway, but at an awkward distance, in the way that you'd hug a child covered in jam. Jess said she could only stay for another half-hour, because she had to get back for Ruby. Close up, she really looked like she was suffering. She should have been in bed. She reminded me of the whippet I'd seen tied up outside the petrol station that morning, all eyes and bones and trembles. I felt the same way about Jess as I did about the whippet. I wanted to give her a big hug, a fleece-lined jacket and a sausage roll.

A few supporters turned up, and a very enthusiastic man showed us around the museum, then we went outside and marched about, looking cross and trying not to let our signs blow away. Jess said she had to go, and as I watched her walk away I thought how small she seemed, and that her shoulders drooped. Kate was more or less how I'd imagined her to be, Evie was exactly how I'd pictured her, but Jess was different. Less confident, less shiny and more vulnerable.

I hung back with Evie when the photographer started snapping away, but Kate strode right to the front, posing with her fist in the air.

'Wow, you're good,' I said, partially hiding myself behind a museum sign.

'Am-dram!' Kate shouted back to me. 'I'm used to dressing up and being daft.'

I noticed that Kate naturally took charge of things – not in a domineering way – but she just clearly liked getting stuff done. If there was a thirty-second lull, she'd say, 'Right, what's next then, do we need to speak to this person, do we have a photo of this, have these people signed the petition, are the signs clear enough from this angle?'

As the protest came to an end, and we were packing up our things, we discussed what we'd do next. Supporters had already been contacting their local Co-ops, and Lucy had set up a meeting at their headquarters in Manchester to discuss their advertising strategy. If we got nowhere with that, perhaps we'd try a different company.

'There's a pub across the road,' Lucy said. 'We could just pop in, have a quick drink and carry on the conversation there?'

All sentiments about the North being friendly are shattered to pieces when you walk into a local boozer dressed as Emily Wilding Davison with a No More Page 3 banner. The pub was busy and people turned and stared as we entered. The frosty reception only became frostier when Lucy answered questions from men at the bar about what we'd been doing.

'Page 3? What's wrong with Page 3?' one of them asked and, as Lucy started explaining our stance on it all, I went to order drinks. That's when I realised I had no idea what any of them would order in a pub. I knew how Lucy felt after watching internet porn, how Evie felt about her body after having children and how Kate rebuilt herself after her divorce. I knew about their childhood fears and the anxieties that woke them up in the night, and yet I didn't know where they went for summer holidays, the toppings they'd have on their pizzas or if they'd rather have lager or wine.

I bought some beers and took them to the table.

'Is this OK?' I asked.

'Of course, you absolute sweetheart!' Lucy said.

We picked up our drinks, clinked glasses and started talking.

Building Blocks

Once, during a conversation with Jess (the topic of which is long forgotten), I said the words, 'It just sort of happened organically,' and she burst out laughing and said, 'Oh my god, you're *such* a wanker.'

But what came next for No More Page 3 really did happen organically. Lucy's meeting with Co-op didn't go anywhere and we felt deflated for a while, until Kate said, 'OK, so that went tits up, what's next?'

What happened next was *The Sun* launched a big bells-and-whistles promotion with Lego. It was plastered over the front page of the paper: 'collect tokens' for free toys.

Max: What a beautiful way to combine children's activities and soft porn, all in one conveniently accessible place.

Evie: This is so disappointing! I love Lego

Kate: It gives me palpitations just thinking about it. The hours I spent picking up Lego pieces

when the kids were little and you'd always miss
one and stand on it, and it would always be one
of those sodding roof bits that are extra pointy. I
can still remember the agony.

Me: Livia loves Lego. Her friend Ling gets the
girly kits to make poodle parlours and stuff, but
Livia will only play with the boys' ones.

Max: I don't have kids so a lot of this stuff
passes me by – but can someone please explain
to me how you can assign gender to bricks?

Lucy told us that a supporter had been in touch, who had
started a petition, asking Lego to stop partnering with *The Sun*
until they drop the topless images. My eyes glazed over when
I saw this. Hypocritical, yes, but I was getting really sick of
petitions. I could see their usefulness – a petition sets a clear
goal that a campaign can be built on – after all, our campaign
was built around a petition. But it felt like everybody and their
grandmother had a petition going about something, and I was
tired of seeing emails about them stack up in my inbox. You
could lose entire afternoons to fracking, chimpanzees, listed
buildings and sewage. You couldn't sign one without signing
the next one, and the next, because the issues were all so
important. But I had petition fatigue. I just wanted a day to
pass without having to sign something.

Kate: So are we sharing her petition? The Lego
one I mean.

Lucy: He. His petition.

Kate: A man?

Me: Really?

Lucy: Yes, he's called Steve. His sons were
pestering him to buy *The Sun* for the free Lego
and he's really angry about it. He hates the way
they're trying to appeal to kids.

I googled the petition and read the blurb. Steve wrote that he grew up with Lego and loved building models with his own kids. He'd always believed it was a brand with really positive values that supported children's development and learning, so he was horrified that Lego were advertising their toys 'just millimetres away from an image that is famous for being one of the most sexist institutions of our time – Page 3 of *The Sun* newspaper.'

I was surprised and ever so slightly suspicious. We often received messages from men, saying they supported the campaign, and quite a few of my male friends had signed our petition. But I hadn't yet come across a man who cared enough to start a petition of his own.

Lucy: I think we should meet him. He's based in
London

Kate: Oh balls, London is miles away

Building Blocks

Jess: I doubt I could come this time – it costs
loads to get to London

Evie: I'm struggling with childcare at the
moment, but I'll try my best

Me: I can come!

We planned to meet Steve to take photos for the campaign. We'd post them on social media and link them to the Lego petition in the hope that the press might pick up on the story. We wanted a strong image. We thought Legoland might be the place, but we didn't want to cause a scene in front of loads of kids having a day out. There's nothing worse than people protesting about something and making you feel bad on your day off, when you've saved up to go somewhere exciting and just want a laugh on a log flume. I remembered seeing the anti-abortion protestors in Hyde Park at Christmas and all the parents trying to herd their children away from the awful banners and signs. It was a Saturday, and the crowds were heading to Winter Wonderland for hot chocolate and ice skating. The kids were bundled up in scarves and mittens and had probably looked forward to that day for ages. There they stood, the pro-lifers, with their blood-splattered, nightmare-inducing photos, attempting to protect the lives of unborn children while scarring for life the ones running around in front of them. Lurking about next to them was a solitary man in a parka with his hood pulled up, carrying a sign that read: 'Things will only get worse.' I wanted to shove the lot of them in the Serpentine.

Killjoy

Kate: I've just checked and Legoland is closed midweek during low season. We could just go on a day when it's shut, get some pictures and sod off?

Evie: Will we be able to get anywhere near if it's closed and all locked up?

Lucy: All we need is a sign. A big Lego sign to stand in front of. We could just take a quick picture and leap back in the car.

Me: Speaking of which, does anybody have a car?

Kate: I'm due a lieu day at work. I could get the day off and drive down if everyone could split the cost of petrol?

Lucy: You superstar, that would be amazing!

Lucy: Maybe we could also swing by Lego HQ. It's in Slough. I've been trying to get in touch but they won't respond. Maybe if we go in person someone will speak to us?

The plans, as usual, became complicated. Steve could only slink away from work for an hour, so he wouldn't have time for Legoland. We agreed to meet him outside News

International instead to take some quick photos, then we'd rush off to Legoland to take a few more. Next, we'd head to Lego HQ in Slough, after which Kate would drop us at a train station and she'd 'bugger off back up North'. But Max had a meeting and wouldn't be able make it, Evie couldn't find a babysitter and Jess couldn't afford the train fare so it would just be Lucy, Kate and me. And the mysterious Steve. We posted our plans on social media, in case any supporters wanted to join us, but we didn't hold out much hope – lurking outside a closed theme park then visiting an industrial estate in Slough wasn't the most enticing day-trip itinerary.

There was freezing fog on the morning of the meet-up, and I stood shivering on the pavement outside News International. I saw a movement in the mist and squinted to try and work out what I was seeing. It was definitely Lucy, but she was carrying something the size of a bear. I couldn't work it out. And then the fog suddenly lifted and I could see her walking towards me, with Kate close behind, carrying a giant cardboard woman. It was a cut-out of a Page 3 model made of Lego – 'Leanne, 22, from Legoland' – complete with 'News in Bricks' caption.

'Where on earth did you get that?' I shouted.

'It's brilliant, isn't it? A friend of mine had it made.'

'Only problem is,' Kate said, 'I don't know how we're going to fit it in the bloody car.'

Another woman arrived soon after. Her name was Rhianne, and she had read our post on Facebook and had come along to show her support. I felt for Rhianne. She had clearly been expecting bigger things, not just three women and a cardboard glamour model, but she didn't let the disappointment show. She had a trusting, open face, like a golden retriever or a cherub in a fresco. She looked healthy and bohemian and freckled and there was a distinct *Darling Buds of May* vibe about her.

'Are you coming with us to Legoland?' I asked.

She looked uncertain and hesitated, 'Erm, well, yeah, I mean I could if there's room in the car.'

'It might be a bit . . . cosy,' Kate said, 'but we'll work it out.'

Steve turned up two minutes later. He was wearing dark clothes and a woollen hat and looked like the kind of burglar you'd draw as a child. I'd expected him to be twenty years older, with maroon trousers and reading glasses, but he wasn't like that at all. He looked like someone who would know what to do with a rugby ball or a gas boiler, and I couldn't imagine him crossing his legs when he sat down or doing anything with fennel pollen. I always imagined feminist men would look like Bill Nighy. Steve didn't. He looked like the kind of bloke you wouldn't mess with, but his eyes were sparkly and full of mischief. I thought he'd be equally impressive in a pub quiz, in a fight or at an MOT centre.

'Alright,' he said, shaking hands with each of us in turn. 'I've only got a few minutes, or they'll realise I'm not at work.'

We took pictures of Lucy with Steve and Lego Leanne, then said a rushed goodbye and Steve legged it back to work. The whole thing was over in five minutes.

'He's not what I expected,' I said as we walked to the car.

'He's quite fit,' Kate said. 'Not to objectify a man who's fighting objectification but, I mean, he *is* quite fit.'

Kate had parked in the Waitrose car park, so we rushed into the shop to buy some croissants so she wouldn't get clamped, then we loaded the car. Lego Leanne was so big we could barely fit her in.

'You two get in the back,' Kate said to Rhianne and me, 'and we'll have to wedge her tits above your head and her arse in the boot.'

After lots of huffing and puffing, Kate manoeuvred Leanne so she rested half on my shoulder, half on Rhianne's, with our heads poking up next to her thighs. It was ridiculous, and she was heavier than expected. If Kate braked suddenly, there was a chance she'd fly forwards and decapitate us. Imagine:

PAGE 3 CAMPAIGNERS KILLED BY
TOPLESS LEGO GLAMOUR MODEL

The Sun would have a field day.

Kate wasn't a stressed-out driver, which was lucky, as she had to do all kinds of manoeuvres through the centre of London. She was chatting about campaign things and every now and then would interrupt herself when we whizzed past a landmark or drove down a Monopoly Street: '. . . I mean, come on, in light of the Leveson Inqui— Is that Madame Tussauds? Sherlock Holmes! Baker Street! And what was I saying? Oh yeah, IPSO pays no attention whatsoever.'

So, we arrived at Legoland on a day when it was closed, pulled up in an empty car park and propped up Leanne beneath the giant Lego sign. We counted to five, threw off our coats and tried to look warm in our T-shirts, but I was sure I was doing the constipated expression again. People on the internet talk about having a resting bitch face – a neutral expression that makes them look annoyed or bad-tempered – but my resting face just looks like I've eaten nothing but white bread and Toffos all week and I'm pained just thinking about the consequences.

I was relieved when we piled back into the car and drove to Slough. It started raining as we pulled into a car park filled with potholes and puddles and we were soaked by the time we found the Lego HQ building. We buzzed the intercom and spoke to the receptionist, who told us that no one was available to talk to us. The door was locked and we couldn't get in, so we stood outside on the pavement in the rain.

'Look!' Lucy said. 'Everybody's staring at us from the windows.'

It appeared that every person who worked in that building was watching us from behind the blinds. It was like the Diet Coke advert, but with a topless cardboard woman and four wet feminists instead of a shirtless man.

'Let us in!' Kate shouted, as they gawped silently. 'I've had a fucking day off work for this, I've driven all this sodding way and they won't even speak to us.'

We propped Leanne against the door, slumped against the wet concrete wall and looked at each other pityingly. I sighed loudly. Rhianne kicked a pebble into a puddle and watched it splash. Kate moved a strand of wet hair out of her eyes.

Lucy has a loud, alarming laugh that comes all of a sudden and at once, like when you turn the hot tap on in Nessa's kitchen. She looked at our glum faces and burst out laughing so manically that it set us all off. It was the kind of laughter that you can't seem to stop, the sort you'd get detention for at school.

We looked up and watched as the office workers slowly backed away from the windows.

The next day I received a card from Nessa:

*I HEARD YOU WENT TO LEGOLAND SO I'VE
FOUND YOUR OLD LEGO KITS THEY'RE IN THE
AIRING CUPBOARD IN CASE YOU WANT TO
MAKE ANYTHING YOU USED TO BE GOOD AT
HOUSES BUT BAD AT ROOFS XXX*

Steve joined HQ. We'd had a discussion about it beforehand. Kate said she thought he seemed nice, but worried that having a bloke in HQ might disrupt things a bit.

'I feel like we've got this amazing space where we can share and talk about things and I don't know how it would work with a man here?'

Max had similar doubts but, in the end, we put it to a vote and we all said yes. Lucy had a good feeling about Steve, and she was keen to expand the team.

'The more we expand and let new people in, the less stress and pressure falls on us individually, plus we'd get fresh new perspectives and ideas to drive things forward.'

So Steve appeared in HQ and introduced himself.

Steve: Hello everybody, I'm Lego Steve. I have
2 boys and a Swedish wife, Anna, who doesn't

get Page 3 at all! I like cycling, keep chickens
and work for a clothing company. They're cool,
I'm not.

Steve: I would love to get rid of Page 3 from
The Sun, and also page 4, page 5, 6 thru to 50
and 1 and 2 and/or Murdoch from its ownership.

Steve: Happy to help in any way I can.

Over the next few days it quickly became apparent that Steve was a) good with numbers and b) keen to be of service. He'd pop up unexpectedly with a statistical fact that he'd drop at our feet like a dog with a chew toy. The rest of the time he'd lurk quietly in HQ, like one of those fish that looks like a pebble at the bottom of an aquarium, and we'd forget he was there. If anything, I think he felt more awkward being with us than we did with him. The day after he joined the team, we were talking about 1980s television personalities who allegedly do unsavoury things on glass coffee tables. It was Kate who started it – whenever she's excited about something, she says, 'Shit the bed!' We were talking about Lego to begin with, but it quickly moved from the bed to the coffee table and just took off from there.

Me: It might not be true, it's just what I've heard

Evie: Well there's my childhood smashed to
pieces

Building Blocks

Kate: How does the table not smash to pieces?

Max: OMG having now googled these stories, I have found out that people do something with frozen poo that I never ever ever needed to know about EVER.

Evie: Did you read the bit about the pipe cleaners?

Kate: No. I got as far as prosthetic arseholes and called it a day.

Steve, lurking about like the pebble fish suddenly surfaced.

Steve: OH MY GOD what have I walked into

Evie: hahahaha

Max: #SorrySteve.

Kate: I think that hashtag might get a lot of use.

As soon as the photos of Lucy with Lego Leanne and Steve were posted on social media, the trolls had a field day, and went for him like a pack of wild dogs.

They used homophobic slurs as insults for Steve, with the most quaint and pleasant of trolls calling him a 'pansy' and the rest of us 'jealous lesbians'. It was incredible to me that people still used sexual orientation as an insult, as if any of us would be offended by being called lesbians. It was like being back at school, when Rachel the class bully would tell me my pencil case was gay. I didn't want to be singled out, but I just didn't know what to do to make my pencil case heterosexual. We deleted the trolls' abusive comments, but I secretly filed away Pansy and the Jealous Lesbians as a potential future band name, just in case anyone needed it.

Steve's petition was doing well, with the signature count rising slowly but steadily. But we needed something to happen to give it a big push.

And that something was the Oscars.

I'd never heard of the bloke who hosted that year's ceremony, but the whole thing was a car crash. He appeared to be one of those comedians who are paid to say controversial things to deflect attention away from how naturally unfunny they are. He sang a song called 'We Saw Your Boobs', naming all the actresses in the audience he'd seen topless in a film. It was really creepy, especially when he bragged about seeing naked pictures of Scarlett Johansson after her phone was hacked and the private photos were leaked online. And all this on a night where women's talent was supposedly being celebrated and rewarded.

'"We Saw Your Boobs" . . .' Evie said. 'It could be *The Sun*'s theme tune.'

Of course, *The Sun* was all over it. They printed a double-page spread with the headline:

WE REVEAL NUDE BABES FROM SETH'S
'WE SAW YOUR BOOBS' OSCARS SONG

alongside a series of close-up pictures of the actresses' bare breasts – stills taken from the films they had starred in. Four of the photos of these 'nude babes' were freeze-frames from rape scenes. One picture stood out in particular; the photo of Hilary Swank taken from *Boys Don't Cry* after her character has been severely beaten and raped. The close-up of this 'babe's boobs' showed Swank's breasts covered in scars and bruises. Over the page was the Lego toy promotion.

> Jess: Great. Children's toys and rape scenes over morning coffee.

> Kate: URGH look at the comments on *The Sun*'s website:

> 'I think Kate Winslet should keep her boobs to herself there awful.'

> 'Angelina Jolie was already saggy then and she was very young!'

> 'Kristin Stewart . . . ewwwwwww . . . put them away. They look as flat as her acting.'

We shared all this with our supporters, and hundreds of people posted comments on Lego's Facebook page. Steve's petition hit ten thousand by teatime.

Killjoy

A week later, Lego issued a response, claiming that their promotional arrangement with *The Sun* had come to an end, and acknowledging the company's awareness of 'a significant level of disquiet' as a result of the collaboration. Newspapers interviewed Steve. 'I take it as a victory,' he said.

In HQ we toasted to celebrate. Jess posted a picture of herself with a big glass of red wine, Max had a G&T in a tumbler the size of a goldfish bowl, Steve had a beer, Lucy was off booze and had something that looked like pondwater in a mug, Kate had prosecco and I made a margarita with extra salt.

Jess: Cheers guys!

Evie: Well done Steve

Max: To Lego brick victory!

Me: Bricktory?

Kate: Go on then – to bricktory!

Guides

Lucy and I were cantering down Buckingham Palace Road, trying not to drop everything. We'd been to an event with Lego Leanne and we were carrying her between us, holding an arm each and swinging her off the ground like a toddler.

We were heading to a roundtable discussion at Girlguiding HQ about young women and feminism. It was hosted by the Girlguiding advocates, a group of members aged 16–25, with a number of high-profile journalists and writers present.

Few things alarm me more than the prospect of a roundtable discussion – debating things in a seating arrangement where everybody is inescapably staring at each other? How utterly awful. I think the best time to talk things through is on a countryside ramble, where everyone is so conscious of not tripping over a molehill or standing in a cow pat that the words flow freely, without any intimidating eye contact and with a pheasant here and there for distraction. But this is what people do in offices: they get a big pitcher of water that no one will dare to pick up and plonk it in the middle of a table. Then everyone sits in a circle around it like a campfire, while one person, who relishes these situations, does all the talking. Two hours later, everyone goes home with a headache and absolutely no idea what's just happened.

So, I wasn't thrilled when Lucy asked if I'd go with her, but I realised that it's impossible to say no to her. She's got big, trusting eyes like the cocker spaniel from *Lady and the Tramp*, and I'd hate to disappoint her.

We turned up an hour late and I ended up sitting at the other end of the table to Lucy, pretending to write important notes in a jotter while various journalists said clever things about the glass ceiling. But I started to pay attention when the Girlguiding advocates began to talk about their experiences of sexism and the struggles young women face today.

'Girlguiding really is the ultimate feminist organisation,' one of them said, and I thought how much it must have changed since my sister was a member in the eighties.

'We just sat in the church hall every week with a woman named Wendy, and planned walks we never went on,' she'd told me. 'The most dynamic thing we did was make popcorn, and then it was just the sort you chuck in the microwave.' She would never have bothered with the meetings at all if it wasn't for the glamour of the uniform. But Girlguiding had clearly evolved. Some of the girls I babysat for were members, and they were always off rock climbing and wild swimming and abseiling down a quarry.

The advocates spoke about how No More Page 3 and The Everyday Sexism Project had made them feel less alone and had encouraged them to speak out.

'You can't be what you can't see,' one of them said, 'and here at Girlguiding, we want to see inspirational role models in the media, who raise our aspirations. Images like Page 3 say that looking sexually attractive is the most important thing. It says that women are for sale – they can be bought and then thrown away.'

They were so confident and full of fire. *If* The Sun *wants youth and freshness*, I thought, *then this is where it's at.*

One of the things we were most proud of at No More Page 3 was how the campaign was embraced by young people. We received messages every day from school kids and teenagers telling us how Page 3 affected them. Laura Bates, the founder of The Everyday Sexism Project, received thousands of statements outlining young women's personal experiences, and she forwarded on to us any that mentioned Page 3. One morning, she sent us a schoolgirl's testimony.

> I'm 16 and have been receiving sexist comments
> from older boys since I was about 13, in school and
> out of it. They shout 'rape!' if they're in a group
> walking down the corridor and see a girl, loudly
> rate girls out of 10 while we walk past, look at Page
> 3 and compare girls to it . . . discuss girls' bodies,
> it happens literally every day . . . I never wear
> skirts to school any more as it'd sometimes get
> lifted in the lunch queue . . . how anyone can say
> it's harmless I don't get! Why can't the editor of
> *The Sun* or a lads' mag spend one day in a school
> and see what girls have to put up with in the

culture they help create. I challenge them to do it and still think Page 3 or their mag is harmless.

We thought that teenagers' testimonies were so powerful that we started to save the messages we received from young people to a document. Within a few weeks it was already ten pages long.

> As a 17-year-old girl, I battle with misogynist attitudes every day, between builders wolf-whistling and making me feel uncomfortable on the street to male teachers who feel it's okay to comment on my appearance. This campaign is so important to me.

> I'm 18 years old, because of Page 3 and pornography I feel pressured to have breast implants. I feel helpless and inadequate . . .

> As a 17-year-old girl I want to see female role models with high ambitions and outstanding careers widely reported on, not the size, shape or buoyancy of a girl my age's breasts . . .

> I am 13 and a strong supporter of the No More Page 3 campaign. The issue is very important to me, I want girls to feel confident being who they are, being strong-willed and I want NO MORE PAGE THREE.

I'm 18, and I'm sick of being told to 'get my tits out like this' while being showed a P3 girl, by old men.

All the boys in my class go into the Co-op after school to look at Page 3. It's really embarrassing.

Was told by my father when I said Page 3 made me uncomfortable 'you're just jealous'.

Some teenagers messaged us regularly to talk about issues that affected them, or just to tell us about school, their friends and their lives in general. Others, like Yas, a sixteen-year-old from London, staged their own No More Page 3 protests. So many young people contacted us to share their art, films, essays, poems, photography projects. They kept everything fresh and energised. On the hardest days, it made us feel that the campaign was worth the effort.

After the roundtable meeting, Girlguiding contacted us again. The advocates had run a poll, asking members how they felt about Page 3; 88 per cent said they thought Page 3 should go and, because the advocates were so passionate about the issue, Girlguiding decided to officially support the campaign. We were beside ourselves with excitement.

'We have the Girl Guides! We have the Girl Guides!' I said to Will as soon as I opened the door. I hadn't seen him in nearly three weeks. He'd been visiting family in Devon and in his absence all of my waking hours had been filled with Lego and HQ and suffragette costumes.

'We have the Girl Guides!'

'Are you holding them to ransom?'

'They've voted to support No More Page 3,' I said, standing aside to let him in. 'Girlguiding has half a million members and they're officially supporting us, isn't that amazing?'

'Actually,' he said, 'that's really impressive. There was an article about No More Page 3 in the paper the other day – Louise, the HR person, was reading it at work. I told her my girlfriend's part of the campaign team and she said she'd sign the petition. I sent her the link.'

I made a concerted effort to talk about other things, to not let the campaign take over the evening completely, but every time Will went to the bathroom or to the kitchen to make tea, I'd quickly check in to HQ to see what I was missing. While we were watching TV, I couldn't follow what was happening on screen. I had no idea who any of the characters were, what they were saying to each other, or why it mattered. All the time, I was smiling to myself, thinking, *He shared the petition with a woman at work!* And then, *We have the Girl Guides! We have the Girl Guides!*

Sleepover

Jess was visiting her mum and stepdad in Croydon.

'That's near me,' I said, 'why don't you come and visit me afterwards?'

It happened to be a weekend when Rebecca and Kevin were away, which meant no *Lion King*, or queueing to use the bathroom, or arguments about whose turn it was to take the bin out. I had the place all to myself.

'You can stay over if you like?'

It was agreed that she would come over around 7 p.m. on the Saturday night and would leave early on Sunday morning, to get back to Shropshire in time to have lunch at Matt's sister's house.

I felt flutters of nerves on Saturday morning, the way I used to feel waiting for a school friend to come for a sleepover in the summer holidays. I hoovered, and laundered towels, and filled the ice tray, and put a new carton of milk in the fridge. And then I stood there with the fridge door open, staring at the shelves. One for Rebecca, one for Kevin, one for me. Rebecca had written her name on a jar of raspberry jam with a permanent marker and had underlined it twice. Kevin's shelf contained a large bar of Dairy Milk and a multipack of Rolo chocolate mousses. I was filled with a deep shame.

Although she was five years younger than me, Jess had a driver's licence and a car with a child seat in the back. She had a mortgage and a variety of winter coats and, at some point in her life, she had walked into a shop and bought a washing machine with a built-in tumble dryer. She owned a wheelbarrow – I knew this from her Facebook photos. Oh god, she probably had a shed as well. And there I was, living like a nineteen-year-old with a single shelf in a shared fridge and an NUS card that gave me 20 per cent off in Topshop. I had £18.72 in my bank account, and I used a sock as a purse. I suddenly feared that, when she really got to know me, Jess would think I was the world's biggest loser.

The doorbell ding-donged at 7.15 p.m.

'Oh, thank god,' she said as I opened the door, 'I thought I'd got the wrong house.' She hugged me and I stood back to let her into the narrow communal hallway. Miran, the woman who lived downstairs, opened her door an inch and peered through the crack to see who I was talking to.

'Hi, Miran,' I said, giving her a small wave, but she just slowly and soundlessly closed the door, as if to convince me she'd never been there at all.

I turned back to Jess. 'Can I help you with your bag?'

'Oh no, I'm OK.'

Despite the heavy holdall, she seemed to be standing straighter, taller than she had been in Rochdale. We climbed the stairs and walked into the kitchen.

Sleepover

'I'm sorry the flat's a bit of a mess,' I said, despite the fact that I had spent all afternoon tidying up.

'God, don't be, my house is a shit tip, everything is still piled up in moving boxes. I don't have anything together. And my child is feral, I'm not even kidding.'

I waited for her to laugh but she didn't, she just sighed, dropped her bag on the table and took her trousers off. I just stood there, staring without blinking.

'Sorry, am I being a weirdo? I just really want to put my pyjamas on. Today has been about fifteen years long.'

It's difficult to be formal with someone who has taken their trousers off, so I just acted as if this sort of thing happened in my kitchen all the time. I was super casual about it.

'Did you have a good time with your mum?' I went to put the kettle on but saw Jess getting a bottle of wine out of her bag.

'This is for you – and these chocolates.'

'Aww, that's nice.'

'Not really, I plan on eating half of them myself.' She handed me the wine. 'Yeah, it was good seeing my mum. Andy – that's my stepdad – is really lovely, but it's all a bit full-on.'

She walked around the kitchen, looking at things as she talked, picking up salt and pepper shakers and putting them down again, touching the edge of the table, as if she was trying to join the dots and work out who I was. All the time, she was just wearing her red T-shirt and black pants. No pyjamas materialised. She pointed to a pile of papers next to the toaster and asked, 'Is this your PhD stuff?'

'It's notes for a conference thing. It's not for a few weeks, but after the last one, I'm doing extra preparation.' I hadn't had time to think about the upcoming postgraduate symposium. I'd been so busy with the campaign, but the date was getting closer, creeping up on me. All PhD students had to publicly present their research in their third year at the symposium, held in the Courtauld's lecture theatre. It would be attended by students, staff and members of the public who had nothing better to do with their time. It was mandatory, and I was dreading it.

'What happened at the last conference?' Jess asked.

While pouring wine, I told her the whole sorry tale about how I ran away just before it was my turn to speak.

'Well, of course you felt out of place at the conference,' Jess said. 'Our culture wants women to be uncomfortable in those spaces. I mean, women weren't even allowed to graduate from a university until when – like, 1920? And working-class women? It's a really recent thing. Being afraid of public speaking is not your own personal hang-up. The world wants you to be afraid to speak.' She took the glass of wine I was holding out for her. 'Sorry, I'm ranting now. It just pisses me off.'

'No, I get it. You're right.'

We clinked glasses.

'I'd quite like to do a college course or something, but I'm just knackered all the time. I'm working from home at the moment, and the only time I manage to get anything done is while Ruby's at nursery, then I pick her up and . . . it's just a fucking circus. It never ends. There's never time to do anything.'

'I don't know how you do it,' I said. 'I look after other people's kids for a few hours a day, and I come home and want to drink heavily.'

'What are the parents like?'

Sleepover

'Nice, mostly. There was this one woman called Sue who was an absolute cow. I know I shouldn't say that. But she really was a cow though, and no amount of yoga made her a nicer person. She put her daughter on a diet and made me take her a carrot as an afterschool snack. The other kids would have a chocolate biscuit or a banana, but she made me give her a raw unpeeled carrot, like you'd offer to a donkey or use on a snowman. And she never, ever paid me on time. But usually the mothers are lovely and understanding and exhausted. But the dads . . . oh, the Dulwich dads.'

'Oh my god,' she said, 'Dulwich Dads should be a category on Pornhub.'

'Nobody would watch it.'

'They fucking would.'

'Every clip would begin with a forty-five-year-old white man in cycling shorts leaning against a kitchen island, flicking through the pages of a Nigel Slater cookery book.'

'. . . and in walks the childminder . . .'

'And he looks her up and down and slowly – with conviction – tells her everything she's been doing wrong with sourdough.'

Jess burst out laughing and spilled wine on the table. She mopped it up with Rebecca's Cath Kidston tea towel, and the stain ran through the repeated pattern of tuberoses.

'Shit, sorry, I've just totally ruined your nice tea towel.'

'It's fine, I'll wash it. It's my flatmate's.'

'I should have used a cloth, sorry. You'd think I'd be more practical since I spend half my life mopping up after a three-year-old.'

'Do you ever wish you hadn't had a child?' I just blurted it out. I didn't mean to. People were always asking me why I didn't have kids, or when I was going to have them, but I had never dreamt of asking someone with children if they regretted them. But Jess didn't appear to be offended, or even surprised by the question.

'Oh god, yes, I think about that all the time. Look – I'm a mother so I have to say this – my daughter means more to me than anything in the world and I'm so lucky to have her. I mean, that's one hundred per cent true, but all women have to say that as a disclaimer, right? But my life is hard and I'm lonely a lot of the time and bored. Bringing up a child is honestly pretty boring most of the time. You're just feeding it and trying to keep it alive and teach it how to use the toilet. It's not the most rewarding thing in the world, at least not at the moment. I often wonder what my life would look like if I'd made different choices. I mean, I'm glad I didn't, but, you know. Do you want kids?'

I shook my head. 'I've always known I don't want kids. People always presumed I'd change my mind, but I never have. I wouldn't even play with dolls as a child. The next-door neighbour gave me one of those dolls that blinks when you move its head. I hated it. I called it Domon.'

'Like "demon", with an extra O?'

'Yeah. I kept trying to lose it. I threw it away and somebody got it out of the bin. I chucked it in the canal, and my auntie scooped it out with a fishing net.'

'Yeah, I think you probably shouldn't have kids.'

'I think that as well.'

'I'm only joking.'

'I'm not.'

Sleepover

She tipped her bag upside down and found the pyjamas at the bottom of the pile. I put the oven on to warm up the pizza while Jess stepped into her pyjama bottoms, slid one arm under the back of her T-shirt to unhook her bra and pulled it out of her sleeve, as if performing a magic trick.

'You're never going to have me over ever again, are you? Taking my bra off in your kitchen. Classy.'

She started fiddling around with Rebecca's digital radio and I imagined the trouble I'd be in if the stations got messed up. I already owed her a replacement tea towel.

'If I'm at home on my own – if Ruby's at nursery and Matt's at work – I have the radio on so loud. I used to be the neighbour from hell when we were in Newcastle, but now . . . well, the nearest neighbours are two miles away. It's so quiet you could hear a pin drop and it drives me mad. Silence makes me want to scream.'

'You'd love living here then,' I said. 'You never get any peace in a shared house with a stone-deaf *Miss Marple* enthusiast living downstairs.'

'Living the dream,' she said, topping up her wine. 'But seriously, I never thought I'd say this, but I miss having neighbours.'

'Is the house totally isolated then?'

'Yeah, completely. It's in the middle of nowhere. It's pretty, the countryside is lovely, and it's good for Ruby because there's space for her to play and run about and . . . yeah. It'll just take me a while to settle in, I suppose.'

She told me more about the house, about the crumbling hayloft where the barn owls nested and the empty fields that surrounded it. Matt had inherited the place last year after his dad died.

'There was always this unsaid agreement that we'd live there one day,' she said. 'And yeah, I mean, we've got more space and everything, but I really miss seeing people and being able to just walk out of the house and go to the shop without having to drive for five miles. And I'm not even kidding, I miss the noise – the traffic, kids shouting in the playground, drunk people walking home after a night out. I genuinely miss it.'

We ate the pizza and drank more wine, and then Jess discovered the Rolo mousses and ate one with a tablespoon. We didn't stop talking until the clock on the microwave said 2 a.m., and Jess said she had to go to bed or she'd be in no fit state to drive in the morning. I'd left blankets and pillows on the sofa but she took one look at it and said, 'Can't I just sleep with you? Your bed looks so comfy.' She made a cute, desperate face, like an extra from *Annie*, and I said, 'Yeah, get in.'

I can't normally sleep with someone else in the room. As a child, at sleepovers, I'd lay awake all night, staring at the ceiling, listening to other people breathing. But I slept so well next to Jess that I didn't even wake up when she left in the morning.

I walked into the kitchen to make coffee and found a note on the worktop.

> *God that was SO fun.*
> *Sorry about the Rolo mousse and the tea towel.*
> *Love youuuuuuuu!*
> *Jess xxx*

For the first time ever, the flat seemed too quiet.

Small Victories

I spent the first week of April desperately trying to catch chickenpox. It was going around Dulwich and all the kids were getting it in their turn. I hugged pox-riddled kids, I dried my hands on their bath towels, I let them rifle through my bag and play with my hairbrush. If I caught it now, I would reach peak contagion by the day of the postgraduate symposium and would have to stay at home. That was the plan. But when I mentioned it to my mum, she insisted I'd had chickenpox in 1987, and was off school for three weeks.

'I didn't know it lasted so long,' I said.

'Well, you were contagious for a week,' she replied, 'but then you had an accident on your roller skates, so I kept you off till Easter.'

It didn't matter. I knew deep down that I couldn't escape the symposium and had been staying up late every night practising my paper. I looked in the mirror and wished I hadn't. I looked like someone who had suffered a month of dysentery at sea. I had mouth ulcers and bad hair and purple shadows under my eyes. Luckily, I didn't have time to dwell on my appearance, because it was the day of the Girl Guides' announcement about supporting No More Page 3. We were expecting a lot of media interest and had a series of interviews lined up already. I logged on to HQ.

> Evie: Are we ready? The Guides will be making their announcement soon. Eeeeeeeek!!!

> Max: We were born ready! The pope's not going to steal our thunder this time!

> Kate: Speaking of which, I've been keeping an eye on religious leaders in case any of them are about to die or retire – the pope appears to have stayed out of trouble and the Archbishop of Canterbury and the Dalai Lama seem to be doing well

> *Lucy is typing . . .*

> Lucy: You're not going to believe this. The interviews have been called off

> Evie: What? Why, what's happened?

> Lucy: There's bigger news: Margaret Thatcher has died.

> Jess: What? WHAT???

Lucy: It's true. It's breaking news.

We all started typing at once, but Kate got there first.

Kate: UNBEFUCKINGLIEVABLE! But I suppose
you've got to admire the woman really. She
screws us over in life and manages to carry on
screwing us over in death.

Despite the Iron Lady's demise, our story was still picked up by the press, albeit in a minor way. News websites had Thatcher's face everywhere with a tiny thumbnail image of a Girl Guide somewhere near the bottom of the page. But Becky Hewitt, the Director of Communications at Girlguiding, was still asked to appear on the news, and we all sat in front of our TV screens to watch, wishing we were all gathered together in the same room. I thought it would just be Becky on the news, but next to her sat Michael Waldon.

Jess: Oh god why

Max: Perhaps the producers included him to
provide the necessary sexist balance.

Jess: But he doesn't even work for *The Sun* any
more – why does he care so much?

Becky explained what had happened; how the Guide advocates highlighted Page 3 as an issue they cared about and voted to support the campaign. They said that seeing images in the paper, where women are treated as objects, has a damaging impact on their self-esteem and confidence. 'What they'd like to see is inspiring role models who lift their aspirations.'

The presenter then turned to Michael Waldon, and said, 'For a time you were certainly partly responsible for putting that picture on Page 3 on a daily basis . . . how does it feel to have the full force of the Girl Guides against you?'

He said he felt depressed when he heard about it, because 'political correctness has even infected the Girl Guides'.

'What this feels like,' he said, 'is a group of middle-class women sat in a room thinking "what can we do to be relevant?" and then thinking to themselves, I know, let's leap on this bandwagon and get our girls involved.'

Becky patiently explained that this is not what happened, that the girls approached *them* about No More Page 3, but he wouldn't listen. He just kept denying it and talking over her, until the presenter had to forcefully tell him to let Becky speak.

Becky got about five seconds of airtime before he butted in again, saying, 'I think there are things that are more important than Page 3.'

'With respect,' Becky replied, 'what *you* think is important to girls isn't the point, it's what the *girls* say is important to them, and we must listen to them.'

'There are things like body image,' he said, and Becky just stared at him.

'How can you disassociate Page 3 with body image?' she asked. He carried on talking over her and she burst out laughing at the ridiculousness of it all, and then it was over.

Jess: How dare this sexist old dinosaur tell the
Girl Guides what they should think is important?

Kate: Yeah but I absolutely loved it! It's the
best interview yet! Becky was amazing and the
presenter too. Waldon looked so out of touch.

Evie: I've been having a Twitter spat with him.
He called me silly. I offered to send him a
T-shirt.

Steve: Send one with a very very tight neck.

My phone started ringing, so I stepped away from my computer to answer it. It was my dad. My stomach lurched with fear. My mum was the one who always phoned, so I panicked that something had happened.

'Dad, what's wrong?'

There was a pause and then he said, 'Joanne . . . Joanne, can you hear me?'

'Yes, I can hear you, is everything OK?'

I could hear a noise in the background, as if he was eating something.

'The *Mail Online*,' he said. 'There's a picture of you and the other girls. It's an article about the Girl Guides and it's a big picture – the one where you're all doing the scout salute. I'm looking at it now.'

I heard more munching.

'Dad, what are you eating?'

'Fish, chips and carrots. We've run out of peas.'

'What's the article like?'

'It's good. I mean, what can they say? Page 3's old hat now, innit?'

I paused. 'What did you say?'

Munch, munch, munch.

'It's old hat now, Page 3. It's time they got rid of it and called it a day.'

I was speechless. I couldn't find a single thing to say. This was the first time my dad had ever agreed with me about *anything*. Saying that Page 3 was 'old hat now' was as out of character and as revolutionary as if he'd donned a beret and leapt on his chair to perform spoken-word poetry.

This is what it's taken, I thought. I've been telling him how I feel about Page 3 since the nineties, and he's dismissed me over and over again, but the second the *Daily Mail* prints a photo with me on it then he's on board.

I didn't say this, and I knew better than to question him about his change of heart. It was best to approach conversations with my dad as if trying to feed a wild fox: treading very carefully and giving him space so he wouldn't feel cornered. One wrong move and he'd snap or retreat and the magic of the moment would be gone. So, I decided to accept his comment as a small victory, to hold it close and to walk away quietly before he noticed I had taken it.

Two days later, I was on the bus on my way to the postgraduate symposium. I was so nervous I felt dangerously sick, so I took deep breaths and stared straight out of the window.

Small Victories

According to the fear book I set on fire, people fear public speaking more than death. I believe this. Standing up in front of people and speaking feels unsafe. I think it's especially difficult for women because, as Jess said, we've been told repeatedly for centuries that we have nothing of value to say; that our brains aren't as analytical, our experiences aren't as valid, that our emotions undermine our reasoning. We're shrill and hysterical. We were taught as children not to show off or draw attention to ourselves. Never to be bossy. To sit with our knees pressed together, not to take up space. And then we're supposed to stand on a platform in a lecture theatre and take up all the space, project our voices to fill an entire room, and tell all the intimidatingly clever people sitting on the staggered seats with notebooks and pens everything we know, in precisely twenty minutes, with slides.

When I arrived at the Courtauld, I locked myself in a toilet cubicle to go over my crumpled notes one last time. The pages had got stuck in the printer – which hadn't worked properly since my parents' cat was sick on it – and some of the ink had smudged.

I suddenly had a vivid memory of being at a holiday camp as a child, watching the kids' talent show in the club room. A little girl in a party dress climbed on stage to sing Cyndi Lauper and froze with fear when she looked out at the crowd. She tugged on the holiday rep's skirt and whispered something. 'She'll only perform,' the holiday rep told us, 'if you all turn to face the doors, shut your eyes and put your fingers in your ears.'

I wished so deeply that I could have done that. That I could have said: 'I'm going to speak about artists in exile in Britain during 1933–1945, but could you all please turn around – yes, you'll have to straddle your seats like Christine Keeler – and just chat among yourselves until it's over and I'm safely on the bus home? Thank you.'

I was the second person lined up to speak, so I sat on the front row, feeling self-conscious. The first speaker was clear and articulate and steady-voiced, and it felt like she was up there for three and a half hours. Each minute stretched endlessly. And then she stopped and a voice was announcing my name and I was frozen to my seat. I just couldn't get up.

An acquaintance sitting next to me gave me a nudge and whispered, 'Just picture them naked,' and something clicked in my head. I thought of all the times I had heard that advice – picture them naked – because if they are naked and you are clothed, there is a power imbalance weighted in your favour. Everything that makes a person formidable and intimidating is stripped away and they are left vulnerable. It was this momentary distraction – mere seconds of thinking about Page 3 and power – that stopped me panicking and got me to the podium.

I cleared my throat, shuffled my papers and started speaking. I said the words in my own voice, and I kept going, right to the end.

Flash Dance

'Right,' said Kate, 'I've made a dance instruction video.'

I clicked the link and set off squealing like one of those miniature pigs you keep indoors.

Kate was marching on the spot in her living room while 'Y.M.C.A.' played from tinny speakers in the background. Dressed in leggings with her hair in a high ponytail, she shouted out words of encouragement, like Jane Fonda in the eighties.

'Just one more time, it's the same routine we did before, OK let's go!'

Oh, sweet Mary mother of Jesus H. Christ, I thought, *this is actually going to happen. We're actually going to do a flash mob.*

It was Kate's idea.

'We need to keep trying new things,' she said, 'to keep the momentum going. How about a flash mob with a 1970s theme, since *The Sun* is stuck in the seventies – the decade they launched Page 3? We could do it on the pavement outside News International!'

The only time I'd seen a flash mob was on TV, on an advert for a bank or building society. It showed crowds of people milling about at a train station, going to work, buying sandwiches, catching heavily delayed First Great Western trains and then, out of nowhere, a big group of terrible people started enthusiastically leaping about to music. I found that sort of thing bone-achingly embarrassing. It was filed in the same box in my head as Christian rock music – in the box named 'please, please, anything but this'.

But Kate had it all planned. First came the message about the music.

'It has to be a 1970s song, something we can dance to, something everyone knows . . . what about "Y.M.C.A."?'

Then came the lyrics.

'Mohan – are you listening to me? I said Mohan, can't you see what we see?'

Then came the recording.

'I've just taped myself singing it, just so you can hear how it fits, but a friend at the am-dram society says I can use their equipment to record a proper version on Thursday.'

And now the choreography. Oh, sweet Lord, the choreography.

I watched the video a second time and wondered if I'd ever get the hang of the routine. During the chorus, Kate bent her arms into the shape of N-M-P-3 and I pressed pause to practise, but I kept doing the N backwards. There was one horribly difficult bit in the third verse, where Kate slid one leg behind the other and coordinated her opposite arm in a single fluid movement – a routine I'd performed successfully once before, on a frozen puddle outside Dorothy Perkins, but it was very hard to replicate.

'You'll get the hang of it,' Kate said. 'I want it to be fun.

We're about to hit one hundred thousand signatures. There are A HUNDRED THOUSAND of us. We should celebrate that!'

We shared our plans and the dance video online and received a flood of warm, encouraging messages. But not everyone liked the idea. A few supporters and a couple of journalists suggested that we were making light of the issue by planning a 'fun' activity.

> Jess: The media so desperately wants us to be serious and offended all the time.
>
> Kate: It bothers me that some supporters think we're making light of it though. That wasn't my intention. It's just that the past few months have been so incredible, but so hard. I just wanted to take a minute to celebrate what we've done. All 100,000 of us.
>
> Me: What, you mean you've found the daily death threats HARD?
>
> Kate: I just think that sometimes when you're dealing with a lot of shit the best thing to do is just get dressed up and dance.

This got me thinking. On the street, random men frequently told us to cheer up. As members of No More Page 3, we were often told to stop smiling and be more serious. At what point could we just be ourselves and laugh and rage and, equally, just dance around looking stupid in ridiculous trousers?

> Me: If we have to be serious until Page 3 ends, then *The Sun* gets to define our experience.

> Me: And the thing is, you're all the funniest, most joyful people I know.

> Me: So Kate, if you want to dance on the street, then I'm right behind you.

> Kate: Thanks love!

> Me: I mean literally right behind you, so no one can see me.

Now that I'd fully committed myself, I thought I'd better find something to wear. Since it was early summer, it wasn't necessary to trawl around fancy-dress stores or vintage emporiums as the shops, catering to the Glastonbury crowd, were stocked to the brim with sparkly hot pants, ditsy-patterned bohemian dresses and hideous platform shoes. Wandering along Oxford Street, I wondered why women attending music festivals were encouraged to dress like children's party entertainers, *Little House on the Prairie* characters or Noddy Holder. I no longer bothered with festivals because they were always full of other people, but if I did, I'd want to dress like Tony Robinson on *Time Team*; trousers with pockets to conceal a useful array of tools, zip-away hoods in case of a downpour and boots that can withstand days of squatting in a rain-drenched furrow filled with slop.

Ultimately, I bought an astonishingly ugly pair of rainbow crochet flares and a truly hideous fringed waistcoat. I was all set.

As the day of the flash mob loomed ever closer, people started dropping out. It appeared that everyone was ill or busy or working, or busy being ill at work. I held them all to my own standards and presumed that they were lying. Of course, there was a chance the excuses could have been real – maybe everyone was *genuinely* taken ill the day before we had to dance in public but, whatever the truth was, it left Lucy, Kate, Evie and me to do the flash mob. Four of us, like the Spice Girls after Geri left.

We had just one group practice, an hour before the performance. Members of Unison, the UK's biggest workers' union, had recently voted to support the campaign, and they offered us the atrium space at their head office in Euston to use for the rehearsal.

Kate was peering out of the window when I walked in, and I saw only the back of her psychedelic, flared catsuit with her long blonde hair tumbling down to her waist.

Evie had brought her daughters, who were chasing each other round and round in a figure of eight.

'They insisted on coming,' she said, with an exhausted half smile.

I went to the toilets to squeeze into my crochet flares and

by the time I returned, a cameraman had set up his equipment and had started filming. He caught the moment that Lucy turned up in a blonde wig, purple flares, a velvet jacket and huge platform shoes. She had travelled on the train like that. I thought that my life would be fifteen times better if only I could adopt Kate's can-do attitude and Lucy's absolute inability to give a shit. If I could just have those attributes, along with Evie's hair, then I'd be wildly happy.

'OK.' Kate clapped her hands like an enthusiastic primary school teacher. 'Let's have a run-through.'

The practice did not go well and was made worse by the fact we were being filmed. It was like being on a very low-budget Channel 5 reality show.

On the tube, I found a space by the door and leaned against the handrail, enjoying a brief moment of peace. I closed my eyes and tried to relax.

'It'd be great to have a bit of footage of you dancing on the train.'

My eyes sprung open in horror. The cameraman was filming.

'Just a few seconds is all we'd need – if you can just do the chorus bit.'

'OK,' Kate said, 'I'll count us in – ready – one, two, three, four –'

Usually, I admired the way that tube passengers committed themselves wholeheartedly to ignoring each other's existence, but this journey was different. People were staring. The woman sitting on the fold-down seat next to the door rested her book on her knee and looked up expectantly.

This is it, I thought. I'm about to dance on the tube. And

then I have to dance on the street. And then I can simply throw myself in a canal later on this afternoon.

We didn't have the music to hand, so Kate sang the lyrics. I glanced over at Evie's kids. The littlest one, Sophie, was eating an apple and staring, wide-eyed. Milly, who was old enough to realise how embarrassing her mother was, pulled her coat over her head and tried desperately to disappear down the back of her seat. We managed to get through the N-M-P-3 bit before the train shuddered into Angel and we stumbled sideways, narrowly avoiding falling onto passengers' knees, as if performing a clumsy, ironic lap dance.

I walked up the steps from the tube feeling horrified, shaken and embarrassed; an emotional cocktail I hadn't experienced since I was chased, on a busy Saturday, through the centre of York by a goose. We rounded the corner to Thomas More Square.

'Shit the bed!' Kate shouted. 'Look at that!'

A crowd of sixty or seventy people were waiting for us. Some had brought their kids, a glamorous woman with eyeliner and a fluffy jacket had brought a little designer dog. There were wigs and garish trousers and a sea of campaign T-shirts. Everyone was laughing, talking, hugging. The mood was celebratory, just as Kate had wanted.

About a third of the crowd danced, while the rest cheered us on. Kate, Lucy, Evie and I stood at the front, but as soon as the music started playing and everyone was marching on the spot, I marched slowly backwards until I merged into the second row. Kate noticed and laughed, but she didn't say anything.

When it was over, I sat on a wall with Evie's kids. 'I can't believe we just danced, like, in the middle of London,' Milly said.

Just a few months ago, I had walked down my own street with my coat zipped up and my head down, wishing I could be invisible, and now I was dancing in a public square in fancy dress. In such a short space of time, these women had turned my small world upside down and had shaken it vigorously, like you would with a handbag with loose change stuck in the lining.

I watched as Kate was interviewed by a reporter.

'Yeah, I choreographed it, I can't believe how many people came. Everybody did the dance brilliantly and nobody fell over. Amazing. It was all just amazing.'

I recalled snippets of conversations with Kate from the past five months:

'I'm knackered, and I've got to be up at 5 –'

'I haven't had a minute to myself all day –'

'I've got to go to the shop, then make dinner, then pick Chloe up –'

'I keep meaning to read that book but the second I get into bed I just fall asleep 'cos I'm so shattered –'

Kate spent all of her time looking after people, and receiving little to no acknowledgement, gratitude or credit for it. She was a person who made things happen for others, and now she was doing something for herself. The flash mob was one thing that wasn't about her patients, her kids, her family or her boss.

I looked at her and saw for the first time what the campaign really meant to her, and to all of us. It was about so much more than Page 3.

The Pineapple

The following day, we held our first strategy meeting at Evie's pub, The Pineapple.

I bumped into Rhianne outside.

'I missed you yesterday at the flash mob,' I said.

'Come on, you know dancing in flares is not really for me, Jo.'

Since the trip to Legoland, Rhianne and I had become friends, bonded by the unique experience of being trapped at close quarters beneath a cardboard glamour model in the back of a Volvo. She lived on the other side of Peckham Rye, and we'd gone for a drink a few times at a pub midway between our flats. The more I got to know her, the more I liked her.

She grew up in a working-class family in a small town near Glastonbury, and she was named after a Page 3 model her parents had seen in the paper.

'Doesn't that just speak volumes about how massive Page 3 was in the eighties?' she said. 'I was actually named after a topless model.'

Rhianne was hardworking and down to earth, she always paid her electricity bill on time and she rolled her eyes when people spent good money on a handbag, but growing up near

Glastonbury gave her an interesting edge. She wore clothes made by Fairtrade community cooperatives, she liked 'proper' music, was often stoned, and had friends who looked like the sort of people who could find an underground water source by waving a stick.

She had recently joined HQ, along with Priya, who I'd met at the first protest. Priya, a trainee midwife, had been too busy with work to get involved earlier in the year, but now she had a bit more free time, she'd told Lucy she was happy to help out in any way she could.

Priya was at the bar when I walked in, paying for a drink. I hadn't seen her since that first protest nearly a year ago, when she'd turned up with the reluctant man in film-director glasses. I said hello and she stared at me for a while, before saying, 'Jo! Shit, sorry, sorry, I'm rubbish with faces, honestly, I'm terrible, I can never remember what anyone looks like.'

She gave me a hug. 'Can I get you a drink?'

'Can I have a Guinness? I'll get the next round.'

'I always think Guinness is a really wholesome thing to drink,' she said. 'As if you're having porridge or something.' She paid, and I waited for the barman to top up my pint, then I followed her towards the stairs.

'You know, I come here all the time,' she said. 'I used to live around the corner. Me and my mates usually sit over there, and do jigsaws. If there's nobody waiting to be served, Ben – that's the guy behind the bar – he'll come over and help us to do the sky 'cos, let's be honest, Jo, nobody likes doing the sky in a jigsaw, it's the shittiest bit.'

I remembered how easy it was to talk to Priya, how warm

and engaging she was, and how nice it felt when she said my name in a sentence.

'Hiiiiiii!' Jess trotted towards us with her arms outstretched, her pointy-toed ankle boots clicking on the floor tiles. She saw me looking at them and made a frustrated growling sound.

'Urgh, they're driving me mad, why did I wear such pointy pinchy stupid fucking boots to London? I could have screamed going up and down all the stairs in the tube. They're murdering my toes. You must be Priya, I'm Jess!'

Kate greeted me by shouting 'Cheeseandham!' with an amused look on her face.

I'd recently told her about the letter I'd received the previous year from Vodafone, addressed to Mrs Joanna Cheeseandham.

'I'll never call you anything else,' she'd said.

Evie appeared in a full-length floral dress with her hair tumbling over one shoulder. She would have looked perfectly Victorian if she wasn't carrying an ice bucket containing a big bottle of gin and lots of miniature tonics.

'I thought this way we wouldn't have to keep going down to the bar,' she said.

Max was sitting at the end of the table in a leather Chesterfield armchair, sipping white wine. Lucy was perched near the window, holding her phone in the air to get reception while searching for something in her bag with her other hand.

When Steve walked in, Kate cheered, then Lucy joined in. He turned and checked there was no one behind him.

'Well, this is a first. Women have never cheered when I've walked into a pub before.'

I moved closer to Jess to make room for him to sit down.

Rhianne dashed over and squeezed in next to me and then Lucy pulled a bit of paper out of her bag and said, 'I have an agenda!'

We settled in our seats as Lucy ran through the list.

'So, in no particular order of importance . . . the MPs' letter.' She turned to Rhianne and Priya to explain. 'Steve has been contacting MPs, asking them to sign a letter to the editor asking for the removal of Page 3. It's going really well, Steve, do you have any idea off the top of your head—'

'Fifty-five Labour MPs have signed the petition, fifteen Lib Dems and three Conservatives, which means, percentage-wise, we've got . . .'

I zoned out as Steve presented a series of figures.

'How can you remember all that?' Kate asked.

Steve shrugged. 'I'm good with numbers. I like stats. I told you, I'm a geek.'

'OK and next – organisations.' Lucy looked at her list. 'So, Unison have recently voiced their support – and they're our biggest national workers' union with 1.3 million members, so that's pretty huge. And Mumsnet have just voted in favour of supporting.'

'How many members have Mumsnet got?' Kate asked.

'Hang on, let me read the blurb. It's the UK's largest website for parents, with 4.3 million monthly unique visitors. Wow. And we've had a lot of Women's Institutes asking us to speak at their meetings.'

'I'm happy to speak at WI meetings,' Kate said, 'but if they want me to make jam, we're buggered.'

'The other news,' Lucy said, 'which is quite lovely and

amazing is that, after supporting No More Page 3, Girlguiding created an activism badge.'

Jess put her hand to her heart. 'I love that so much. I love that so many girls are being encouraged to speak out about issues they care about.'

'I know,' Lucy said. 'It just makes my heart go to mush. I really think that No More Page 3 could be the gateway issue that leads these young women into all kinds of incredible campaigning. It's giving them a taste of activism. It's just brilliant.'

Rhianne was always rolling cigarettes. She'd roll one and place it in lieu of a pencil next to her notebook, then she'd go outside and smoke it, come back in and start rolling again. I thought it must be nice to have something to do with your hands while you talked, and an excuse to go outside whenever you needed a break. Slowly, the conversation moved away from the campaign to other things. We'd break off into twos or threes, having conversations of our own, before drifting back to the group. I sat between Jess and Rhianne and the three of us talked about grandparents and ghosts and uncomfortable shoes, and it was easy, as if we had been friends for years.

We overheard Lucy talking about the books she'd written and drifted into her conversation.

'My novels were classified as chick lit, and I hate that term. I love the genre, but I hate the term. And I feel like it limited what I could write about. I wanted to write a story about a woman who has an abortion but I was told it was a no-no. Then I wanted to write about a woman who has mental health issues, and I was told to make the character more "every woman" – I was like, well, me and my friends talk about mental health issues – who IS this every woman? I just felt that the experience of being a woman is a lot more interesting and complicated than I was being allowed to explore in my books. And the cover art. Oh my god. They'd send me the design and I'd be like: why have you put a cupcake on my cover? There's no mention of a cupcake in the book – the character doesn't talk about cupcakes, I can take or leave a cupcake – so, erm, why are you putting a cupcake on my cover? And then it would come to the next book, I'd be like "please don't put a cupcake on my co— oh. You've put a cupcake on my cover. Again."'

We overheard Kate, at the other end of the table, talking about her ex-husband.

'He would get really aggressive and start throwing things around. We were having this row and he smashed this giant mirror we had in the bedroom and there were just shards of glass everywhere and I thought this is it, I can't do this any more.'

Jess, who had been talkative all afternoon, went quiet. She sat back in her chair, swirling the gin around in her glass, blinking, and not saying anything.

Rhianne notices things. She can pick up subtle changes in the atmosphere of a room. She suddenly grabbed her roll-up and said, 'I'm going outside for a smoke. Come with me if you want to stretch your legs.' I got up to follow her and Jess came too.

We stood outside the door and rubbed our arms to keep warm. Jess looked at us both and smiled and I saw her shoulders relax.

The Pineapple

She told me years later that at that moment, while we were standing on the kerb surrounded by all the noise of Kentish Town, with the sun setting and Rhianne blowing smoke rings into the air, she decided, *I will tell them. At some point, I will tell them everything.*

PART THREE

Bigger Things

Quite a Storm

We were queuing in the security line outside the Houses of Parliament. I'd drunk too much coffee and kept hopping from foot to foot. It felt as if we were about to catch an early-morning flight, and I kept anxiously checking my bag, searching for a passport or boarding pass that wasn't there.

'Next!'

We approached the desk and the security blokes looked us up and down.

'You can't go in wearing that,' said the one with the beard.

I looked at Rhianne and Lucy, confused. I thought dress codes were reserved for court hearings and Halloween parties, not for Parliament?

'Your T-shirts,' he said, 'you can't enter the building wearing them.'

'Why not?'

He gave a long, exasperated sigh. 'Clothing bearing political slogans is banned in Parliament. You'll have to take them off or put something else on.'

'This is my own personal opinion,' Lucy said, 'it's not really—'

'Cover it up or take it off.'

'So, Page Three is allowed at Westminster,' Rhianne said, 'but No More Page Three T-shirts are not?'

'Cover it up or take it off.'

We all glanced at each other. Part of me hoped that Rhianne or Lucy would just rip off their T-shirt and prance around in their bra, but neither of them did.

'I'll have to ask you to hurry up.'

I was wearing a dress under the T-shirt, so I just took it off and stuffed it in my bag. Rhianne, who was wearing a bright-red vest, did the same. Lucy rolled her eyes and put her jacket on, buttoning it up to the top. It felt like we were being reprimanded for wearing trainers with our school uniforms.

'If at any point you put the T-shirts back on, you'll be asked to leave.'

'We won't,' I said.

'You'll be asked to leave *immediately*.'

'Yeah, *alright*.' Rhianne walked quickly away before she could lose her temper.

We were at Westminster to watch Caroline Lucas speak about Page 3. Caroline, MP for Brighton and Hove, was a supporter of the campaign, and was arguing that *The Sun* should not be widely available across the parliamentary estate while it continued to print topless images. There were laws in place prohibiting the display of pornographic material in the workplace but Caroline, like so many women, regularly saw Page 3 in her place of work, because it appeared in a newspaper. It felt like a pivotal moment; our small grassroots campaign being discussed at Westminster.

I didn't know what to expect. Despite walking past Big Ben a thousand times, I'd only ever seen the inside of the Houses of Parliament on the news. As soon as I walked through the doors, I started talking in whispers.

'What are you doing?' Rhianne asked.

'I don't know,' I said, very, very quietly.

I was awestruck, made small by my surroundings. It was a structure built to intimidate, like a gothic cathedral or a grand stately home. Men in suits strode by, the soles of their expensive shoes echoing across the vast rooms. There was a smell of old wood and leather and every part of me was desperate to get out of there as quickly as possible.

I thought of Clare Short, and how courageous she was to stand in the Commons and talk about Page 3 back in the eighties.

We'd recently met with Clare Short to talk about the campaign, and about the bill she raised 'to make illegal the display of pictures of naked or partially naked women in sexually provocative poses in newspapers' in 1986. She received threats and abuse, *The Sun* called her 'Killjoy Clare' and mocked up images of her as a Page 3 model, but she also received thousands of supportive letters from women, some of which were reproduced in the book *Dear Clare . . . This is What Women Feel About Page 3*. In the book's introduction, she explains how her bill came about.

One Friday, she had cancelled her weekend plans to stay in the Commons to help block Enoch Powell's Unborn Children

(Protection) Bill. In order to prevent this bill from being considered, opponents had to ensure the debate for the preceding bill dragged on and on, taking up so much time that Powell's couldn't get a look in. This preceding bill aimed to change the law on obscene publications, and was introduced by the grandson of Winston Churchill, a man, unimaginatively, also named Winston Churchill. His bill listed specific violent or sexual images that he sought to ban, including many that, as his detractors pointed out, frequently featured in war reportage, medical textbooks and sex-education teaching material.

Like any woman forced to ditch weekend plans because of Enoch Powell, Clare Short was annoyed. She was particularly annoyed because many supporters of Churchill's bill had suggested that most women, angry at society's ever-present threat of sexual violence, would welcome such a ban.

She hadn't planned to speak but, fuelled by her irritation, she got to her feet and said that if the Commons really wanted to respond to women's anger, they should introduce a bill to remove 'Page 3 pornography' from the press. Afterwards, Clare received numerous letters from women who had heard about her ad-hoc speech, and wanted to encourage her to go ahead with the bill.

The regulations surrounding Ten Minute Rule Bills are so complicated and convoluted, it makes the operating manual for my printer seem breezy, educational and fun.

To kick things off, the MP must address the Speaker in the style of a BBC period drama, saying: 'Mr Speaker, I beg to move that leave be given to bring in a bill . . .'

If they are granted permission, the MP must walk to a white

line on the floor of the chamber, holding a pretend bill, bow once, walk five paces forward, bow again, then walk to the ceremonial mace – a massive golden truncheon with a crown on top – and bow a third time. A lot of fancy footwork.

When I mentioned this to my sister, she said, 'So, why are MPs always so rubbish on *Strictly Come Dancing*?'

After this rigmarole, Clare had to secure a slot to present her bill, which involved spending the night in a sleeping bag on the floor of the antechamber to the Public Bill Office, to ensure she was first in the queue in the morning.

She presented her bill three weeks later, in a crowded House of Commons. A number of male MPs openly laughed and jeered. Clare was one of only twenty-seven female MPs in an establishment built for men, which included a rifle range but no crèche facilities. It would have taken so much courage and strength to stand up and speak against Page 3 in that environment, particularly in light of the fact that her father had died just the previous day. She proceeded in presenting her bill, because she thought it would be a better tribute to her father to carry on than to give up.

The vote on the bill revealed ninety-seven in favour and fifty-six against, which meant that Clare's bill would join the queue of other Private Member's Bills, but there would be little time to take it further before the Parliamentary session ended in June, at which point the bill would die. But Clare persisted because she believed the bill was worth pursuing, if only to raise the issue and see it widely discussed.

And nowhere was it more widely discussed than in the pages of *The Sun*. Readers were encouraged to write in for a free

'Stop Crazy Clare' car sticker, and *The Sun* approached male MPs who had voted against her, asking them to appear on Page 3 with their favourite model. Clare wrote in her book that four or five MPs actually did this. She also received more than fifty letters from men, the forefathers of today's internet trolls, who had raided the craft cupboard and glued pictures of her head onto porn stars' bodies. Some threatened her with violence, others said she was too ugly to rape. All this while she was rushed off her feet working for her constituency and grieving for her father.

But there was a good side too. The supportive letters from women began arriving by the sackful. Women wrote to say they agreed with her, to thank her for raising the issue and to let her know that they were furious at the way she had been treated. Women of all ages, from all backgrounds wrote; women who had experienced sexual violence, women who'd had mastectomies, women who regularly saw Page 3 at work or at home. Twelve women wrote to say they'd had Page 3 mentioned to them while being raped. One woman said she had gone to the local police station to report a sexual assault and, upon seeing a Page 3-style calendar hanging on the wall, had gone home, feeling sick to her stomach, without reporting the incident.

So many letters arrived that Clare asked her mother and sisters to help her read and sort them. They read five thousand before they stopped counting.

We spoke to Clare about the letters she received, and compared them to the thousands of emails and messages that had been sent to us at No More Page 3. Almost thirty years had passed since Clare's bill, but the experiences and opinions shared by the people who had contacted us were strikingly similar. Decades had gone by and society had changed, and yet the new generations of women and girls who were speaking to us were echoing the words of their sisters, mothers and grandmothers who had spoken out before them.

Although no legislation was passed as a result of Clare's bill in 1986, or the reissued bill of 1988, Clare continued to speak out against Page 3, and *The Sun* continued to attack her for it for almost twenty years. In 2004, *The Sun* ran the headline,

FAT, JEALOUS CLARE BRANDS PAGE 3 PORN

and mocked up a Page 3 image of her – superimposing her head on a topless model's body, mirroring the behaviour of the men who'd sent her hate mail. They used News in Briefs to call Clare 'a jealous old battle-axe' and printed a line-up of eight topless models with the headline 'This one's for you Clare.' They also sent a double-decker bus full of topless models to the home she shared with her eighty-four-year-old mother, and chased her down the street, trying to take photos.

Clare spent a long time talking with us at the meeting we'd arranged. She bought us all coffee and laughed with us, and sighed and shook her head when we talked about the traumatic experiences supporters had shared with us. When each of us spoke, she would look us in the eye and, if we paused or hesitated, she would smile and nod encouragingly.

'I know it feels like the end goal is the important thing,' she said, 'but that's not it. The most important thing is what's happening now – the conversations, and the collective effort of all the people who have signed the petition and spoken out.'

She said that when one person speaks out, it paves the way for another to speak out too. There's a little ping of recognition when people realise they're not alone in feeling the way they do.

'It was the reaction of thousands of women throughout the country that made the debate significant,' she wrote in *Dear Clare . . . This is What Women Feel About Page 3.* 'Together we caused quite a storm.'

I was thinking about this, while standing with Rhianne and Lucy inside the Houses of Parliament, waiting for Caroline Lucas to speak.

When it was time to go in, we lined up like we were marching into a school assembly, straight-backed and proper. We slid along a row of benches, not saying a word. That's what the building requires of you, to behave as if your headmaster is watching.

It's not surprising that there are so few working-class MPs. When you go to school in a prefab, or study at a 1970s polytechnic that looks like the office of an ailing insurance company, buildings like this make you feel intimidated and inferior. But if you'd gone to a school with deer parks and croquet lawns and Grade I-listed interiors, you'd be used to all the pomp and grandeur. It wouldn't seem weird at all.

Caroline Lucas walked in wearing her No More Page Three T-shirt. I wanted to cheer so hard. Rhianne and I quickly put our T-shirts back on, and Lucy unbuttoned her jacket so hers was on view. She was leaning so far forward in her seat she was practically on the floor. She couldn't sit still and kept wriggling around like somebody at a wedding reception who is desperate to get up and dance.

Caroline began to speak, and the room fell so quiet you could hear a low electric hum coming from the power cables.

'There are few things more important than ensuring that every member of our community feels safe in their own home, in their own workplace . . . and school. Sadly, for far too many women and girls in the UK, this is simply not the case, and there is strong evidence that media sexism is playing a significant contributory role.'

Caroline went on to state the facts; that in Britain sixty thousand women are raped every year and two women a week are killed by a current or former partner. That a YouGov poll for the End Violence Against Women Coalition found that one in three girls had experienced unwanted sexual touching at school, and that an NSPCC study revealed that one in two boys and one in three girls believe that there are some circumstances in which it's OK for a man to hit a woman or to force her to have sex. She also referenced a review commissioned by the government, *Sexualisation of Young People*, which found evidence to suggest a clear link between the consumption of sexualised images, a tendency to view women as objects and the acceptance of aggressive attitudes and behaviour as the norm.

She was interrupted mid-flow by Jimmy Hood, who was chairing the session, asking her to cover up her T-shirt, which was 'not in line with regulations' and 'may cause offence'.

She picked up a copy of *The Sun*, opened it at Page 3, held it up next to her and said, 'It does strike me as a certain irony that this T-shirt is regarded as an inappropriate thing to be wearing in this House, whereas apparently it is appropriate for this kind of newspaper to be available to buy in eight different outlets on the Palace of Westminster estate.'

Rhianne squeezed my hand, and Lucy nodded furiously.

She threw her jacket on and continued, pointing out that *The Sun* contained pictures that would be illegal if displayed on workplace walls due to equality legislation, and calling on the government to take action if *The Sun*'s editors did not stop publishing topless women on Page 3 by the end of the year.

And then suddenly it was all over, and we filed out of the room. Outside in the hall, a crowd had been watching the debate on a monitor screen. Laura Bates, the founder of The Everyday Sexism Project, was standing next to Steve who was dressed head to toe in Lycra, with a red mark across his forehead from his bike helmet.

'Why are you two out here?' Lucy asked, running towards them.

'They wouldn't let me in,' Laura said. 'It was full capacity. But then I met Steve and we stood out here and watched it together.'

We slowly dispersed out onto Parliament Square. I took deep gulps of fresh air, and I started talking at a normal volume again.

The image of Caroline Lucas wearing the No More Page Three T-shirt in Parliament swept across the media. Every time I searched for something online, I'd stumble across an article with Caroline's picture asking, 'Has Page 3 had its day?' Happily,

The Sun did not respond by sending a bus load of glamour models to Caroline's house, nor did they mock up a topless photo of her in the paper. In fact, they didn't do anything at all; they carried on as normal, pretending the whole thing hadn't happened. Of course, Michael Waldon weighed in, appearing on the news with Caroline and telling her to focus on bigger things. He was infuriating in the interview, talking over her and dismissing her opinions, but we were on such a high we didn't really care. Even my mum, who usually dismissed politicians as 'all the same', was caught up in the excitement of it all.

'That Caroline Lucas is wonderful,' she said.

'And what did you think of Michael Waldon?'

'I thought he seemed totally out of touch. And he certainly likes the sound of his own voice.' She paused for a moment and then said, 'Actually, he reminds me a bit of your dad.'

High Art

The next few weeks got busier and busier and things became increasingly surreal. I'd take Livia to school in the mornings, then focus on the campaign for the rest of the day. It consumed almost all of my time. The requests we received were no longer just for interviews or comments, but for increasingly bizarre things. Did we want to have a strategy meeting at Alastair Campbell's house? Would Max give a presentation at the European Guiding conference in Berlin? Did Lucy want to speak at Glastonbury? Would I like to talk about street harassment for a German documentary? How about performing the flash mob on a West End stage? To make things even stranger, my dad appeared to be genuinely interested in what we were doing. He'd send text messages saying, *Good bit about the campaign in the paper today*, or, *Your mate Lucy's just been on Channel 4. I've recorded it for you.* He appeared to have convinced himself that he'd always thought the campaign was a good idea, in much the same way that he now insisted he had never voted for Tony Blair.

In the middle of another hectic week, *The Sun*, without any sort of fanfare, appointed a new editor.

High Art

Jess: Who is he then?

Lucy: He was the editor of *The Scottish Sun*.
David Dinsmore.

Steve: Described as 'a *Sun* man through and
through'.

Jess: Imagine being described like that and not
throwing yourself under a bus

Lucy: There are rumours that he's scrapping
News in Briefs

Evie: I hope he does. I've always thought News
in Briefs is the worst bit.

Kate: I've got mixed feelings. On the one hand
this new editor might start acknowledging us.
That would be good. But on the other it really
buggers up the YMCA lyrics.

Me: Dinsmore are you listening to me?

Kate: Doesn't work.

Kate: Never thought I'd miss Mohan.

After taking over as editor, David Dinsmore made a series
of small but significant changes. First, he scrapped News in

Briefs, then Page 360 – a feature on the website which allowed viewers to 'take her for a spin', rotating the model and pausing at their preferred angle.

> Me: I can't believe News in Briefs has gone.

> Kate: And Page 360! It always felt like a cattle auction, turning the woman around to inspect her from every angle

> Evie: And there's been no Page 3 idol competition this year

Page 3 Idol was *The Sun*'s annual contest, where 'girls aged 18+ with natural breasts' were encouraged to send in topless photos. These photos were printed and published online, and readers were encouraged to judge the girls' bodies to decide who was the best. It was *The Sun*'s way of recruiting girls from their own living rooms.

We wondered if Page 3 was slowly being dismantled bit by bit, like a Christmas tree being taken down and put away in the loft.

Our burgeoning hopes were dashed when David Dinsmore was interviewed on LBC Radio about his appointment as editor. The interviewer inquired about the future of Page 3 – was it safe?

'It is, it is, yes, I can tell you that,' Dinsmore replied. 'This stuff at the British Museum is far more explicit and raunchy.'

He was referring to a new, age-restricted exhibition of nineteenth-century Japanese erotic art that had opened in

London for visitors over the age of sixteen. *The Times* had written an article about it, reproducing an image from the exhibition, which Dinsmore claimed had 'given the editor of *The Times* the opportunity to put a naked Japanese lady on Page 3 which, as we know, is a good way of selling newspapers'.

I looked up the article and saw the image he was referring to.

'Hmm,' I muttered. 'Interesting.'

It was a nineteenth-century woodblock print showing a hirsute woman rapturously receiving the intimate attentions of a pair of octopuses.

> Kate: Am I high or did Dinsmore just compare Page 3 to a picture of a fisherwoman getting head from a mollusc?
>
> Max: Maybe this Page 3 rebrand is going further than we thought.

The radio interview put us in an unusual position because, when we were asked to respond to Dinsmore's comments, we found ourselves saying combinations of words we never expected to say, ever, like 'octopus sex' or 'tentacle erotica'.

But Dinsmore wasn't the first person to compare Page 3 to fine art. The Page 3 issue was often turned into a debate about 'high' versus 'low' art. People frequently said to us, 'You can walk into a museum or gallery and see naked women, what's the difference between those paintings and Page 3?' Michael Waldon's *Huffington Post* piece about the campaign was illustrated with Picasso and Modigliani nudes. A Page 3 fan tweeted us an image of Manet's *Déjeuner sur l'herbe* saying, 'So this is OK and Page 3 is not?'

> Kate: it drives me mad when people compare Page 3 to fine art

> Kate: I've never been on a bus and had a man next to me looking at a Leonardo saying, 'Look at the rack on the Virgin Mary'

> Evie: Jo you're our resident art historian, what do you think?

I said that painted nudes and Page 3 pictures both reflected the attitudes of their cultural epoch, showing us how women were viewed and valued. And the truth was that, despite everything I was studying, I wasn't entirely comfortable with a lot of the art that I saw. The truth was that most of my trips to galleries went something like this:

Oh, oh good, here's another room of paintings of women done by men.

I love the Old Masters, who's being raped in this one? Proserpina? Europa? The Sabines? Medusa? Orithyia? And what is she being raped by this time? A man, a swan, a bull? By the wind? She's being raped by the weather? Well, it keeps it interesting, I suppose; one can get very bored with the more traditional rapes. I just love the depth of colour on that dress that's being torn off.

And what's over here? Oh, yes, another painting of a woman getting out of a bath, and there's an undressed twelve-year-old – Balthus, what a treat – and what's this? Naked Tahitian girls, painted with the skill and vigour that only a syphilitic sex tourist could possibly achieve. Before we go, shall we have a look at Eric Gill? I love the line on those prints of his naked teenage daughter, you know, the one he raped repeatedly throughout her childhood, along with her sisters and the family dog. It's definitely OK though, because his work hangs in churches and cathedrals, otherwise looking at it would feel weird!

Of all the examples of artistic nudes that David Dinsmore could have used, the Japanese woodblock print was the furthest from Page 3 that I could think of. The image was all about a woman receiving pleasure, a theme that doesn't crop up too often in the history of western art.

> Lucy: Look at her! She's having a great time! I'd love it if this was on Page 3!

> Jess: Men would be too intimidated by the octopuses.

> Max: #molluscfragility

> Kate: Today's been fucking weird.

Babycam

It was the hottest July in years and London sizzled. Commuters were stranded at stations as train tracks buckled in the heat. Office workers with skin the colour of cooked prawns shuffled through the city, holding tiny battery-operated fans up to their glowing faces. People moved slowly in the mornings and barely at all in the afternoons, exhausted after draining their energy reserves running away from wasps at lunchtime.

My hair did things that I don't understand and can't explain. Each day, it became more triangular in shape, flatter at the scalp and wider at the bottom. My face was pink (Pantone 191 C), apart from two white circles around my eyes where my sunglasses had been, and my dad took to calling me Chi Chi, after the panda he'd seen at London Zoo in the sixties. The only people who didn't look sunburnt, angry and frazzled were the women who appeared on the covers of most newspapers, most days; women in bikinis or cut-off denim shorts with sun-bleached highlights, snapped laughing on Brighton beach or reclining on a picnic blanket in Hyde Park.

Aside from the heatwave, the other big news was the Royal

Babycam

Baby. Kate Middleton, newly restyled as Catherine, Duchess of Cambridge, would soon give birth to the future king or queen, and the tabloids were shamelessly obsessed with her womb.

They guessed the gender. They guessed the name. They guessed the godparents. They made terrifying photofit images of what the child might look like at the age of five, eight, twelve, forty-seven. They expressed 'concern' over whether the Duchess was too thin to carry the Royal Baby, whether her roots were too grey since she'd stopped dyeing her hair, whether she should be wearing *those heels* in her condition. The tabloids swarmed around her like the interfering relatives you see once a year for fifteen minutes at Christmas, offering fawning praise, harsh judgements and backhanded compliments in quick succession. Intoxicated with Royal Baby fever, newspapers dispatched journalists and photographers to lurk outside the Lindo Wing of St Mary's Hospital, where the Duchess was expected to give birth at some point in the coming days or weeks. Reporters and members of the public with patriotic hats set up camp on the pavement outside the hospital, armed with sleeping bags, flasks and biscuits. *The Sun* had a 'Babycam' fixed on the entrance to the Lindo Wing, livestreaming on their website twenty-four hours a day.

From the coverage, you would have thought we all were awaiting the second coming of Jesus Christ.

> Evie: The poor woman, they won't leave her
> alone. That Babycam is creepy

Me: And pointless. I mean, it's not like they're
going to get footage of her staggering in agony
out of the back of a taxi, is it?

Jess: God they'd love that

Max: I feel sorry for the camera people, having
to camp out outside a hospital to film
A CLOSED FUCKING DOOR

Jess: And the people watching the livestream.
Endless real time footage of a closed door.

Max: A closed fucking door.

Jess: Sorry. A closed fucking door.

We were made slow and stupid by the heat. Whole minutes
passed before Evie typed her message.

Evie: Oh my god I've had an idea!

Evie is one of my favourite people in the entire world, and
I often think I would do anything for her. But when she asked
me on that boiling afternoon if I would like to meet her at
Paddington station in an hour and a half, I looked out of my
window and saw the heat rising in waves from the pavement,
and then I looked at the fan on my desk, slowly, beautifully
oscillating from left to right and back again, and I knew that

nothing could induce me to get on a bus, followed by the tube, changing lines at Oxford Circus. I put down my Calippo and wrote, with a twinge of guilt, that I was busy.

The others were also too busy to meet Evie, and it was suggested that we wait until the weekend, when it would be cooler and we'd all be off work and able to meet up, but Evie didn't want to wait. She was worried that the Duchess of Cambridge would go into labour and it would be too late. 'You never know,' Evie said, 'she might eat a big curry tonight and then that's it – we've missed our chance.'

She roped in her friend Camille instead, asking her to come to a pub in Paddington for a drink after she'd finished her shift at the bank. When she arrived, Evie passed her a campaign T-shirt and told her the plan. She messaged us from the pub.

Evie: Camille's just got here, we're just having a drink

Evie: God I'm nervous, going to have a tequila shot

Evie: I might just have one more tequila shot

Evie: OK oh my god OK. We're on our way

We were all glued to our laptops, flicking between HQ and *The Sun*'s Babycam.

Kate: This is more exciting than Andy Murray in the Men's Final at Wimbledon

Steve: I wonder if she's finished the tequila yet?

Lucy: They're on!!!! Oh my god, look!!!!!!

I switched to the Babycam just in time to see two women walk purposefully to the door of the Lindo Wing and turn to face the cameras. I actually screamed. Then a policeman wandered over and started talking to them and they disappeared off screen.

Jess: Nooooooooooo

Lucy: Shit do you think they've been moved on?

Kate: Wait! They're back!!!

Evie suddenly reappeared right in front of the camera in her No More Page Three T-shirt, her friend Camille lurking at a distance behind her, looking uncomfortable and embarrassed, like a teenager with her mother on parents' evening. I could hear a man's voice. I turned the volume up and heard him say, 'Nah, this isn't *The Sun*'s camera, you've got the wrong one darlin'.'

Evie was looking around. Someone out of view was shouting something to her. I saw her look at her phone. We all started typing at once.

Evie: Can you see me? There are loads of
different cameras here – tons of people filming.
Some of them told me this IS *The Sun*'s camera
but he's telling me I'm wrong.

Babycam

Jess: He's lying to you! We can see you!

Me: You're on the Babycam!

Evie: You can see me? Can you hear me?

Lucy: Yes!!!! Don't move!!!!

Evie's expression changed as she read our messages. She grinned, put her phone in her back pocket and shouted to Camille: 'It *is* this camera, he's lying to us.'

Camille anxiously whispered something. Evie later told me that she'd said, through clenched teeth, 'I can't get arrested, Evie, I'm going to Lovebox this weekend.'

And then the Babycam went blank.

Kate: They've turned it off! The fuckers have
turned it off!!!!!

I refreshed the screen, but nothing happened. That was it then, it was over.

I went into the kitchen to stand in front of the fridge for a while. I thought that if I took the shelves out I could probably fit inside, but that would mean moving Rebecca's jam and I was expressly forbidden from touching it. I held some Lurpak against my face for a bit, then strolled back to my laptop. The Babycam was live again, and Evie was right in front of the camera, mid-rant.

'– men in their suits or football kits actively doing stuff and then seeing the women posing, standing still, posing – just there to look pretty – it's an absolute disgrace that women are treated like this when there's so much more to us than what we look like. We need to be heard. We need to be treated as people.'

I could hear the cameraman laughing, but she just carried on talking.

> Jess: AAAAAAAAAAHHHH can you guys hear this? She's a LEGEND!

> Steve: Taking down *The Sun* – live on their own website

> Lucy: Evie you are a HERO!!!!

The cameraman moved the camera away and Evie followed it, still talking. Then he tilted the camera up, filming the hospital windows above her head, but we could still hear her.

'So this man, who has his back to me now, has averted his camera because apparently I'm more offensive than pictures of naked women in the newspaper. Maybe if I took my top off he might turn around – maybe I'd be worthy of attention then – or maybe I've just got too much to say and he's frightened of hearing a woman's voice?'

'It's off air,' the cameraman said. 'We've taken it off air.'

> Me: Evie he's lying again – we can hear you!

Babycam

Jess: Did you hear that? The guys behind the
camera sneering, and saying 'tart'?

Me: Don't give up Evie, you're doing an
AMAZING JOB

Lucy: Look at this comment from someone who
has just signed the petition:

'I am watching the live feed of the Lindo Wing
and this woman is making a compelling stand
against the nudity that is in this paper and even
though I'm American, I totally agree with her!'

Lucy: Lots of people tweeting too

The whole thing had the air of a 1980s telethon; Evie broadcasting live outside a city hospital while the messages rolled in: 'Marie from Swindon says you're doing a great job, keep it up!' But not everyone approved.

Jess: Have you seen these messages from
people who say Evie is spoiling their view on the
Babycam?

Max: I'll say it one more time. It's a CLOSED
FUCKING DOOR

I looked at the clock. Evie had been speaking for two hours. She'd spoken about the girls who'd contacted us to share their experiences of growing up with Page 3, she'd talked about breastfeeding, workplace harassment and sexist news. A female police officer had watched from across the street, nodding in agreement. Every now and then, Evie stopped mid-rant to speak to journalists or passers-by who had approached her for a chat. After speaking to a reporter, she turned back to face the camera and said: 'If *The Sun* got rid of Page 3 it would set a precedent for other newspapers to follow and maybe, just maybe, we could live in a world that was a bit more equal.'

And she paused, looked across at Camille and burst out laughing.

'Well done!' Camille shouted, and then people started clapping.

> Jess: Oh my god they're clapping!!! Can you hear them all? People outside the hospital are applauding her!
>
> Lucy: I'm clapping too!!!
>
> Kate: I've been cheering solidly for two hours

Evie grabbed Camille's hand and they walked away, holding on to each other. As the Babycam focused in on the closed door, my heart felt fluttery and light.

It was the best thing I'd seen on TV in ages.

Bruises

Suddenly everybody wanted us to repeat the flash mob. Requests poured in for us to do it again and again. Supporters organised flash mobs of their own in different towns and cities. Kate danced on stage with trade union members at the Unison AGM, in front of hundreds of delegates, to officially announce their support of the campaign. And then we were asked to perform the flash mob on stage at the Garrick Theatre as part of the comedy benefit, Stand up for Women. We had inadvertently become a 1970s dance troop. We were the Pan's People of feminism.

For some reason, the organiser of the benefit wanted us to get there at 2 p.m., six hours before the performance. We arrived and quickly realised that the theatre was the hottest place in Britain, hotter even than Nessa's house, and she'd had the radiators on since 1973. I was in a terrible mood. I had a head-ache and the carpet in the theatre smelled like a damp tent. I was bloated and short-tempered and had cramps and I felt like a boiled ham.

The organiser bustled into the room. She clapped her hands together.

'Right, well if you want something to do, you could put

your costumes on and head over to Covent Garden to hand out flyers.'

Covent Garden in peak tourist season, on the hottest weekend of the year.

Jess and Evie looked at each other.

'Well, it's really hot,' Evie said, 'and we'll need to get some food and a drink, but I suppose we—'

'No,' I said.

Jess stared at me.

'Sorry, no,' I said again.

It was the first time I could remember resolutely refusing to do something I didn't want to do.

The organiser mouthed 'OK' and trotted off in search of Lucy.

Jess said, 'What's up with you?'

'Oh, it's just . . .' I sighed and sat down heavily. 'I just don't feel great. I'm having . . . I mean, it's just a bad period, that's all.'

'Oh, darling, why, what's happening?' She tucked a stray strand of hair behind my ear and looked deeply concerned.

'No, I mean it's literally a bad period. I've got cramps and I'm bloated and this zip is digging into my back.'

'Oh my GOD!' she shouted, shoving me harder than expected. 'I thought something terrible had happened! You're so dramatic!'

She laughed and then her phone pinged with a text message and, as she stared at the screen, her face changed.

'Everything OK?'

She put her phone back in her pocket and said, 'Yeah, yeah, everything's fine. Matt's just being a dick, that's all.'

Bruises

We went to get lunch. I was sat in the corner, next to Max. As everyone ordered coffee, water, lemonade, Max ordered a glass of Sauvignon Blanc.

'What size?' the waiter asked.

'Large please. Very large. Well,' she said, turning to me, 'if we've got to dance on stage we might as well do it pissed.'

'I'll have the same,' I said to the waiter.

'How's the PhD going?' she asked.

'Not great. Well, OK, maybe. I don't know. I shouldn't be doing it.'

'Imposter syndrome,' she said.

'You always say that, but it's not, honestly. I have no idea what I'm doing.'

'Then, you know what they say, fake it till you make it.'

'Did you fake it before you made it?'

'I'm ALWAYS faking it.'

'And it seems to have worked for you?'

'Well,' she said, 'I work hard. Twice as hard as most of the men, because I have to, to prove myself. And I'm judged, I know I'm judged, for being a single woman in her forties with no kids. It's almost expected that I'll take on extra work because I've got "nothing better" to do. It's absolute bullshit. You have to have a thick skin. I don't really, but I pretend I do.'

'I've got the world's thinnest skin,' I said. 'I care way too much what everybody thinks. If I'm in a room with someone who's angry or sad or anxious, I feel it straight away, and then I take it all on. I absorb everybody else's emotions.'

'You can't do that. If you do that, you take on everybody's shit until there's no space left for your own. And you need to focus on your own stuff. That's the most important thing. Just keep faking it. Keep pretending and then one day it'll be real, and you actually won't care so much what other people think.'

It had taken a while to get to know Max. She wasn't as open as Lucy or as easy-going as Kate, and she'd told us that she doesn't let her guard down easily.

'I've never had a big group of female friends,' she said in HQ. 'This is all new to me.'

But although Max wasn't as forthcoming as some of the others, she was a great listener and she was trustworthy and loyal. She was like a fierce older sister who would look out for you at school. She wouldn't necessarily hug you if you were feeling sad, she'd just efficiently plot the downfall of the people upsetting you, while drinking a very strong martini.

'You know,' I said to her, as we sipped our very large glasses of very cold wine, 'I was intimidated by you at first. You scared me a bit.'

Max smiled and said, 'I'll take that as a compliment. I mean, what could be better than being a scary woman?'

We slinked back to the theatre and started getting ready in a big shared dressing room with lights over the mirrors, then we sat in the audience and waited for our cue to rush on stage and launch into the dance.

Max and I were both really tipsy. I can't remember getting onto the stage, but Max almost fell over and I lost confidence, forgot all the moves and just flailed my arms around. On all the photos, we are a blur at the back, as if moving at a completely different speed to everyone else. There's one photo I like in particular: it shows Lucy, Evie and Kate standing under the spotlights looking at each other in a disbelieving 'this is INSANE' sort of way. It perfectly captures the spirit of that time, of all the bizarre situations we found ourselves in, and those quiet moments when you suddenly take stock and say, 'Can you believe this is happening?'

Jess stayed at mine that night. We started the journey back to Dulwich in high spirits, fuelled by adrenaline and rum and coke, but good humours were difficult to sustain on the night bus.

'How long does this take?' Jess asked, fanning herself with a dirty newspaper she'd found on the floor. 'I feel like we should be in Southampton by now.'

Instead of the typical London double-decker, the number twelve to Dulwich was a bendy bus – a single-level, double-length vehicle that was articulated in the middle and moved like a python that had swallowed a vibrator. I saw countless people vomit on that bus. Passengers would board, scan their Oyster cards and behave like a normal commuter for seven or eight minutes, before becoming increasingly clammy and panicked, their faces taking on the pallor of a Victorian ghost child.

When we finally reached our stop, we got off the bus and walked to the flat like veterans of the Crimean War. I took deep breaths and made – what I expected to be – light conversation.

'How's work going?'

'I'm not working any more, am I?'

'I thought you were working from home?' We walked up the path and I searched for my keys.

'I ended the contract, but I'm kind of regretting it now.' I saw Miran peeking from behind her living-room curtains and quickly unlocked the door, ushering Jess into the hallway.

'Why did you do that?'

'I didn't want to. It was Matt, putting loads of pressure on me. He's been wanting me to stop working for ages.'

'Because you didn't like it?'

'No. I mean, look, I didn't love it, but I needed the work. I needed something to do that wasn't about the house or my husband or my child.'

We walked quietly up the stairs and into the kitchen. Jess sat at the table as I ran the tap, waiting for the water to get cold.

'So why doesn't he want you to work?'

'He says we don't need the money, that I'm exhausting myself for nothing – that it's time that could be spent with Ruby or sorting out the house. Ever since we got married, he's been saying, "You don't need to work so hard now," as if he's rescued me from my fucking life. He doesn't get that I need my own money. I've left so many jobs because he's made me feel guilty for working. It's fucked up.' She took a long drink of the water I'd placed in front of her on the table. 'It's only when I stand back and look at my life that I see how ridiculous it is.'

We looked at each other for a moment and then she shook her head and looked away.

'Don't ever get fucking married.'

'How many times has he made you do this before? Quit jobs, I mean?'

'Oh, like every time.'

'Every time you've had a job?'

'Yeah, every time.'

I started to say something, and stopped.

'I know,' she said. 'I know. It's really messed up.' She pulled her phone out of her pocket, glanced at the screen and placed it face-down on the table. 'I've got eleven missed calls and I don't know how many text messages. This is what he does whenever I go anywhere. He needs to know exactly where I am all the time. When he used to work away, he'd insist that I text him a photo of myself in bed with my pyjamas on and my make-up off every night, so he'd know I wasn't out with my friends. He only stopped doing that when I had Ruby, because he knew I couldn't go anywhere then.'

I stared at her without blinking. 'That's insane.'

'I know,' she said. 'he's always been controlling. I used to just go along with it all because I was scared of him.'

'He never physically – he never hurts you, does he?'

She took a deep breath. 'He used to drink. He had a drink problem. Half of his family are alcoholics, not that it's ever talked about. He's stopped now, he's teetotal. But, yeah, things weren't great when he was drinking. He'd sometimes get so angry, he'd just suddenly flip and be totally out of control, smashing stuff around the house, or throwing things at me. That's how it started. Then gradually it got worse, like he'd push me around, or grab me by the wrist so hard I'd have bruises. He hit me a couple of times when he really lost it. The more he drank, the worse he'd be. I'm not making excuses for him – he didn't hit me *because* he was drunk, but when he was drunk, he didn't care about the consequences. That was the difference. He'd fly into a rage whether he'd been drinking or not, but when he was sober, he'd usually stop himself before he went too far. He stopped being physically violent to me when he stopped drinking a few years ago, but then he just hurt me in other ways instead, like, after we'd have a row he'd sometimes storm out of the house and lock me in – he'd take my keys and make sure the windows were locked so I couldn't get out. That was the worst thing he did actually, because it would really freak me out not knowing when, or if, he was coming back.'

The words tumbled out of her, as if she couldn't hold them back any longer. I just sat there, trying to take it all in.

'When I met him, I was so confident and loud and outgoing and that's what attracted him to me, and then as soon as we were married he started trying to dismantle all that and make me into something else. He wanted me to dress differently and have different friends and to stay at home, and to be a completely different person, basically.

'I tried to leave him once, but it didn't work. He's got all the money, that's the thing. His family have money and mine don't, so there's always this imbalance.

'After I left, he promised he'd change and we went to therapy and everything. Fuck knows where he found the therapist though. She'd come out with all this new-age bullshit, and it was just so blindingly obvious that she was on his side. She agreed with everything he said, and then I brought up the money issue. I said he has to have control over everything, he has to make all the decisions and he has all the money. And you know what she said to me? She said, "Money is just energy – that's all it is, it's just energy," and I said "OK, well he's got all the fucking energy then," and she just gave me this hard stare like you'd get at school if you acted up.

'The only good thing to come out of it was she told him that he had to trust me more and let me go off and do things, and without that I probably wouldn't have been able to do any of the campaign stuff, he wouldn't have let me. I mean, he still watches everything I do, but—'

'That petition signing,' I said. 'When he went with you to the petition signing, and you posted that photo on Facebook –'

'And everyone thought he was there to support me? No. He was there to keep an eye on me. I barely spoke to anyone that whole day, because I knew he was listening to everything I said.'

My chair scraped across the floor as I stood up to hug her. I saw that she was trying not to cry.

'It's OK,' she said, 'I'm OK.' She pulled a tissue out of her pocket and blew her nose. 'It was the Reeva thing that made me think about it all. It just messed me up. Did you hear about that voicemail?'

I shook my head.

'Reeva Steenkamp left this voicemail message for him, for Pistorius, saying, "I never thought I'd need protection from the person who is supposed to be protecting me." And when I heard about it, I felt like I'd been punched in the stomach, because I've said those words. I've said near-identical words, and this woman is dead and she's saying the words I say. And then at The Pineapple. That last time we were there, when Kate was talking about her ex-husband smashing that mirror and it just hit me, like, what's happened to me – what's happening to me – it's not OK, and it's not normal and I don't deserve it. And I was just sitting there thinking, if they knew, if any of them knew my situation, how fucked up it is . . . It just forced me to think about it all.'

'You've got friends in Newcastle,' I said. 'And family, right? Couldn't you stay with them while you find somewhere?'

'I've never told them about any of this. I don't want them to know. And I have a three-year-old – I can't just turn up at my cousin's house and sleep on her sofa.'

'I'll help you,' I said. 'Everyone will. We'll work something out.'

'I know, I know, but how? I've got no money. I've got no job now. What about Ruby? She adores her dad.' She looked at me.

'I know what you're thinking, but he's a really good dad. Honestly, he adores her. It's me – he's like that with me, but not with her – he'd never lay a finger on her. And it's not always bad. I'm making it sound bad, you know, I'm telling you the worst things. It's not like that all the time.'

Jess sat down, resting her head in her hands, and I thought of my sister, when she left her ex-husband and was alone with her two-year-old daughter, no money, no job, a council house found under emergency circumstances. She was so beaten down, so exhausted, and the house was empty, with peeling paint and no carpets. Nessa came over, and she and my mum and my sister all painted the tiny house together. Nessa, my mum, my sister and her daughter, four generations of women, filling that house with the future. My mum babysat while my sister went to university. Three buses there and three buses home every day, hours of travelling and studying. She hadn't made it to university at eighteen, but she got there in the end.

Her graduation photo was the one family picture that hung on the wall at my parents' house. She was a success story. She escaped that marriage and built a new life for herself and her daughter. But it all started with a group of women standing together, painting an empty house.

I wanted to do that for Jess. And I knew the others would want that too.

I met Rhianne at the pub on Peckham Rye. We sat in the beer garden and she chain-smoked as we talked. She leaned back to blow the smoke away from me, but it always blew back in my face. 'Sorry,' she'd say, waving away the smoke with her hand. 'Sorry, what was I saying?'

We were talking about Jess. Rhianne had spoken to her on the phone, and Jess had told her about the situation with Matt.

'I'm so worried about her,' I said.

'Me too.' Rhianne took a swig of beer, stubbed out her cigarette and said, 'He's clearly a total arsehole.'

'She put new photos of them up on Facebook the other day. Did you see? They were having a picnic with Ruby.'

'His stupid smirking fucking face.'

'I hate him. I've never even met him and I hate him.'

Rhianne started rolling another cigarette. When she had finished, she positioned it next to her wallet and her ancient Nokia flip-top phone, everything lined up, just so.

'We've got to get her away from him,' I said. 'We've got to do something.'

'I know, Jo, but the truth is we can't do anything unless she *wants* us to. She just doesn't seem ready to leave him. We've got to give her time.'

'What if there isn't time? What if he really hurts her?'

'She said he doesn't hit her any more.'

'What a great guy. He doesn't hit her any more.'

'Hey, I'm on your side. I want her away from him as much as you – but I just think that if we go in there telling her what to do it'll push her away, and she'll stop telling us anything at all. She has to be able to trust us.'

'What day did you speak to her on the phone?'

'Tuesday.'

'Have you been in touch with her since?'

'I've messaged her, but she's not replied.'

'Same. She hasn't replied to me either.'

Almost a week had passed since Jess stayed over. She'd sent me a message the following day, after she'd got home, saying, *Sorry for dumping all that on you Jo.* I replied right away, saying, *Tell me anything, call me anytime,* but that was the last time I'd heard from her. I'd sent texts, Facebook messages, I'd tried to call her, but she clearly didn't want to talk. She hadn't been in HQ, but she'd been online at some point to change her profile picture to the photo of the family picnic; the three of them huddled together, laughing at the camera as if everything was just perfect.

'She probably feels vulnerable after sharing so much,' Rhianne said. 'Or, I dunno, maybe she feels guilty for telling us about him.'

'I just want her out of there, now. He's separated her from her family, her friends, the people she worked with. She's totally isolated there.'

'What do you want to do, turn up at the house and insist that she leaves?'

'Yes.'

Rhianne sighed. 'It feels like an emergency to us, right? But to Jess it's just routine. It's her daily life. They've been married for what, ten years? Eleven years? She's used to him treating her like shit, it's all she knows. And I don't think she's in a position to just get up and leave.'

'I know you're right,' I said, sighing. 'But what are we supposed to do, just pretend everything's fine?'

Rhianne lit another cigarette and thought for a moment. 'I feel like the best place for her is HQ. It's a place where she's loved and appreciated and respected. And listened to. I think we just carry on as normal and wait until she wants to talk, and then be there for her. We've got to make it clear that we love her unconditionally, regardless of what choices she makes or what she feels able or unable to do. And you know what else matters? We have fun together. We make each other laugh. God, she'll need that.'

And so, we carried on, business as usual. Instead of asking Jess how she was, or how things were at home, we sent her funny messages to make her laugh. She responded then, and her relief was palpable.

'I know you're worried,' she said, after a volley of light-hearted messages, 'but things are good at the moment. Me and Matt are getting on and, yeah, stuff's fine.'

'Good,' I said, 'I'm so glad things are better.'

But I didn't feel better about any of it at all.

Yas

I got off the train at Kentish Town and made my way to The Pineapple at a pace faster than Nordic walking but slower than jogging; a type of rushing that requires a series of long strides followed by a short trot, and then more strides. The trains had been delayed again, and I didn't want to miss the start of the campaign meeting.

I rushed into the upstairs function room, where everyone was gathered in the usual corner, and as I said hello, I spotted a person I didn't recognise sitting quietly in a chair pushed further back than the rest. It took me a while to remember that Lucy had invited Yas to join us.

Yas, sixteen and still at school, had first contacted us a few months earlier.

My parents are Sun *readers*, the message had said, *so I see Page 3 all the time at home. And I hear on average three rape jokes a day at school – I know because I started counting them.*

That sentence made a knot form in my stomach. I remembered sharply how threatening school could be and how unsafe

I often felt in classrooms and corridors. I felt an overwhelming desire to protect Yas, even though we'd never met, even though I knew it was impossible to shield another person from the harshness of the world.

Yas wrote a blog and shared the link with us, and I read all of it in one go. The posts were about activism, anxiety, gender and cultural identity, and were tender, complex and beautifully written. Back then, when we first met, Yas hadn't yet come out as trans non-binary, and was still excavating and exploring their identity, and questioning the experiences that had shaped who they were in the world, what was inherited and what was learned. Back then, Yas used feminine pronouns and tried to feel comfortable with the words 'girl' and 'woman', even though they never felt quite right.

I stood in front of the mirror, Yas wrote in a blog post. *'She' I'd say out loud, and shake my head. 'He' I'd say out loud, and shake my head too . . . The language doesn't feel right to me.* Yas wrote that they often felt like an 'odd half', like the half-creatures in the comic books they loved – centaurs, mermaids, werewolves and valkyries. They wrote about their childhood love of super-heroes, and how they wanted their body to be powerful, strong and muscular and flat. As a child, they would stand in front of the mirror and hit out at their reflection, pretending to be a boxer. Yas wrote so honestly of how they struggled when their body softened and curved after puberty and how they strived to look more androgynous, but felt pressured to dress like a girl. Yas also wrote about their Cypriot family, especially their grandmother, who would speak in English and Turkish, some-times drifting into Greek and praying in Arabic. It was all so searching and raw and the things Yas said grabbed at my heart. I had read so much about their life that when I met Yas in person, I wanted to ask about school and friends and relatives, but they seemed quiet and introverted and I didn't want to make them feel uncomfortable, so I just smiled and asked if I could get them a drink.

'A coke or something, maybe?'

'No, thank you, I'm fine with water.'

'Really? Are you sure, I can just pop down to the bar –'

'No, it's fine, honestly. Thank you.'

Priya plonked down in the next chair. 'Hi Yas, I'm Priya. Is it alright if I sit here?'

I saw Yas visibly relax as Priya started conversation in that easy, engaging way.

'I heard you organised a No More Page 3 protest,' she said. 'I wish I could have been there. I went to one that Lucy organised last year – that's where I met Jo – but I haven't done anything since. I've been so busy with work and everything. But your protest sounded amazing.'

'It was fun,' Yas said quietly, 'we asked people to write down why they wanted No More Page 3, then we took the pieces of paper and made them into origami flowers. We made this big bouquet and delivered it to the editor.'

I thought that Yas's style of protest mirrored their personality. Gentle, creative, peaceful, unique.

We had discussed the possibility of inviting Yas to join the team, and our only reservation was their age. We were on the receiving end of so much abuse on a daily basis, and we didn't want a teenager to be exposed to the trolls.

'But Yas will get all that shit at school anyway,' Jess said. 'School is brutal. Plus, Yas already does loads of campaigning stuff, right, for other causes?'

I had read on Yas's Facebook page that they were involved with anti-bullying charities, mental health awareness and animal refuges. They did stuff for LGBTQ+ organisations and homeless shelters as well. I didn't know anyone so socially conscious and self-aware when I was a teenager; at sixteen, my idea of social injustice was having my fake ID refused at Yates Wine Lodge. But Yas was different.

We really wanted Yas on board and we talked through our concerns, but the decision wasn't ever really in our hands anyway. Yas appeared to have decided that we all belonged together, in the way that a neighbourhood cat will suddenly decide it lives with you now.

'Yas will be safe with us,' Lucy said. 'Always.'

The theme of the campaign meeting was education. We'd been invited to speak at a number of schools and universities, and Jess had spent the past few weeks rushing from one event to the next. At first, I was worried that she was doing too much and would burn out.

'Honestly, I'm not keeping busy just to distract myself because my life is shit,' she told me. 'I feel good about myself when I do campaign stuff. It makes me feel better. Like I matter.'

She told me about a talk she'd done a few weeks ago at a secondary school in Middlesbrough.

'So, this teacher, Julia, arranged for all these incredible

speakers to run workshops with her sixth-form students – these really inspiring activists and campaigners and writers – and she did it all in her own time, for no extra pay. And she's this formidable, brilliant woman and she gives off this teacher energy, you know, like you wouldn't mess with her. Then after I spoke, I went to say thank you and shake her hand, and she just said, so casually, "You're coming to my house for a drink, right?" And we just sat around at her place, talking and laughing and drinking wine, and we came up with all these ideas for lesson plans and activism packs we could send out to schools.'

We built a new website with a section dedicated to schools, colleges and universities, providing free downloadable resources and ideas of how to get involved with the campaign.

In just a matter of months, twenty-six universities and colleges contacted us to say they had voted to stop selling *The Sun* on campus or providing it in their common rooms, including the University of Sheffield, University of Manchester, London School of Economics and a number Oxford colleges. At the same time, the National Union of Teachers announced their support of the campaign, followed by the Association of Teachers and Lecturers and the National Association of Headteachers. The talks we had done in schools and the planning Jess had done with Julia, the formidable teacher you wouldn't mess with, had lit a fuse that had led to explosions of activity in institutions and on campuses across the country.

Lucy's nieces and their friends, all undergraduates, had stepped in to help with social media, reaching out to student unions and blogging about their experiences of student life. They brought a certain glamour to HQ with their bodycon dresses, high heels and long swishy hair. If Simon Cowell ever set eyes on them, he'd have them in a girl band within fifteen minutes.

'I love all the pictures they post,' Kate said, 'where they're all dressed up to the nines drinking cocktails.'

'I know,' Lucy said, 'they're so young and they're having so much fun. I keep messaging them, saying, "OK, remember – eat some vegetables and drink some water".'

Student life wasn't all fun though. We received so many messages from young people who had been harassed or assaulted on campus. Jess had been liaising with the NUS, and had agreed to speak at their national summit on lad culture.

I looked at her across the table. She seemed energised and happy. She spoke a lot, and made notes in a small hardback book. If she caught my eye she'd wink or smile or blow a kiss. Seeing her on such good form made me relieved and confused at the same time.

Yas stayed quiet for most of the meeting, but when we were talking about lesson plans and the curriculum, they leaned forward in their seat and said, 'Did you know the guidelines for SRE haven't been updated since 2000?'

'What's SRE?' I asked.

'Sex and relationships education,' Yas replied. 'We're taught nothing about consent, nothing about online bullying. Like, there's no mention of porn or sexting or anything – there's nothing about the internet whatsoever. It was created for a totally different generation and it just isn't addressing the issues we face now. It needs to change. Schools are failing us. They're supposed to prepare us for the world, and they're not doing that.'

'That's so interesting,' Lucy said. 'So, these guidelines were written before internet porn was really a thing?'

Yas nodded. 'And you know there's a statistic that says a third of teenagers actually believe that porn teaches them how to be in a relationship – and the average age that children start viewing internet porn is eleven. I've been in lessons where boys, like, really young boys, have been watching porn on their phones in the back of the classroom.'

'I can't imagine what it must be like to be at school now,' I said. 'I mean, boys used to bring in Page 3 and every now and then they'd get hold of a porn magazine, but *watching porn on their phones in class?*'

'It happens quite a lot,' Yas said. 'And like, sex education at school isn't addressing any of it. For us, SRE was basically our maths teacher wheeling out this old TV and putting this VHS tape in from, like, the eighties, and it was just this like, heterosexual, cisgender, nuclear family talking about sex. It was so awkward and weird and didn't answer any of our questions at all.'

When Yas finished speaking, they shrunk back into their seat, like a turtle disappearing into its shell, but their words hung in the air with a gravity all of their own.

The final thing we discussed that afternoon was *The Irish Sun*. Earlier in the week, it had been announced that they were dropping Page 3. The editor explained that the decision reflected 'the cultural differences in Ireland', which did little to address why those cultural differences were suddenly so glaringly apparent now, after Page 3 had been in the paper for over forty years. Page 3 was set to stay in the UK version though, because the editor insisted it was a 'hugely popular pillar of *The Sun* in the UK'.

Lucy was optimistic, as always. 'I honestly think Page 3 is on the way out,' she said.

Steve took a sip of his pint. 'Did you see the article this morning?' He picked up his phone and read aloud: 'A spokesman for *The Irish Sun* confirmed the paper has received a few phone calls inquiring about the change, which took effect on Monday, but only one reader has asked for the return of topless models.'

Kate laughed. 'Only one person has complained?'

'Can you imagine,' Max said, 'being that one loser who is so angry to find there are no tits in the paper that you stop everything and write in – to demand they're brought back?'

I leaned over to grab a handful of chips from the plate in front of me. 'Apparently, thousands of people complained when KitKats changed wrappers.'

'To be fair though, they were better before,' Kate said. 'Everybody preferred the foil.'

'The way you could run your fingernail down the groove in the middle,' Jess said, with a sigh of nostalgia.

Steve looked from Kate to me to Jess. 'How have we gone from Page 3 to KitKats?'

'You know,' said Lucy, moving on, 'I really think this could be it. I reckon they're watching to see what effect dropping Page 3 has on sales of *The Irish Sun* before doing it over here.'

'I agree,' Kate said. 'I think it's getting serious. I think we've got to really push now. It's time to turn it up a notch.'

'Let's do it,' Max said. 'Go big or go home.'

'Well, I mean, we've got to go home,' Kate said, 'because we don't have a bloody office.'

'OK, fine,' Max replied. 'We'll go big *and* go home.'

Go Big and Go Home

'Look!' I said, nudging Will and pointing across the road. 'Look over there!'

'Is it David Beckham?'

'What? No – why would it be David Beckham?'

'I see him around here sometimes. You see loads of famous people in Primrose Hill.'

Our favourite Sunday-morning activity was buying coffee and pastries and walking for miles and miles around London, people-watching. We saw all kinds of interesting things; a woman pushing a pram containing a doll with a cracked face, a man in gym gear doing pull-ups on a climbing frame while kids waited patiently to play, a miniature poodle wearing glittery red shoes like a tiny, woolly Judy Garland.

'It's not David Beckham,' I said. 'It's the woman outside the deli.'

He turned to look across the street. 'Who is she?'

'I don't know.'

'So, why am I looking at her?'

'Wait till she turns around – see! She's wearing a No More Page Three T-shirt!'

Go Big and Go Home

Will looked underwhelmed and disappointed.

'But don't you see?' I said. 'I've never seen her before in my life – she's just a random person, wearing our T-shirt.'

Two days later, Max said she'd seen somebody wearing a campaign tee on the tube on her way to work. Then a supporter from Belfast sent us a photo of her standing next to a woman with bright-red hair. They didn't know each other, but had both turned up to the same bar wearing No More Page Three T-shirts.

Me: It must be the Caroline Lucas effect. She wore the T-shirt at Westminster, and now everybody's wearing them.

Steve: I sometimes wear mine to train in. A woman high-fived me the other day as I ran past her in the park.

Steve: I told my wife and she said I'm becoming unbearable.

Evie: Did you see the picture Gemma Chan sent us, of her wearing her T-shirt on the train?

Jess: I LOVE HER. She's supported us from the very beginning.

Kate: Have you noticed though how we no longer have to spend all our time approaching people to ask for help? They come to us now.

It was true. Each week, we received messages from supporters who had made campaign films or music, staged exhibitions, created photography projects, conducted research and written dissertations. The singer, Miss Baby Sol, made a No More Page 3 song, Sabrina Mahfouz and Hollie McNish performed poems, Sarah Maple made art. A number of hip-hop artists signed the petition under the umbrella 'Hip Hop respects women'. Bridget Christie collected her Edinburgh Comedy Award in a campaign T-shirt, Russell Brand tweeted a photograph of himself holding one up to his chest, Jo Brand name-checked No More Page 3 in the pantomime she was appearing in. Jennifer Saunders signed the petition and Juliette Lewis shared our web link with her followers.

Then we received the news that the National Assembly for Wales had formally agreed to support No More Page 3. The decision was reached following an Individual Members Debate that gained cross-party support, brought forward by Rebecca Evans, Labour Assembly Member for Mid & West Wales. In a press release, Evans said that the continued presence of Page 3 in a national daily unrestricted newspaper, 'only serves to undermine the good work that government, the third sector, trade unions, teachers, parents, and many others are trying to do every day to build a country where we are all treated equally and with respect, and where young people grow up with healthy expectations of themselves and of others.'

By this point, we were used to people getting in touch to offer their support and to share their projects and ideas. We were even used to politicians contacting us; one hundred and fifty MPs had now signed our letter to the editor, but we never expected an entire parliament to support us.

We were in shock for about two weeks. We just couldn't believe it. We'd walk around distracted, burning toast, leaving emails unsent, picking things up and putting them down again, forgetting what we were supposed to be doing.

'OK, enough of this,' Kate said after a while, 'when are we all moving to Wales?'

That autumn, Scottish Parliament also passed a motion to support No More Page 3. During their debate, the Minister for Equalities, Shona Robison, said:

'The Scottish Government believes that achieving gender equality is one of the key building blocks that are required if we want to create a more successful Scotland. The routine reduction of women to their appearance – or a particular appearance – or to a combination of body parts is a barrier to achieving that aim.

'Like all Members who are here, I applaud the work of the No More Page 3 campaign. In just over a year, it has managed to encourage thousands of women and men to take a stand against negative, demeaning and limiting portrayals of women.'

We watched the debate livestreamed. Jess cried all the way through.

'I've got my diary here in front of me,' Kate said. 'Shall we just pick a date when we're all moving to Scotland?'

A few days later, I met Will and his mum for brunch; a meal that didn't exist in Rotherham, where people ate breakfast at breakfast time, and then went to work.

Will seemed more and more interested in the campaign, and we talked about it a lot. An increasing number of men were speaking out against Page 3 culture, including creative, funny, interesting people in the public eye. Doc Brown wrote a comedy rap in support of the campaign, Chris O'Dowd tweeted *Alright, we've had our fun, but we're grown ups now, right? Let's lose this dumb Page-3 shit.* Neil Gaiman signed and shared the petition. Billy Bragg offered to write a song. Male journalists wrote articles, male supporters ordered T-shirts. Seeing other men support the campaign gave Will permission to support it more vocally.

It also helped that his mum was interested in No More Page 3. A former journalist, she'd been supportive from the very beginning, always interested in what was going on, always ready to hear what we'd got planned.

'I've been keeping up with all you've been doing,' she said, when she arrived. 'Hats off. Very impressive. Has anyone at *The Sun* responded at all?'

'No,' I said. 'They pretend we don't exist. The only person who ever responds is Michael Waldon.'

'Who?'

'He's a former deputy editor of *The Sun*. He's a nightmare.' I complained about him for fifteen minutes, while we ate buttery toast and drank the last of the coffee in the pot.

'He likes to call himself The Wolf,' I said, 'because, well, I don't know why, but a lot of men who are total arseholes seem to like comparing themselves to wolves. But I call him The Shih Tzu, because he reminds me of my friend Paul's dog, Tinker, that used to just run around in circles and yap whenever a woman spoke in the vicinity.'

Months later, I would have reason to obsess over this conversation, revisiting every word I said over and over, but at the time I thought nothing of it. What did it matter what I said about Michael Waldon? I wasn't intimidated by him. He was just an annoying man on TV and Twitter who disliked the campaign. He had nothing much to do with my life at all. I could, and did, say whatever I wanted.

#KitOn

'The problem with the name No More Page 3,' Lucy said one afternoon, 'is that it focuses on what we *don't* want. I still think it's great – it's punchy and memorable and to the point. But it doesn't give any indication of what we actually want to see instead.'

We talked about this endlessly. We wanted to see women celebrated and critiqued in the media for the things they say and do, not for what they look like. We wanted to read articles about female politicians, actors and leaders that didn't focus on their hemlines, their weight, their age or their roles as mothers and wives. We also wanted to see more column inches dedicated to women's sport. We knew that, statistically, women's sport received only around 5 per cent of overall media coverage, roughly the same amount of space dedicated to men's darts. Studies told us that 64 per cent of girls in the UK drop out of sports by the age of sixteen; that 80 per cent of girls feel they do not belong in sport and 72 per cent of girls aged 11–21 say a lack of media coverage of women's sport leads them to being treated unfairly. We wanted to address this. We wanted to see women celebrated for what their bodies can do, rather than for what their bodies look like.

Lucy: You know how we've been talking a lot lately about women's sport?

Lucy: Well, we've been contacted by a women's football team – Cheltenham Town Ladies FC. They've had their funding cut and they desperately need money to pay for a new kit. They've asked if we'd consider sponsoring them, and having No More Page 3 emblazoned across the new strip.

Lucy: I love this idea. I love it I love it I love it.

Lucy: What do you all think?

I had always truly, deeply hated football. When I worked in pubs in Rotherham, I used to dread match days, when the fans would drink and fight and, occasionally, throw chairs through the windows. I'd go home and find little bits of glass embedded in the soles of my shoes. Whenever big tournaments rolled around – the European Championships, the World Cup – I always wished that I could live underground until it was all over, like a mole or a badger. I associated football with aggressive packs of drunk men, shouting nonsensical strings of words and waving flags. It all felt a bit *Lord of the Flies* to me.

Will played on a couple of local teams, and was always telling me how aggressive the other players were, about their banter and laddish behaviour.

One morning, on our Sunday walk, I stopped to smell the

most beautiful flowers trailing over a garden wall. Their petals were bright yellow, and their middles were fluffy like a teddy bear's paw.

'You have to touch this,' I said, 'it's so soft.'

Will turned around and leaned towards the flower, but then he suddenly snatched his hand away and swore loudly. I thought he'd been stung by a bee.

'Are you OK?' I asked, inspecting his finger.

'I play football with them,' he said, pointing to a car that had just zoomed past.

'So?'

'They saw me TOUCH A FLOWER!' He was horrified, and said he'd get loads of hassle for it.

'So, football is so macho that you can't play if you've done anything so wimpish as touch a flower?'

He didn't respond.

'If only it'd been a cactus, you might have got away with it,' I said.

The only girl I knew who played football was Livia. She was the only girl on a team of boys, all of them at least two years older than her. It's a testament to how good she was that ten-year-old boys wanted her on their side. She always wanted me to play with her after school, and for five minutes she'd enjoy kicking the ball as hard as physically possible in my direction and watching me run away from it, but she'd quickly get bored. 'It's like playing football with a mouse,' she told me. She could never get anyone to play with her. Her friends did ballet or gymnastics and they thought football was a boys' game.

I thought about Livia when I read Lucy's message. I imagined for a moment how things would change if female football players were plastered all over newspapers, billboards, TV, pencil cases. There would be a whole generation of girls growing up thinking it was a game for them, and wanting to play.

Kate: Wow! I love this idea so much! Footballers playing in a No More Page 3 kit!!!

Me: This is possibly the only thing that could ever get me interested in football.

Jess: It feels like we've come full circle. It was the reporting of women's sport that kicked off the whole campaign – with the Page 3 model taking up more space than Jessica Ennis.

Lucy: God I loved the Olympics. Seeing those powerful women doing amazing physical feats of endurance. I adored watching them stand on podiums and win medals. I was so inspired. I bought new trainers and everything.

Lucy: I only wore them around the house but the thought was there.

Max: *The Sun*'s coverage of women's sport pretty much consists of photos of Anna Kournikova going shopping. It's a joke. I love the idea of footballers wearing a NMP3 kit.

> Evie: I think it's really important that we do everything we can to help Cheltenham Ladies. How much money do they need? Can't we scrape it together between us?

> Lucy: They need £2,000.

> Evie: OK. We definitely can't scrape it together between us.

The campaign's only income came from the sale of T-shirts, which were made and printed in Britain, making them costly to produce. We donated a percentage of all sales to Women's Aid and, if anything was leftover, we used the money to fund our website and campaign expenses, but we were usually in the red.

> Yas: What about crowdfunding? I bet our supporters would want to help.

> Kate: I know sod all about fundraising, but I'm sure people will get behind this.

> Lucy: Let's do it!!!

We set up a crowdfunding page with the goal of raising £2,025 to cover the cost of the new football kits, complete with No More Page 3 logo. We wrote a message to supporters, telling them about Cheltenham Ladies FC and the difficulty they'd had finding sponsorship. We also shared a *Guardian* article written by Anna Kessel, about the history of women's football in the UK.

Kessel wrote that women's football used to be very popular, citing a women's game played at Everton on Boxing Day in 1920, that drew a crowd of fifty-three thousand spectators. A year later, the Football Association decided to ban women from playing on FA-affiliated pitches, on the grounds that football is 'unsuitable for females and ought not to be encouraged'. The ban was only lifted in 1971, the year after Page 3's launch.

When the crowdfunding page went live, the team's captain, Kirsty Dunleavy, told us that all the players were very supportive of the campaign and were delighted at the prospect of No More Page 3 sponsorship.

'We believe this will not only be good for the club,' she said, 'but for the promotion of women's football in general.'

And then we sat back and watched as supporters shared a link to the fundraising page with the hashtags #KitOn and #Page3NeedsSendingOff.

Kate: Shit the bed! The page has been live for 57 minutes and we've reached our target!!!!

Lucy: We sponsor a fricking women's football team!

Lucy: How AMAZING is this???

Max: And people are still donating

Although we had only asked for £2,025, supporters donated more than £10,000.

We asked Cheltenham Ladies if there was anything else they needed with the extra money. They replied, 'Please could we have a big bag of footballs?'

This was wonderful, but also somehow heartbreaking. The top UK women's football players earned approximately the same amount per year as the top male players earned *per day*. We'd all heard about the prima-donna demands of certain male footballers and there we were with a women's team, asking them what they wanted, and they replied, 'Some footballs, please.' They only asked for footballs and the kits to play in. All they wanted to do was to play the game.

The leftover money was used to sponsor Lee Craigie, a Commonwealth cyclist, and Nottingham Forest Ladies FC, who'd suffered funding cuts to their own team, along with their seven girls' youth teams.

> Me: I'm surprised by the effect this is having on me. I always thought I hated football, but I suppose it wasn't really the game I disliked, but the lad culture that went along with it. All the drinking and fighting and aggressive behaviour.
>
> Max: And how every time there's a big match, *The Sun* have a football-themed Page 3 with a topless model in tiny shorts and long socks, as if women's football is just a sexy fancy dress theme.

Jess: It feels subversive. Seeing women running
around, sweating, competing, not giving a shit
what they look like. I love it.

Every time we received a photo of one of our football teams playing a match, or Lee Craigie training in Scotland, we burned with pride.

It was around that time that newspapers stopped referring to No More Page 3 as a campaign, and started calling it a movement.

Midlife Crisis

It is a law of physics that for every action, there is an equal and opposite reaction.

For all the energy, time, love and effort that we poured into ending Page 3, *The Sun* put an equally stoic effort into keeping it alive.

David Dinsmore maintained that Page 3 was a pillar of the newspaper, and was a good way of generating revenue. After all, *The Sun's* sales doubled within a year of Page 3's launch and, as Marina Hyde wrote in her article about the Reeva Steenkamp reporting, *Sun* editors could estimate precisely how much money a picture of a semi-naked woman would bring in each day. They knew that women's bodies were profitable, and they didn't want to risk losing readers.

But mounting pressure from the public, from organisations, unions, teachers, students, MPs and entire governments suggested that Page 3 could not continue indefinitely in its present form. The growing opposition was clearly becoming a headache. Murdoch had hinted at changes to come with his notion of glamorous fashionistas, and News in Briefs, Page 360 and Page 3 Idol seemed to have disappeared without a trace.

Midlife Crisis

It appeared that *The Sun* wanted to adapt Page 3, to frame it differently, to suggest the purpose of the photos was something other than pure titillation. They wanted to dress Page 3 up as something else, without dressing the models.

After being around for more than forty years, Page 3 was having a midlife crisis.

Early one morning, in the quiet hour before she left for work, Max shared a link to a *Sun* article, written by a body-image campaigner, arguing that Page 3 models presented a healthier body type to the stick-thin fashion models found in glossy magazines. Page 3, the writer insisted, promoted a healthy body image.

> Kate: Are they having a laugh? Most of the
> Page 3 models are a size 8, but with massive
> knockers.

> Me: Oh, but they have a size 14 model,
> remember? They like to mention that fact at
> every opportunity, to show how staggeringly
> diverse Page 3 is.

> Max: Coincidentally, the body-image campaigner
> is also a journalist who regularly writes for *The
> Sun*. She's on their payroll.

> Kate: So, this is the new angle they're going for?
> Page 3's purpose is NOT to give blokes a boner

at the breakfast table, it's for women's mental
health and self-esteem?

At a media event, David Dinsmore reiterated the message, stating that Page 3 is good for 'positive body image'. *The Sun* printed another opinion piece on the subject, with the headline:

WHY WOMEN SHOULD WORSHIP PAGE 3: IMPASSIONED PLEA ON BODY SIZE

As if Page 3 was doing some kind of community service for women. This message was slightly undermined by a different *Sun* article outlining a plastic surgeon's 'scientific formula for perfect breasts', which featured an annotated Page 3 image. Fractions and percentages were scrawled across the model's chest, pointing out the twenty-degree 'upwardly slanting' angle of her nipples, and the 'convex 55 per cent lower pole' of the breast beneath the areola. 'The more breasts deviate from these measures the less attractive they are regardless of size,' the article said.

Kate: Brilliant! So in addition to all the usual
body insecurities, women now have convex
poles, nipple meridians and deviant tits to worry
about. I'll just add all that to the list then.

Kate took part in a university debate, and found herself sharing the stage with the body-image campaigner who wrote for *The Sun*. She spoke first and declared herself 'actively pro-Page 3'.

I watched the livestream of the debate, and had to constantly shove chocolate digestives into my mouth so I wouldn't shout at the screen.

The body-image campaigner said that *The Sun*'s models were 'happier and healthier and less pouty than the ones you will see in any other publication' and insisted that 'they range in size from a size 8 to a 14. None of them have breast implants. The ones who are smaller have a smaller chest, the ones who are larger have a larger chest, just like in life.' I nearly choked on my chocolate digestive.

Happier, healthier . . . natural . . . it sounded as if she was marketing free-range, RSPCA-approved turkeys.

And what she was saying didn't add up. We had taken note of the models who had appeared on that year's Page 3 calendar; all *The Sun*'s favourite, most popular 'girls'. We looked up their biographies on their agents' websites, which listed their dress sizes: Leah, size 6/30FF, Keri, size 6/30E, Samantha, size 8/32F, Nicki, size 8/30E . . .

The models were clearly gorgeous, and of course there was nothing wrong with featuring women of their size, but to suggest that Page 3 represented the average woman was ridiculous. Where were the older women, the larger women, the disabled women, the trans women, the women of colour? A researcher told us that only four Black women had ever appeared on Page 3. Four, in over forty years. What did this say about what our society considered to be sexually attractive?

I had spoken to women who said that Page 3 should stay, because there were bigger issues to worry about. I had spoken to women who said, 'If you've got it, flaunt it!' I had spoken to women who said that they supported the models in pursuing their chosen career path. But during the thousands of conversations I'd had, not one woman ever said to me, 'Page 3 should stay because it makes me feel good about myself.'

Yas sent David Dinsmore a lot of letters. They were busy studying for their exams, but still found the time to write to him most weeks. Sometimes, Yas politely suggested alternative content for Page 3, mocking up potential pages, all hand-drawn. Ideas included news features, profiles of female athletes or politicians and fundraising drives for charitable causes. *The Sun* sometimes linked Page 3 to charities, and had recently raised money for Help for Heroes via a series of themed Page 3 pictures, featuring models posing in T-shirts far too small for them that ended just beneath their armpits. Yas didn't understand why the models had to be topless to raise money, and sent Dinsmore an alternative Page 3 idea, featuring a clothed woman wearing a vest and a pair of jeans, raising her arms in the air to show unshaven pits. It was to illustrate the fundraising campaign Armpits for August, which encouraged women to stop shaving for a month to raise money for polycystic ovary syndrome. It was the women's version of Movember but, unlike Movember, people often pulled a face and pretended to vomit when it was mentioned.

A few weeks after Yas had posted the letter, Page 3 miraculously featured a model raising money for Armpits for August. Unlike Yas's suggestion, however, the woman was topless. It was the usual Page 3-style image, except *The Sun* had censored the model's armpits with little symbols saying 'Armpits for August'.

Jess: Oh. My. Fucking. God. Let me get this
right. They've printed a photo of a bare breasted
woman and have censored her ARMPITS

Yas: Yeah. Like that's the offensive thing about
Page 3 – the woman's body hair.

Me: Celebrating natural beauty. What a joke.

Sun readers shared their reactions online in the comments section:

Gross.

Get a shave, love.

I'm all for charity, but this is a bit much.

In one image, the model was raising her arms above her head, as if to show off her underarm fuzz – except she was wearing a cardigan.

Me: In over forty years of Page 3, this must be
the only time a model has been asked to put a
cardigan on.

Yas: Yeah, it just really wasn't what I had in
mind when I wrote to Dinsmore

Throughout the month of August, *The Sun* informed readers how they could support the cause. At the end of the month,

I checked the fundraising page to see how much money our biggest national newspaper had managed to amass.

The grand total was £222.89.

> Me: A kid at my school once raised a hundred
> quid doing Penny for the Guy, and that was
> in the eighties when the pits were closing and
> nobody had any money. And it wasn't even for a
> good cause – the cash would've been spent on
> fireworks to be thrown at old people and cats. He
> got a hundred quid for a stuffed pillowcase with a
> face drawn on it and chucked in an old pram.

> Max: £222.89 works out at approx 1p donated
> per 100,000 readers.

> Me: Surely, they could have doubled that amount
> just by doing a whip-round in the staff canteen?

It had been said over and over that Page 3 drove newspaper sales; that if they dropped it, it'd seriously hurt their bottom line. Since the models were flogging so many papers for them, couldn't *The Sun* have donated a bit of cash for the cause?

> Jess: It's amazing what happens when a Page
> 3 'lovely' steps out of the beauty standards box
> for a brief moment

> Kate: Yeah. They hand her a cardigan, give

her two pence and tell her to come back next
month, when she's had a shave.

Evie: It really feels like they're trying to rebrand
Page 3 though, doesn't it? We'll have to watch
closely to see what they do next.

We could not have guessed in a million years what *The Sun*
would do next.

Between December and January, Muchelney, a picturesque
Somerset village, had been severely flooded. It was all over the
news. Residents were trying to leave their homes in rafts and
boats to access food and emergency items.

The Sun responded to the disaster by sending a Page 3
model in a dinghy down the flooded streets. The model
looked absolutely freezing in a tiny red T-shirt as she drifted
aimlessly, holding a four-pack of Foster's lager in one hand
and a couple of copies of *The Sun* in the other. Their moti-
vation, apparently, was to 'cheer up' the stranded citizens of
Muchelney.

Me: Imagine you're trapped in a bedroom, with
filthy brown water lapping against the stairs. All
you can do is look out of the window and hope
that help will arrive . . .

Me: . . . And then, you see a disillusioned,

shivering woman with a can of lager drifting
across the cul-de-sac in a small inflatable boat.
What could possibly cheer you up more than
that?

Me: Yes, a sandwich would be nice, or a safe,
dry place to sleep or help rescuing your cat out
of that tree, but a nineteen-year-old posing in
a dinghy with a copy of *The Sun* would be the
best-case scenario.

A video appeared online, showing local people responding
furiously, insulted that *The Sun* was using their misery and
misfortune as a promotional exercise.

Max: I feel so sorry for the model. But I wonder
who the four lucky lads were that got the lager?

Steve: *The Sun* were once the leaders. They
were in tune with popular sentiment. Imitated.
Feared. They had the best headlines, the best
publicity stunts. In 1997, nearly 4 million people
bought it. Now look at this and laugh. Or cry.

Even *Sun* readers appeared to find the stunt pathetic. On
The Sun's website, one bloke commented, *Let's face it, the
Foster's was the most insulting thing. Watered down beer. In a
flood.*

★

A few months later, I was on a mission to return overdue books to Senate House Library, and was ambling contentedly along the London streets, eating a warm croissant, pausing to look at shop windows. I was Holly Golightly, in a hoodie, with a Tesco carrier bag. It was one of those March mornings that promises spring. There was early blossom on the trees in Bloomsbury Square, daffodils shivered against wrought-iron railings and, though it was cold enough to see your breath, the sky was dazzlingly blue.

It was a perfect morning. And then I saw the cover of *The Sun* at a newsstand.

PAGE 3 VS BREAST CANCER

I reluctantly bought a copy, and read it as I walked through Russell Square.

The Sun had teamed up with breast cancer charity, Coppafeel, to launch an awareness-raising campaign called Check 'em Tuesday, Page 3 appeared as usual but at the bottom of the page was a small section about symptoms, reminding women to check their breasts regularly. Readers could sign up to get text reminders, prompting them to 'coppafeel'.

I felt ten different emotions at once. I scuttled to the library and hid in the social studies section, logging on to HQ.

Lucy: Their campaign is going to run for six
months. Every Tuesday, Page 3 will collaborate
with Coppafeel.

Killjoy

Me: So on Mondays, Wednesdays, Thursdays
and Fridays Page 3 is for men, but on Tuesdays
it's for women?

Yas: Obviously it's great that *The Sun* are raising
awareness of breast cancer, but why do they
have to involve Page 3?

Jess: It doesn't even make marketing sense –
young women are not Page 3's target audience

Evie: But I don't think *The Sun* are doing this for
women, or why would they do it via Page 3? I
think they are doing this to rebrand Page 3. To
say it's good for women.

Me: To say how can you criticise Page 3? It is
saving women's lives.

Max: Oh god. I'm just picturing the future
headline: 'Page 3 saved my life'.

Kate: Have you seen *The Sun* are encouraging
readers to tweet pictures of themselves checking
their breasts?

A number of women had shared images of themselves
performing a self-examination, and a number of men had
posted supportive comments, offering their assistance in the

procedure. *Want a hand?* asked several helpful chaps. *I'll help you check* another bloke said, *#crackingset.*

A few male Z-list celebrities jumped on the bandwagon, posting photos of themselves squeezing imaginary breasts, encouraging blokes to 'help the ladies out'.

Any excuse to coppafeel! another man said.

That day, we received a number of messages from women who had been diagnosed with breast cancer, or had survived it in the past. These women were deeply upset that sexualised images of topless women were being used to highlight breast cancer. Many of the women who had contacted us had undergone breast surgery or had mastectomies, and they found the Page 3 collaboration very upsetting. We spent the whole day discussing all the benefits and pitfalls of the campaign in HQ.

Lucy: I met Kris, the founder of Coppafeel recently. We were at an event together. And she's an incredible person. She's warm and kind and inspirational and just really very lovely. We had this great conversation about Page 3 actually. She asked me if I'd think differently about it if Page 3 used its platform for good. They must have been discussing the collaboration then.

Lucy: And the thing is, I can totally see why a small charity would want to team up with *The Sun* – what a fantastic opportunity to reach a huge audience. But I just wish *The Sun* had

promoted the charity in a different way, in a way
that didn't involve Page 3.

We issued a statement, offering our congratulations to Coppafeel for securing a partnership with the UK's biggest newspaper, and applauding *The Sun* and the models for raising awareness. We said that we hoped their campaign succeeded in encouraging women to check their breasts, but we stood firm in our belief that Page 3 was not an appropriate way to raise awareness of breast cancer.

Kris Hallenga, the founder of Coppafeel, responded with a statement of her own, stressing that her charity only employed a staff of six, and the partnership with *The Sun* would raise awareness to over a million young people – an opportunity too important to pass up. She also wrote that she'd received a respectful response from the No More Page 3 campaign, 'women who I admire greatly'. We were really touched by that.

A few months later, *The Sun* ran a front-page story about a woman who had read about Coppafeel, checked her breasts and found a lump. The headline read:

PAGE 3 SAVED MY LIFE

Kate: Surely the headline should be: 'Coppafeel
saved my life?'

Max: I'm thrilled for the woman who caught her
symptoms in time. But seriously, I called this in
March.

★

Midlife Crisis

Late spring became early summer and Page 3 became all about football. It was the run-up to the 2014 World Cup and the papers were wall-to-wall coverage. On the opening day of the tournament, Page 3 featured a topless model perched awkwardly on top of a giant replica of the World Cup. I always presumed the World Cup trophy would be a chalice or an urn with handles on the side – the sort of thing that would sit on the mantelpiece, and would end up filled with old keys, bits of Blu Tack and glacier mints covered in fluff. But the World Cup was actually a wobbly golden thing that resembled a gilded goblin claw clasping a magical orb. It looked like an energy healing lamp you'd buy in Hebden Bridge, and wasn't the kind of thing you'd want to sit on.

Kate: It looks less like she's sitting on the World Cup and more like it's wedged up her arse.

Max: What a brilliant way to celebrate the opening day in true British fashion. The World Cup is UP HER ARSE.

Me: Remember the hymn 'He's got the whole world in his hands?'

It fits perfectly.

♫ She's got the World Cup up her arse ♫

Evie: It'll be stuck in my head all day.

Killjoy

As if a topless woman with the World Cup up her arse wasn't sexist enough, *The Sun* also offered a model as a prize in their Fantasy Football League. Players would be entered into a prize draw to win 'a date with a Page 3 girl'. The blurb said, 'We might even let you pick which one, so feel free to start your research now.'

Jess: Holy fuck.

Jess: They're offering a woman as a prize.
'We might let you pick which one', as if you're
buying a bag of pick 'n' mix sweets at the
cinema.

Max: So Page 3 is for charity, for self-
esteem, for emergency flood relief, for cancer
prevention . . . and now it's a dating service for
lonely football fans? The rebrand is going well.

Kate: The advert also says: 'Don't listen to your
girlfriend when she says size doesn't matter. The
bigger your Mini League is, the more prizes you
can get your mitts on.'

Kate: It's all aimed at men. Even virtual,
imaginary football is just for the lads.

We crafted a letter of complaint to the Advertising Standards Authority, encouraging supporters to do the same. Even the footballer who starred in *The Sun*'s World Cup TV commercial contacted us to offer his support. The ad showed the football freestyler performing clever tricks with a ball, entreating the England team to #DoUsProud.

'Page 3 is more than harmless titillation,' he wrote in his message to us, 'it's a bastion of sexism. It rubber-stamps the idea that women's bodies are commodities, available for consumption.' He thought that *The Sun* should finally get rid of it for good. 'It's a golden opportunity for the newspaper to #DoUsProud.'

Following an investigation, the ASA announced that they had upheld our complaints, after receiving over a thousand letters, and were banning *The Sun* from running the promotion.

'Maybe next time,' Kate said, 'they can offer a weekend in Blackpool or a new toaster as a competition prize, instead of a human woman.'

All we could do was hope.

The Longest Day

During all the campaign's twists and turns, life carried on in all its mundanity and brilliance. I looked after Livia and made excuses to avoid my university work. I took long walks with Will and drank wine in the park with Rhianne and spoke regularly to Jess, who always avoided talking about Matt or home or feelings.

Rebecca stuck a letter from the landlord to the fridge, announcing that our contract would not be renewed, so we'd have to find somewhere else to live in two months' time. Rebecca had decided to move in with Tom, Kevin was moving in with Louise. I had no idea where to go next. I didn't feel ready to live with Will, whose tiny shared flat in Queen's Park wasn't big enough to accommodate me anyway, and I didn't want to take up Natasha's offer of being a live-in childminder, knowing that if I moved in I'd never have a minute off. I couldn't use the toilet in that house as it was without Livia repeatedly kicking a football against the bathroom door. I'd never be able to relax. Nessa sent a card, saying she'd heard that Mayfair was a nice place to live, but I didn't have the heart to tell her that a flat in that part of London would be £45,000 a year above my budget.

The Longest Day

It was all quite stressful and I just wanted to run away for a while.

> Jess: We should meet up. Just go somewhere to chill out and destress.

> Lucy: Why don't you all come and stay with me for a weekend? A change of scene might be good?

> Kate: I would bloody love that!

> Lucy: We could set up camp beds in the house, or you could bring tents? We could go for walks in the woods and swim . . .

Lucy lived in a commune in the rolling countryside, with ten other people.

'It's beautiful,' she said when she first moved in. 'We have chickens and a herb patch and a yurt, but I just tried to clean the Aga and accidentally dismantled part of it, and I don't know how to put it back together. I fear I may be a bit urban.'

She had settled in and had survived the freezing winter where her teeth chattered in her ice-cold, unheated bedroom, but now it was summer it was, she said, quite heavenly.

We tried to find a date when we could all make it but, as usual, it was impossible. Evie wouldn't be able to leave the kids, Priya was too busy at work and Steve would be doing typical weekend activities with his family. And then there was Max.

Max: I'd love to see you all, but Max doesn't camp.

Lucy: I hear you! I could make you a bed on the floor in my room perhaps?

Max: Thanks for the offer, but Max doesn't sleep on floors.

Max took care of herself as if she were a rare tropical plant that needed specific conditions to survive. The right amount of sun, excellent wine, the sort of mattress that is considered an investment. I envied the way she so clearly stated her requirements, and the way everybody just accepted it. She even got away with referring to herself in the third person. I'd never get away with anything like that. Although I loathed absolutely everything about camping, I knew I'd end up in a sleeping bag all the same.

We settled on the weekend of 21 June.

Lucy: Let me just double check with everyone here. There'll be lots of people coming to celebrate Midsummer's Eve, so it'll be really busy, but it should be OK.

Midsummer's Eve celebrations? Where does Lucy actually live, I wondered, in a toadstool? Were her ten housemates elves?

Me: What do the celebrations entail?

Lucy: All kinds of things. People might dance or
make love in the woods, then come back to the
house.

I sent Jess a private message.

Me: I don't think I can go that weekend after all

Jess: Hahaha nice try but you're coming. I'm
driving down. I'll pick you up in the van.

Jess had bought an ancient van. She told me that the door
was falling off and the exhaust sounded like a cheap firework,
but she'd bought it with her own money, the last of her savings
from her old job, and she loved it because it was hers.

Jess: It's an experience travelling in the van.
Just bring a bag in case you feel sick.

The plans progressed, and I tried to discover as much as
possible about where we were going, so I could mentally
prepare myself for the trip. I found out that the commune was
a big country house with substantial grounds, owned by eco-
warrior hippy types who ate food out of bins and spent a lot
of time wandering about without clothes on. It sounded suspi-
ciously like the subject of a Louis Theroux documentary.

Lucy: By the way – no need to bring a
swimming costume unless you want to. We

usually swim naked, but please bring one if
you'd feel more comfortable.

I had a sudden, painful flashback to a long-ago holiday in
Lanzarote, when a naked German pensioner stood directly in
front of me on the beach and repeatedly bent over to examine
shells.

'Good for him,' I'd said.

And bad for me, I thought.

I sent Jess another private message.

Me: I really can't do that weekend

Jess: Yes you CAN!

I realised that Max was the only person who might have
skipped the naked swimming in favour of reclining on the
grass, in jeans, with a gin and tonic. But she wasn't coming. I
packed a swimsuit, a towel and all the booze I could find in
the cupboard.

Jess: I'll pick you up at 12. No excuses!!!

When Jess told me that her van was falling apart, I thought
she was exaggerating, like when my dad would say the car was
a tip because there was a Twix wrapper and a rubber band in
the glove compartment. But when she arrived to pick me up,
two hours later than planned, I saw that it really was falling

apart. The door nearly came off when I opened it, and there were sweet wrappers, phone bills and coat hangers all over the place. Something jabbed into my thigh and I realised I was sitting on part of a hoover pipe.

'Oh, just chuck it on the floor with the rest of the stuff,' she said.

It was boiling, so I started rolling the window down, but it jammed after opening an inch. It refused to move any further and rattled precariously when we went around corners. It's a good job it was the longest day of the year, because apparently the headlights didn't work either.

She careered down country lanes and I attempted to point out skylarks and oast houses, but we were going so fast they passed by in a blur. She apologised for being late, and told me that Matt didn't want her to leave. Suddenly, she started crying and pulled into a lay-by at the side of the road.

'I'm sorry, Jo,' she said. 'I just don't know what I'm doing.'

We sat there for a moment, with the radio playing. She didn't look at me, so I didn't look at her, in case the spell was broken and she stopped talking. It was the first time she'd spoken about him in months.

'I'm just really weak, I let him bully me. I must just be a weak person.'

'That's rubbish,' I said. 'You're not weak. You do everything for Ruby, every single day. You look after your mum. You stand up and speak out about what you believe in, even though you know you'll get a ton of abuse for it. You told us what was happening at home. That was an incredibly brave thing to do.'

'Yeah, but I didn't do a fucking thing about it.'

'Maybe you weren't ready then.'

'Yeah, maybe.'

We were quiet for a while, and then I said, 'You caught that furry albino moth that time, and put it outside.'

'Yeah,' she said. 'That was actually pretty heroic.'

She wiped her eyes and went to put her hands on the wheel but, instead, just let them drop. 'Oh god, I must look a total mess.'

'You look gorgeous,' I said, stroking her hair.

'You're a good friend, and a good liar.' She took a deep breath, put on her sunglasses and started the engine.

Lucy's house looked like the kind of place you'd pay £10.50 to visit, or £15 if you intended to see the gardens as well. There was a line of cars parked on the driveway, and people were milling around in the sort of clothes that gap-year students wear when they've been in Thailand too long. I spotted Kate walking past the house, a camping mat rolled under her arm. I shouted and she turned around, smiled, and ran over to the van.

'You're here! About bloody time! We've just done yoga, over there, by the . . .' she waved her hands around, trying to grasp the word, 'by the . . . moat?'

'It's a ha-ha,' a passer-by said.

'Well, it looks like a moat,' Kate replied.

The place was huge. Lucy showed us around. It was a house filled with shafts of light, lengthening shadows and dust motes. There were oak doors, creaking floorboards and fireplaces almost big enough to stand up in. It would have made the perfect set for one of those films about a mysterious orphan or a ghostly governess haunting the shit out of the nice family who have just moved in. I stayed within touching distance of Lucy at all times.

Despite the size of the house, all of No More Page 3 was standing around in the kitchen, sipping cold drinks and talking very quickly. As Jess hugged everyone, she closed her eyes with contentment. I kept mine open, unable to look away from the ten thousand dead flies glued to lengths of sticky paper hanging from the ceiling. They were plump and fat, like currants in a Christmas pudding.

'I suppose they had to kill the flies,' Assad said, when I told him about it later. 'They would've been after the food in the bins as well.'

Down by the pool, people were wandering about naked. I made intense eye contact for fifteen minutes then slinked away to find a quiet hedge to be alone in, like a cat after it's been sick. Yas, who I'd seen walking around the gardens, had also disappeared.

'Where's Yas gone?' I asked Rhianne, who happened upon my hedge.

'Up a tree,' she replied.

'What?'

'Yas likes climbing trees.'

I wasn't surprised, because Yas always did surprising things and I'd learned to just go with the flow. I'd got used to saying, 'Yas has painted their face to look like a tiger? Absolutely, why not?' 'Yas is performing spoken-word poetry in a bar in Soho?

Sure.' 'Yas has launched a campaign for better sex education in schools in collaboration with *The Telegraph*? Of course they have!'

Although I must admit, even I was surprised by the last one. Yas, at school in the daytime and in and out of HQ in the evenings, had somehow found the time to set up a petition, calling on the prime minister to 'urgently convene a working group of young people, teachers, professionals and online experts' to re-write the SRE guidance to reflect the influence of the internet on how people view sex and relationships. The petition gained over ten thousand signatures on the day it went live. Yas messaged us during breaks from lessons.

> Yas: This is so wild – in between classes I'm talking to journalists and Sky News!

> Yas: And I just phoned in to Nick Clegg's radio show and spoke with him live on air. I was so nervous! He asked me why I care about this so much, and I said that without any proper advice, teenagers are turning to online pornography for answers – and this is giving very warped and unrealistic perceptions about sex, which is damaging our understanding of how to interact with one another.

> Kate: You bloody superstar!

> Max: Only Yas could end up speaking to the deputy prime minister during a school lunch break

Yas: And he said he agreed with me that the
SRE guidance should be updated!

Me: At this rate, you'll be prime minister one day
Yas.

A few months later, the Department for Education revealed that it had convened a group of experts to draft new guidance to teach pupils about violence against women and the dangers of porn and sexting, which would be emailed to all headteachers to use in conjunction with the existing teaching materials. Soon after, *The Guardian* had named Yas their 'best hope for the future (UK)'.

I sat on the grass and rested my head on Rhianne's shoulder. 'Our best hope for the future is up a tree,' I said.

'Yeah,' Rhianne replied, looking up at the branches of nearby elms and oaks. 'I'm just slightly worried about how our best hope for the future is gonna get back down again.'

We held a strategy meeting in a conservatory, all crowded round a big table. When it got too hot, we relocated to the lawn, just like we used to at primary school on the last days of term before the summer holidays, when we'd leave the stuffy classrooms and have lessons on the grass.

'So,' Lucy said, 'where we're at currently . . .' She read from a list of supporting organisations.

'We've got . . . Girlguiding UK, who have over five hundred thousand young members, Mumsnet, which is the largest UK website for parents, the British Youth Council, representing approximately two hundred and twenty young organisations, the Girls' Brigade with around twenty thousand members, UK Youth and Ambition, who work with a million young people and eleven thousand youth clubs . . . then there are the teaching unions, combining over five hundred thousand teachers, lecturers and head teachers . . .'

She turned the page over and carried on.

'Unison, our largest union with 1.3 million members, the Royal College of Midwives, the Royal College of Nursing—'

Kate whooped.

'Then, of course, we've got Rape Crisis, Women's Aid, the End Violence against Women Coalition . . . National Assembly of Wales, Scottish Parliament, one hundred and fifty cross-party MPs . . .

'And now we've now got twenty-eight universities and six Oxford colleges that voted to stop selling *The Sun* on campus or providing it in common rooms.'

Everybody appeared to exhale at once.

'Wow,' Kate said. 'When you read it all out like that, it's pretty fucking impressive.'

Lucy looked as if she was about to sneeze, or cry. We were all emotional and we all had hayfever.

'I know,' she said. 'I'm feeling really choked up about it. All these people who want to help. And now we've also got the campaign in Germany.'

A student named Kristina Lunz had contacted us to say she'd been inspired by No More Page 3 to launch a sister campaign against Germany's *Bild* newspaper, asking that the topless 'BILD-Girl' photos be scrapped. We'd also heard from a government worker in Costa Rica, who told us she wanted to protest against a similar feature in their national newspapers. Media outlets in more than thirty countries had written about the campaign. It had struck a chord with people all over the world.

Rhianne casually brushed aside a giant wasp, which quickly flew into Jess's hair.

'Get it out!' she said, jumping to her feet and swatting at her ponytail with the back of her hand.

Lucy got to her feet too and, when the wasp had gone, she said, 'You know what? I'm gonna say it. I am going to stand here and say that Page 3 will be gone within a year. I would bet everything I have on it. There might be a struggle ahead, but I am convinced we will win and it'll be gone within a year.'

Kate, who was taking notes, said, 'Should I add this to the minutes?'

'Yeah, write it down,' Jess said. 'We can frame it as a memento next year, when Page 3 is gone for good.'

We took a break and Kate stretched out on the grass in full sun, basking like an iguana. Jess curled up in the shade. She'd suddenly started with toothache.

'It keeps coming on every few days,' she said, 'but I haven't got a dentist yet in Shropshire.'

I searched in my bag and pulled out some ibuprofen. 'Here,' I said, tossing them across the grass towards her.

'You total babe.' She threw two tablets in her mouth and swilled them down with a swig of water from her bottle. 'Urgh.' She pulled a face. 'That one got stuck.'

I had a sudden, overwhelming rush of love for her. Real friendships are small miracles.

You choose that person over and over, not because of familial ties or mortgages or vows, but purely because you *like* each other. Because you'd rather spend time with that person than with anyone else.

'What?' she said, looking at me watching her. She was holding one hand to her face, covering the painful tooth.

'I was just thinking that I would rather clean a toilet with you than do something fun and glamorous with someone else.'

'That might be the nicest thing anyone's ever said to me,' she said, lying on her back. 'I hardly ever clean my toilet.'

'Are you feeling any better, love?' Kate came over and positioned herself with her legs in the sun and her head in the shade.

'Yeah . . . I might have a nap.'

'Good idea,' Kate said, closing her eyes, listening to the birds. 'Let's try not to think for a bit.'

That night, Jess and I stayed up long after everyone else had retreated to their sleeping bags. We were way too drunk to go to bed. I'd planned on having just a couple of beers but, since Jess had severe toothache and was married to an arsehole, it seemed like a good idea to keep drinking, to obliterate all the pain. For that one night, it worked.

We drank wine straight from the bottle in a hollow beneath a hedgerow. We found a canister of nitrous oxide in an old repurposed ambulance and inhaled it, laughing until we fell to our knees. We saw the milky way, and watched bats swoop in circles. We went skinny dipping in the moonlight.

The Longest Day

'Look how bright Venus is,' I said as I floated on my back, watching the clouds sweep across the trees.

Jess got in after me and shouted, 'OH MY FUCKING OH GOD OH FUCK SHIT IT'S SHITTING FREEZING I'VE GOT CRAMP MY LEG MY LEG MY LEG.'

We couldn't find our clothes in the darkness and we lost the path, tripped, and landed, naked, in a massive patch of nettles and thistles. We cried drunk pained hysterical tears.

'Isn't it weird,' Jess said, the following morning, hunched over her cup of coffee, 'how things can be absolutely terrible and fucking hilarious all at the same time?'

Inheritance

Jess dropped me off at the flat on her way back to Shropshire, and I was so filled with nervous hangover energy that I paced back and forth between the kitchen and the living room, dusting bookshelves, washing dishes, taking out the recycling. I couldn't sit down, because if I sat down, I would think, and then I would feel worse. I was anxious about Jess, and the anxiety was so big it spilled over into other areas, making everything seem dangerous and looming and impossibly huge. Things that hadn't worried me a week ago troubled me now. Things like the fact that I'd soon have to find a new place to live, and had recently received my very last scholarship payment and had only a matter of months to finish a thesis I had barely started writing. I had been so busy, I had put it all to the back of mind, not wanting to deal with any of it.

I messaged Jess. *Let me know when you're back home. Hope the journey's going OK.*

She'd be halfway there by now.

I suddenly needed to hear my mum's voice. She picked up on the first ring.

'I knew it'd be you,' she said. 'I was just going to peg the washing out and I thought, I'll wait a minute, because our Joanne's going to ring.'

She always did this. All my life I had watched her stop in the middle of things – suddenly putting down the iron or the potato peeler, and walking purposefully to the phone, just in time to reach it as it started ringing.

If ever I was in any sort of trouble, she'd know. When my brother had an accident on his bike, she held her stomach saying, 'I feel sick, something's happened,' and paced up and down until she got a phone call from the hospital. 'I knew it,' she said. 'I knew something was wrong.'

She didn't believe in psychic powers or ghosts or astrology or magic. She just believed in connections between people. 'Of course I'd know if something was wrong with one of you,' she'd say matter-of-factly, as if this was something that happened to everybody.

'How was your weekend?' she asked now on the phone.

'Fun,' I said, 'but I feel unsettled. Really anxious.'

'I know. I've been feeling like that, like something's going to happen.'

I told her I'd come home next weekend for a visit, and she said, 'We'll see you on Saturday then, if not before.'

I saw her on Wednesday, at the hospital. She'd known. She hadn't known that Nessa was going to fall and break her hip, but she'd known that something was going to happen.

I sat by Nessa's bed. She was sleeping. I looked anywhere other than at her face, which seemed colourless and cold. I looked around the room. The beds were all taken by other elderly women. Nessa had been worried by the thought of a mixed ward.

'There won't be any men?' she'd said. 'I don't want to be around any men.'

There were two small fans balanced on tables but the breeze didn't reach the corners of the room. The air was stale with a strong smell of antiseptic and sweat. The woman in the next bed started screaming and my mum walked over to her slowly and calmly, and took her hand in hers. The woman shook with sobs.

'I don't know where I am,' she said. 'I want to go home.'

'Your daughter was here this morning, remember?' my mum said gently. 'You're in hospital because you've been poorly.'

'Am I? Is that where I am?'

My mum stayed to comfort her, and I looked at Nessa as she opened her eyes.

'Hello, darling,' she said quietly. 'You didn't have to come.'

'Of course I did, I came as soon as I could. I just threw some clothes in a bag and caught the first train.'

My mum came back and took her seat by the bed.

'The poor woman,' she whispered, 'she keeps forgetting where she is.'

We fell into a routine. Members of the family would visit in the morning or the evening, but my mum and her sister would stay all day. She'd come home late at night, and I'd make her pasta or scrambled eggs and she'd eat silently, staring at the wall. We'd turn off the TV, stop the microwave before it pinged. My brother took the battery out of the clock with the ticking second hand. All noise was too much. She couldn't handle it.

In the evenings, I'd quietly close my bedroom door, draw the curtains and crawl into bed. I'd feel too tired to read, but I'd log into HQ to see if anyone was around. Someone always was. One night, Jess, Rhianne and Evie were all online and we talked for hours. It was hot and sticky and the thunderstorms that had been predicted never came to clear the air. None of us could sleep.

Jess: Any change?

Me: No.

Jess: How's your mum?

Me: Exhausted. She does everything for everybody, and never seems to have a minute for herself.

Jess: Mine too

Rhianne: My mum works a 65-hour week, does all the housework and cooking and is the emotional cushion for all of us.

Rhianne: But still, my mum is in a place better than her mum was. My gran had to put up with beating, stealing, drunkenness and gambling

from my grandad. That was the norm for so
many women.

Jess: God our families sound so similar

Evie: My parents had to sneak my nana out
of her house and onto a plane to start a new
life in Ireland away from her abusive husband.
Whenever I went to see my grandad, I wasn't
allowed to tell him where nana lived.

Me: When Nessa was born, her father stood
on the stairs with a gun and threatened to
shoot the doctor if he attempted to enter the
'birthing room'. He wouldn't allow a man in
there. Imagine being in labour with no medical
assistance, no pain relief, no electricity – and
meanwhile, downstairs, your husband is
threatening to shoot the doctor.

Me: We're the first generation of women to have
any real freedom, aren't we? My mum wouldn't
have been allowed to apply for a credit card in
her name until the law changed when she was
in her thirties. Did you know women could be
legally refused service in a pub until 1982?

Jess: I never get over the fact that marital rape
only became illegal in the '90s.

Inheritance

Evie: We're still feeling the repercussions. Real change takes generations.

Rhianne: You're right. We've got better lives now, better health, more opportunities. But all the violence and shame and trauma that our grandmothers and mothers faced – we inherit it, don't we?

After we said goodnight, I stayed awake in the dark, thinking about this inheritance. Thinking that it's our duty as daughters to take every single thing we can from this life, to squeeze out all the experience, adventure and joy, in recognition of all that our mothers and grandmothers didn't have, in honour of all they couldn't do.

Endings

Nessa died at 6.30 a.m. the following morning. After the telephone call, I started cooking. I couldn't even begin to process what it meant to have no Nessa, no grandmother, that entire generation of my family, gone. So, I chopped vegetables mechanically, waiting for my mum to come home.

We had so many people to tell.

'It's a good age,' they said over and over, as if talking about expensive whisky. Eighty-eight is a good age. You couldn't really hope for much more.

My mum didn't sleep more than an hour for the next five nights.

'It feels wrong,' she said. 'Getting ready for bed, turning the lamp on, feeling comfortable. I don't want to feel comfortable.'

Her grief was a heavy, solid thing. It set into her joints and stooped her back. She walked as if trying to stand up against gale-force winds.

In the weeks after her death, Nessa was in everything, everywhere. I'd put the kettle on and suddenly she was there, stirring her tea with the silver scallop-shell spoon, the picture so clear in my mind, so perfectly her. Bags of her things mounted up in the hall, and I'd pause to hug blankets, jumpers, scarves, holding them up to my face to inhale their smell. My mum seemed suddenly aged, and yet I felt like the years had fallen away; I was uncertain and frightened, like a child. I didn't speak to anyone for a while, but then, the day before Nessa's funeral, I phoned Jess.

'How are you feeling?' she asked.

'I'm OK. I mean, I'm not, but. This is what happens, isn't it? Grandmothers die. She was eighty-eight.'

'It doesn't matter if she was one hundred and eight,' Jess said. 'You're still allowed to be heartbroken.'

'It's funny,' I said, 'how we're not supposed to care *too* much about our grandparents. How we're expected to put them in a home, see them every other weekend, if they're lucky. Their deaths are used as homework excuses, you know, "I haven't done the essay because my grandma died." But she meant the absolute world to me.'

'Which is why you have a right to feel awful.'

'I keep telling myself how lucky I am. I keep reminding myself of all the terrible things that happen to people; the Holocaust, Rwanda, Hurricane Katrina, the war in Iraq. Did you know there's a woman who lost her husband and children and both her parents in the tsunami? She was in Sri Lanka, I read about her in the paper. And remember the Bali bombings? Two of the girls who died, we booked their flights at the travel agency I used to work for. I remember them coming into the office, so excited. They were so young, friends on an adventure together. We had to arrange for their bodies to be flown home.'

'It doesn't work like that though, there isn't a hierarchy of grief.'

I was quiet for a moment and then I said, 'I think there is.'

'Well if there is, fuck it. You feel how you feel. You loved someone so much and she died. It doesn't honour who she was to you to deny how you feel. Yes, terrible things happen on a massive scale, but that doesn't take away your own pain.'

'Life scares me, Jess.'

'Oh babe, it scares me too.'

On the day of the funeral, all I could think about was the dress. Don't spill anything on the dress, don't cry all over the dress, don't stand near the person smoking in case the smell clings to the dress. I'd bought it in the sales but I couldn't afford to keep it, so I left the tags in the back and just pulled it on, over a T-shirt. I wanted to look nice, for Nessa.

I hated the service at the crematorium, the minister talking about Nessa as if he'd known her, reading out a list of her qualities as if it was a shopping list. Then afterwards, back at the house – how weird it was being in Nessa's house, with every bit of it jam-packed with her. The cushions she had plumped on the sofa. The photos she had put in frames. The little keepsakes we had brought back from holidays, dusted and put into place.

The couple from across the street sat in easy chairs, drinking brandy. The woman's eyes narrowed as she studied every single object in the room. 'Funerals are so expensive,' she said, holding out her glass for a top-up.

Endings

'Not for our Joanne,' my brother said, nodding in my direction. 'She's even taking that dress back to the shop.'

The look of absolute shock on that woman's face was the one bright moment of the whole day. It was a look that even Meryl Streep would struggle to get right – a perfect balance of incredulity, disdain, judgement and superiority. I wanted to kick my brother hard on the shin, but my shoe would've flown off, so I didn't. That was the other problem with my outfit – not only did I have two cardboard tags sticking into my upper back all day, but I was wearing clunky heels from Marks & Spencer that made me shuffle about like a pregnant llama.

We were all exhausted in the car on the way home. So tired and empty. We didn't speak for ages.

'Barbara's face,' my mum suddenly said, 'her face, when she heard the dress was going back to the shop!' And she let out a peal of laughter that shot through the car like a comet.

I spent my last night in Dulwich alone in the flat. Rebecca and Kevin had already moved out, and almost everything I owned was packed in boxes, ready to be piled into the removal van tomorrow. Up until two weeks ago, I still didn't have anywhere to go, but just as I was getting desperate, Assad phoned. He'd been offered a job in Kent, and wondered if I'd like to rent somewhere with him. We quickly found a little flat above a dress shop in a picturesque village in the Darent Valley, close to where he would be working. There were antique shops and country pubs and a duck pond on a roundabout.

'This'll be the whitest place I've ever lived,' Assad said, 'but let's give it a go.'

I said goodbye to the kids I looked after. 'You're coming back though, right?' Livia asked, and I said of course I'd come back and visit, but she understood the tone of my voice, and went up to her room and wouldn't let me in.

Assad helped me to pack up the flat, and spent hours fixing my bedroom wall, putting Polyfilla in the holes where my pictures used to hang. Rhianne turned up, unexpectedly.

'I'm here to help you,' she said. 'If those carpets aren't clean you won't get your deposit back.' While I packed my London life into boxes, Rhianne scrubbed the stairs so vigorously her face went pink, and Assad cleaned the windows. I stopped for a moment and watched them, thinking this is true friendship, but they both glared at me for not doing anything, so I started clearing the bookshelves.

The next morning, I did a final check of the flat while waiting for the removal van to arrive.

I noticed a piece of cardboard that I'd stuck over an air vent to stop the draught. I peeled it away from the wall and stopped in my tracks. It was the back of a greetings card; the card Nessa had sent when I'd first moved to London. I felt a sharp pain in my chest at the realisation that I'd once treated this card as a throwaway thing, secure in the knowledge that I'd receive more and more over the coming years. I hugged it, I kissed it, I whispered, 'I'm sorry I took you for granted,' and finally, I opened it.

YOU'LL BE MOVING OUT TODAY HOPE IT ALL
GOES WELL DON'T GO LIFTING HEAVY BOXES

Endings

*YOU'LL HURT YOUR BACK JUST WATCHING THE
CHELSEA FLOWER SHOW IT'S RUBBISH HOPE
YOU SETTLE INTO YOUR NEW PLACE I'LL BE
WITH YOU IN SPIRIT DARLING XXX*

PART FOUR

Clarifications and Corrections

Whisky in the Shed

It was late morning, and I was sitting in a gloomy pub in Edinburgh, drinking a real ale with a risqué name. It was one of those places you rarely see these days, with yellowing anaglypta wallpaper, badly painted dado rails and sticky, patterned carpets. The other customers were mainly old men playing dominoes or gazing blankly at the wall. I sat by the window, trying to peer through the dirty frosted glass to watch people trip on the cobbles outside. I was supposed to be speaking soon, about No More Page 3 at an event at Scottish Parliament, but I'd lost my nerve.

'Just think,' my mum said on the phone that morning, 'less than a year ago you ran away from that conference and look at you now – speaking in Parliament.'

'It's not a big thing,' I said. 'It's an event to encourage young people to get into activism.'

'It *is* a big thing,' she replied. 'Look how far you've come.'

But as I sat there in the pub, I feared history was repeating itself, and I was certain I'd end up running to the station and catching an early train back to London.

It had been a difficult few weeks. We'd moved into the new

flat in the Kent village that was the whitest place Assad had ever seen, and had tried to settle into new routines. Assad worked long hours, so I spent most of my days alone, missing Livia and my London friends.

'Perfect time to get your thesis finished,' my dad said, and I tried, I really did. There was so much work to do, but I felt so anxious and empty that it was almost impossible to concentrate. We didn't have any furniture, apart from a tiny sofa and a pair of dining chairs, so I fashioned a desk out of moving boxes weighed down with books. In the evenings, I'd dismantle it and reconfigure the boxes to make a foot stool and a coffee table. It was like living in a giant game of Tetris. Jess was avoiding my calls, and I was worried about her, and I missed Nessa so much. My throat felt tight and sore from the floods of tears I'd been holding back, worried that if I started crying, I wouldn't be able to stop.

I volunteered to attend any campaign events we were invited to, not because I wanted to go – I didn't want to do anything – but just to get me away from the Tetris room. I said yes to Edinburgh because the train journey would take a long time, and I'd have the distraction of packing a bag and planning my day. I just wanted to escape myself for twenty-four hours.

I was about to go to the bar to get another drink when my phone buzzed with a text message: *Let me know where you are – I'll come and meet you and we can go to the event together.* It was Laura Bates, the founder of The Everyday Sexism Project.

Laura had joined HQ. It was Kate's idea. She had been

volunteering for The Everyday Sexism Project, moderating comments on the website and social media channels.

'Laura gets the worst of the trolls,' Kate said, 'and she has to deal with it on her own. And it's not just the usual "you're fat and jealous with shit tits", she gets psychos saying they're going to dismember her. I was wondering if she might like to join HQ, just so she's got a space where she can vent and talk about this stuff, and we can support her?'

Everyone stared when she walked into the pub to meet me. I don't think that boozer had ever had anyone like her in it. Despite spending so much time arguing that women should not be judged on their appearance, I couldn't help but acknowledge that Laura was ludicrously beautiful. Her hair was long and shiny and soft and her big brown eyes were like pools of melted chocolate – the Swiss kind that is dark and fine and rich. She was petite and delicate, all arms and legs. She was basically Bambi in a blonde wig.

She came in with a flurry of compliments and apologies; she'd been so looking forward to finally meeting me properly and she was so very sorry she was late. Her bag kept slipping off her shoulder and she suddenly threw it on the floor and kicked it in annoyance and something about the way she did this made me think: *I love this woman.*

'We should probably get going,' she said and, as she walked towards the exit, she tripped over a chair leg and then pulled the door handle when she should have pushed. It was so clumsily endearing that all thoughts of running away evaporated, and we walked together, side by side, down the Royal Mile.

★

The Scottish Parliament building is very modern and grey with lots of glass and sharp-edged metal, like a housing estate in space, but inside everything is covered in polished plywood and the effect made me feel like I was on a cruiseliner in the seventies. I kept expecting a Shirley Bassey impersonator to drift down the stairs.

We were led up to the event room, which had desks arranged in the giant nightmare circle, where everybody was staring uncomfortably at everyone else. The mandatory pitcher of water that no one would ever touch was plonked in the middle of the table, and a video camera had been set up to record everything. I looked towards the door, and then back at the camera. I didn't want to be on film running out of the room, so I sat down, horrified, as the lights dimmed and an MP started speaking. I couldn't escape.

Laura's talk was brilliant. She said that women hold less than a quarter of seats in Parliament, and only four out of twenty-two Cabinet positions. That only eighteen out of one hundred and eight High Court judges are women. That the National Gallery's collection of over two thousand artworks contains paintings by only ten women. That the Royal Society has never had a female president and only 5 per cent of the current fellowship is female. That women write only a fifth of front-page newspaper articles. That women directed just 5 per cent of the two hundred and fifty major films of 2011. People made surprised little gasps and whispered 'no' or 'wow' after each point.

When it was my turn to speak, I stood numbly on unsteady legs, clicked through Powerpoint images and said a series of words, with no idea where they had come from or where it was going. Afterwards, I sat in shock with no recollection of anything I'd said. I had panicked so much I'd somehow blanked out the entire experience.

During the break, I hid in the toilets for a while, and then ate tiny pieces of quiche with Laura. A woman walked over to her and said, 'Your talk was incredible, really affecting.' Then she turned to me and said, 'Yours was good too – I liked the bit about drinking whisky in the shed.' I attempted to smile at her and thought, *I have to go home. Now.*

Laura and I had booked the same train back to London, and had to leave early to get to the station on time. We said hasty goodbyes, left the room and immediately got lost in the parliament building. It was eerily deserted, with no one around to ask where the exit was. After walking down a series of cruiseliner corridors we found a door, surrounded by spiky gates.

'How do we open it?' I asked, searching for buttons and handles. 'It shouldn't be this difficult. If they really want more women in parliament, they should make it easier for them to enter and exit the building.'

'I'm glad I went,' I said to Assad when I got back home. 'Because I feel like I've made a new friend. Me and Laura laughed all the way back to London. But the talk was awful. I was awful.'

'Mate, don't be so hard on yourself. I bet you were really good.'

'I wasn't. I just thought that I wouldn't feel so nervous by now – that after doing so many speaking things it'd get easier and I'd get better at it, but it doesn't and I don't. If this was a book, this would be the point when I overcome my fears and triumph.'

'Not gonna lie, it's really weird that you always think of everything that happens as if you're reading it in a book.'

'OK, a film then. If this was a film, I'd overcome all these obstacles and face my fears.'

'Yeah, you'd give your talk and then one person would start clapping and then the whole room would start clapping.'

'Yeah, exactly.'

'I know the sort of film. But you know, people have different strengths. Some people will find it easier to talk.'

'Well, what are my strengths then?'

'Well, animals like you, they seem to really trust you, and you always remember people's birthdays.'

'So, cats like me and I've got a diary.'

'Come on,' he said, 'you know what I mean. Besides, you're not gonna go from having a phobia of public speaking to suddenly being the best speaker. It doesn't work like that. It's a –'

Please don't say it's a process.

'– process,' he said. 'Sometimes you'll take one step forward, two steps back. It's a –'

Oh god, I thought. *He's going to say it's a journey.*

'– journey. Anyway, you know what they say. Feel the fear and fuck up anyway.'

'Is that what they say?'

'I'm pretty sure that's what they say.'

The Sausage Counter

Once, many summers ago, I walked across the grass in bare feet and stepped in an old cat-food dish filled with slugs.

I responded like the *Wizard of Oz* witch, melting in a puddle of anguished screams.

'It could be worse,' my dad said, but I was having none of it.

'How could it be worse? What's the worst thing *you've* ever stood in?'

'A dole queue,' he replied.

I remembered this one morning in early September, as I was waiting in line in the Job Centre foyer, and realised he was right. This queue was the very worst thing you could stand in.

The room was airless and rank with a flickering overhead strip light, the sort that is tinted blue to make it difficult to inject heroin. There were security guards everywhere speaking urgently into walkie talkies, as if auditioning for a part on *The Wire*. The 'back to work' posters on the wall showed people laughing at a computer screen or smiling gratefully at a spanner, while all the real people in the room looked demoralised, exhausted and like they wanted to burn the place down. A very official-looking woman was checking names against a list and shouting, 'Do you have your documentation?'

It was like visiting time at Belmarsh.

I had an appointment at 12.15 with a job coach. I was thinking of quitting the PhD. I was sick of academia – of the conferences and lectures and of trying pathetically to write a thesis – and I was also sick of putting myself through the terror of speaking at campaign events.

'I think I just want a normal job,' I said to my mum on the phone. 'I'm tired of trying to do things that I find so hard. I'd like to go to work in the morning, eat a sandwich at one, come home and have a bath and get paid at the end of the month.'

'If you say so, love,' she said. 'But you've never wanted anything normal.'

'Name?' the woman with the clipboard barked. 'You're with Yvonne.' She pointed to a cramped desk, in a room packed with cramped desks, and I nervously walked over and perched on a plastic chair with a padded seat that let out a small whoosh of air when I sat on it. Yvonne didn't look up, she just carried on typing. It became awkward after a couple of minutes and I shuffled in my seat, in case she somehow hadn't realised I was there.

'I'm just finishing something,' she said without taking her eyes off the screen.

An age passed before she finally glanced at my CV, scanning the list of jobs I'd had; shop work, childcare, hospitality, travel, academia, teaching, office work.

'I don't see what you'll get in that field,' she said, without specifying which field. 'We'll have to widen your job search. You don't have a driver's licence?'

The Sausage Counter

I shook my head. She clicked a key with her long taupe nail.

'Let me see . . . sales . . . sales . . . you could try this one in telesales. It's in Croydon.' Click . . . click . . . 'No, actually they want someone younger, school-age, ideally.'

She carried on clicking the keys and I started rapidly losing hope.

'There's a retail role in . . . where is it, Ashford – you could get to Ashford on the train. Let's have a look – oh, it's a butcher's counter; they say experience is preferred, but it's not essential.'

Anyone could look at me and know without question that I would be a terrible butcher, but even if butchery was my absolute passion in life – if it was the very reason I got out of bed in the mornings – to travel every day for eighty miles to fulfil a twenty-hour contract would mean I'd spend my entire wage on train travel. I didn't even bother to mention that I'd been vegetarian for most of my life and had never even handled a raw sausage.

'I'll print you the job details,' she said, before turning to the woman at the next desk and saying, 'Lynn, how do I print again, is it control and P?'

I looked at her and thought: *Yvonne can't save me. Yvonne can't even print a butcher's phone number.*

Almost twenty years had passed since the school careers advisor had tried to dissuade me from going to university, encouraging me to work in a shoe shop instead. I had worked so hard in so many jobs, staying up late studying, writing essays on trains, revising for endless exams, over and over, for years, and here I was. All that effort to progress from the shoe cupboard to the sausage counter.

I thought of Charlie, the Home Counties PhD Arsehole, and knew with absolute certainty that he wasn't currently being advised to take up a butcher's apprenticeship. I imagined the career options he was considering. A junior research fellowship at Oxford perhaps. A year at the Sorbonne. A post-doctoral thesis, a book deal, a curatorship at a national museum.

I'd worked so hard, I'd got the grades and I'd won the scholarships, but in my head, I was still in a council house in Rotherham, worrying about the rent, the future. The way I saw myself had barely changed in twenty years, despite all the things I'd done. Every barrier I had broken through remained intact in my head.

Priya messaged as I was getting on the train. We kept in touch regularly. She left me funny voice messages and sent photos from her daily commute, of men taking up loads of space on the tube. They'd stretch their legs across two, sometimes three seats, and then chuck their rucksack in the middle of the floor. 'I'm taller than most of them,' she said, 'and I've usually got more bags, and yet somehow I manage not to sprawl myself across the entire carriage.'

Priya had been to visit me in Kent, and I'd gone to Kentish Town a few times to meet her at The Pineapple. We'd find an empty table, buy drinks and snacks and just talk while we did jigsaws. We learned a lot about each other by doing jigsaws.

I opened Priya's message. *Do you fancy meeting up tomorrow?*

I'd love to see you, I typed. *But I might not be very good company. I'm not feeling great at the moment.*

The Sausage Counter

A text pinged back. *I don't only want to see you when everything's going well. I also want to see you when everything's rubbish.*

Are you sure?

Of course, she replied. *That's what friends are for.*

Expectations

We met at St James's Park and walked around the lake, looking at the pelicans. One of them stared at us aggressively and didn't look away.

'I don't trust that one,' Priya said. 'It looks like it could peck the shit out of us.'

We broke eye contact and hurried out of the way.

'So how are you, Jo?' she asked.

'Fine, how are you?'

She stopped and turned to look at me. 'Are you really though, because I actually want to know how you are, and I get the feeling you're not fine.'

'I'm pretty tired,' I said. 'I think I feel . . . I just think I feel a bit lost. And angry. I keep feeling so, so angry.'

'I'm not surprised,' she said. 'Grief does that. It makes you tired and it makes you sad and sometimes it makes you filled with rage.'

'But I'm so frustrated. I'm angry with myself. For being pathetic, and for failing.'

'What do you mean?'

We sat down on a bench and Priya leaned in and looked at

me with such careful attention that it made me suddenly fear I was going to cry.

'I went to university,' I said, 'not because I wanted to go or because I wanted to be qualified to do a specific job, but just to prove that I could do it, to prove that I was worth something because, well, no one outside of my family had any expectations that I would do well, and I wanted to prove them wrong.'

'Yeah,' Priya said, 'I get that.'

'You know, in year 11, so many girls were pregnant in my class that some of the teachers would just take breaks in the middle of lessons, so they could all just get up and stretch and walk around and go to the toilet. The format of lessons had to change, because so many of the children were having children. And then, the year I did my GCSEs, it was reported that a high number of fourteen- and fifteen-year-old girls at my school were getting pregnant by twenty-one- to twenty-five-year-old men. So, you know what was done to tackle this? They started giving fourteen-year-olds dolls to look after, to try and convince them not to get pregnant. So instead of addressing the actual issue – that men were raping children – they made it the girls' problem and handed them these dolls that were programmed to cry every twenty minutes to keep them awake all night. Girls who needed the help of social services and the police – who needed teachers to encourage them and believe in them. Those girls never knew they were important. They were never told that full, exciting lives were waiting for them. They were treated like trash. And I remember thinking, are girls at Marlborough and Cheltenham Ladies' College given dolls to take home at weekends, instead of piles of French homework and physics revision and textbooks on Chaucer?' I took a deep breath and then let it all go.

'I've worked so hard to prove that I can keep up with the students who went to better schools, but I can't. I'm not as clever as they are. There are massive gaping holes in my education. I don't really know how to think critically or how to debate. I never know how to pronounce anything.'

I paused, but Priya nodded, to encourage me to carry on.

'I've got three months to write an eighty-thousand-word thesis. I've probably written a third of it. And I don't see how I could ever pass the viva – it's an exam that lasts for hours where experts in your field grill you about everything you've written. I can't even do a ten-minute presentation to a room of feminists about tits in the paper.'

'Jo, listen.' Priya grabbed my hand and held it. 'The first thing I want to say is, you can definitely do it. I have absolutely no doubt that you can finish the thesis and pass the exam. If you decide you want to do it, you can definitely do it. Secondly, being different to the other students is a good thing. That's your strength. You've had experiences they'll never have, and you know things about the world they don't know.'

'Thanks, Priya. You're a good friend.'

'I mean it. But I just wish you'd gone to my school. Yeah, it was a bit shit, but some of the teachers were brilliant and most of the other pupils were nice. I mean, there were some bell-ends at my school, you know, bullies and stuff, but it was a minority of bell-ends.'

'That could be the title of your childhood memoir: *A Minority of Bell-ends.*'

Expectations

'Yeah,' Priya said. 'They were a minority. Most people I liked. School, for me, was like a big social thing. I didn't go there to learn stuff, I went there to hang out with my friends. School was like a pub, without the alcohol. But . . . well, I mean, sometimes with the alcohol. I didn't turn up for any of my GCSEs except English language and English literature. They were the only exams I actually did.'

'Really?'

'Yeah. You know, loads of stuff had happened at home and I was in foster care at the time, so nobody thought I'd succeed at anything. But I had this brilliant English teacher who always pushed me and told me I was clever, and she really believed in me and I liked her, so I turned up for those two exams, and you know what? I got an A-star in both of them.'

'So, hang on a minute,' I said, 'you only got out of bed for two exams and you got the highest possible grades in both of them?'

'Yeah. I like to tell people that I got all A-stars in my GCSEs. Which is true. I just don't tell them that I only did two. Do you want to walk for a bit?'

We stood up and slowly made our way towards The Mall.

'I don't want to keep banging on about everything,' Priya said, 'because I know you're tired. We should actually maybe go and get a coffee and a piece of cake or something. Let's do that. But yeah, I just wanted to say, the thing you said about not feeling confident giving a talk to a feminist group. Well, all I'll say is that in my experience, some of these feminist circles – not all of them, but some of them – can make you feel really uncomfortable and out of place.'

'Yes!' I said. 'A couple of weeks ago I went to this gin and feminism book club thing in Hampstead – they wanted someone to come and talk about No More Page 3 and I went, well, for the gin. But it was all really wealthy people wearing the kind of shoes that would cost more than my rent, and I felt like a commoner who was just there to provide entertainment. I was led into the room like a petting-zoo goat hired for a children's birthday party.'

Priya laughed. 'I'm sorry, Jo, that's really shit. But I'm not surprised. In some feminist groups there's a lot of – let's be honest – pretty well-off people going on about gender theory and really liking the sound of their own voices. A LOT of middle-class white women actually. And I'm not saying there's anything wrong with that – just that it can make people who aren't middle-class white women feel really unwelcome.'

'Can I ask, how do you really feel about No More Page 3?'

'The thing that I find interesting about HQ is that it's mainly working-class women, and you don't find many spaces like that, not in feminism anyway. But Page 3 is an issue that mainly white feminists are interested in, right? I mean, Page 3 itself is such a white thing. It's almost always a white woman on it. You know, when I used to see Page 3, I didn't think, "Oh that's what I should look like", because it was physically impossible for me to ever look like that – I'm never going to be white, so I can never look like that – so I always thought it had nothing to do with me. But then I started thinking about it in terms of representation and *why* it had nothing to do with me and that's what I think is important – who is absent from the media and why.'

'I spoke to this lovely woman named Meera,' I said, 'at a petition signing. She told me she was British Punjabi and she hated Page 3. She said she'd always hated it, but she also hated the fact that there'd never be a woman like her on it. She said, "Women like me only make the papers if we're murdered or marry a terrorist".'

'Well, yeah, but to be honest, most of the women who are murdered don't make the papers. Not women who look like me anyway. That's the thing, Jo, because if I was to separate everything, then race has played a bigger part in my day-to-day life than gender has. There was so much racism when I was growing up. We'd be shouted at on the street all the time. People actually used to put dog shit through the letterbox. I know it's a bit of a cliché, but they actually used to do that. And I'd think, why would you do that? That's bad for both of us – you have to actually pick up the shit to put it through the letterbox; how is this good for you? In fact, there was so much racism where we lived that the authorities moved us all to different floors in the block of flats, that's how they dealt with it – they put us on one floor and the white people on another.'

We stopped at a cafe, and carried on the conversation sitting by the window, watching people walk and cycle past.

'I think I told you,' Priya said, 'that I was raped when I was a teenager?'

I nodded.

'Well, there's a lot of shame in my community around rape. You're not supposed to talk about it. But I've been talking about it a lot lately. I didn't tell you at the time, but a couple of months ago, I was at the train station and this group of men on the platform were making rape jokes, and I was just overcome with rage and suddenly started shouting at them. And then I couldn't stop thinking about it, so I started interviewing women, rape survivors, about their experiences, and it's been so interesting.'

I listened as she told me all about it.

'After I was raped,' she said, 'there was a lot of great counselling available, which helped emotionally, but there was nothing to help survivors to reconnect with their own bodies, or to help them to navigate sexual experiences. So, I've been talking to women about this, and so many have told me they feel vulnerable accessing healthcare, like cervical screening and sexual health checks and stuff, because being examined is so traumatic. I've felt this way, like, being examined by a doctor just reminds me of all the forensic testing I had to go through and it's really upsetting. You know, one in five British women has been sexually assaulted, so this is such a widespread issue, and nobody is talking about it. So many survivors are not getting access to healthcare and something needs to be done about it. I want to do something about it.'

'What will you do?' I asked.

'I don't know yet, Jo. But something. I'll do something.'

I replayed the conversation over and over in my head during the days that followed. I felt proud to be Priya's friend. Her courage and determination in the face of all the things she had overcome inspired me. I took her advice.

I messaged HQ, saying I was sorry, but I wouldn't be around for a while because I had to finish my thesis.

Expectations

'Don't apologise,' Lucy said, 'we'll be fine – just focus on your work. Good luck! We love you.'

I deactivated my Facebook account. I built the Tetris desk and stopped turning it into a coffee table in the evenings. I worked non-stop for weeks, barely even noticing as summer stretched into autumn. Priya was in touch regularly to ask how it was going. Evie messaged me every few days. *You can do it! What's your word count now?*

Assad made breakfasts and dinners and left small offerings around my room: a plate of toast, a chocolate biscuit, a sandwich. He'd appear every now and then in the doorway, rustling a paper bag of grapes, in the way that people shake a box of rabbit-flavoured biscuits to let the cat know it's time for tea.

I wrote and wrote until the words on the screen made me dizzy. I knew some parts of the thesis so well that the passages would spring into my mind, familiar as song lyrics, but I'd catch a glimpse of other paragraphs in other chapters and I'd think, *Did I even write that?*

I printed out four copies; two for the examiners, one for my supervisor and one for me – over two thousand pages – and stacked them in high piles on the floor.

I stepped back to look them and burst into tears.

I couldn't believe I had done it.

Will and I went to the coast to celebrate, staying in a B&B that had net curtains on the windows and porcelain shire horses on the mantlepiece. Above the communal breakfast table was a painting of a springer spaniel looking wistfully at a hot pie. A couple from Bristol ate bacon and eggs across from us, and shared a long story about the congestion on the M5 and how much they had paid for a bag of M&Ms at a service station near Taunton. The owner of the B&B liked to chat.

'I like to chat,' she said, lingering by the miniature cereals, 'yes, I like to talk to my guests.'

She talked about her ex-husband, the rising cost of light-bulbs, and eggs. Every now and then, her conversation would trail off and she'd wait expectantly for one of us to respond but, as soon as we started to speak, she'd immediately talk over us.

'How's the egg, is that alright for you? My son-in-law won't touch eggs, and it's difficult, you know, because everything has got egg in it. He's not vegan or anything like that, he just can't stand the texture or smell of eggs – and it can be any kind of eggs, fried, poached scrambled.'

She went quiet and I started to say something, but she quickly said, 'Omelettes . . .'

It happened again with 'boiled eggs', so I left it at that, and we sat there in silence.

When the Bristol couple had gone and the owner had disappeared into the kitchen with their empty plates, Will said, 'You must be so happy now the thesis is handed in.'

'I can't quite believe it,' I said. 'But I've still got to get through the viva.' The date had been set for 6 January, and I was sick with nerves just thinking about it. 'Let's change the subject,' I said, 'or I'll start to freak out.'

'Mum's got a new boyfriend,' he said, sipping the last of

his coffee. 'She wants me to meet him, so I think it must be serious.'

'Who is he?'

'I don't know anything about him. But she seems really happy. We'll probably all meet up at some point in London.'

'I'll be in London next week,' I said. 'There's a protest in Parliament Square.'

'For No More Page 3?'

I nodded. 'I went into HQ for the first time in ages yesterday, and there are so many new people and there's so much going on. It was like going back to school after being off sick, and you've missed the introductory algebra lessons and everything is written in a language you don't understand.'

'You'll settle back in,' Will said, 'you'll see. After a while it'll feel like you've never been away.'

Rebels With a Cause

It was the biggest protest we'd ever had. Parliament Square was packed. There were protesters chanting, reporters asking questions and photographers shouting directions. I was overwhelmed by the noise, the crowd, the camera flashes. Lucy and Yas were talking to reporters and Max was leading the crowd in protest songs. I thought back to the first protest, with the photographer saying, 'We'll just have to crop it creatively'. There was no need to crop any pictures creatively now. There were too many people to fit in a single frame.

I spotted Evie chasing after Milly and Sophie and I ran over to help her round them up like a border collie.

'Congratulations!' she said. 'I knew you'd do it! So, do you have loads of free time now?'

'I've found a job,' I said. 'Freelance research work. It doesn't pay very well, but it's interesting and I can work from home, and it'll tide me over until something else turns up.'

'That's great news. It'll take the pressure off a bit to have money coming in.'

We smiled at each other. I was so happy to see her.

'I was just thinking,' I said, 'about those early protests when barely anyone turned up.'

Evie laughed. 'Oh god, can you believe we did all that stuff? We must have been mad.'

'*We* were mad? You hijacked the Babycam!'

'Sometimes I just think about that and burst out laughing.'

We picked up our stuff and started following the others as they headed towards Southbank.

'I'm thinking of going back to university,' Evie said, 'to do an MA. It's something I've secretly wanted to do for years, but I never had the confidence to apply.'

'Do it!' I said. 'If you can speak for two hours livestreamed on the internet, you can sit in a classroom or attend a lecture.'

'I think you're right. We've done so much over the past couple of years that I sometimes think I can do anything. Oh god, Jo, look – the Christmas market's here! Is it too early for mulled wine?'

After my second cup of glühwein, I spotted Priya and gave her a big hug. She'd messaged me a few weeks ago to say that she'd started an organisation, My Body Back, to support survivors of sexual assault and was working with a healthcare trust to launch a clinic at a London hospital. It would be the first ever NHS clinic to provide specialist health services for survivors.

We sat on a wall in a patch of November sunshine, and I asked her a million questions at once. She tried her best to fill me in.

'Before women arrive for an appointment, they'll provide information about their trigger points – like, one woman was told by her rapist to "relax and it will be over quicker", and then a doctor said the same words during a smear test, and she was completely traumatised. We want to tailor the experience as much as possible to meet individual needs, whether it's music playing in the room, or aromatherapy or a massage to put the patient at ease. We basically want the women who come to us to be in control of the situation, and to be able to build up to the examination as slowly as they need to.'

'Priya, you're completely, utterly amazing,' I said. 'What you're doing will help so many women.'

'It'll help me too,' she said. 'They're services I need myself.'

'And you're looking after yourself, right? You're not taking on too much?'

'Well, I could do without getting death threats every week . . . but, yeah, I'm OK.'

Priya received not only abuse online from trolls but also threats of acid attacks. She was in constant contact with the police, and suffered from anxiety as a result of all the threats, but she carried on and refused to be silenced.

I travelled back to Kent via Dulwich, to drop off a card for Livia's birthday. Walking past my old flat, I paused to look at the bay trees that had been placed either side of the front door and smiled, imagining how furious Miran would be. She didn't like change, or ornamental plants. It felt strange to walk across Peckham Rye, and I felt a jolt of homesickness as I remembered all the times I'd sat on the grass with Rhianne, drinking wine or beer from cans while she smoked roll-ups and made me laugh. I sat on a bench in the walled garden and, after a while, an elderly woman sat down next to me. We started talking, and she told me about the Italian prisoner-of-war camp that had stood on the Rye in the forties, and the houses that were wrecked by V-2s when she was a little girl.

'William Blake saw a vision here,' she said. 'He saw a tree full of angels. And they say Boadicea is buried here somewhere. Or Boudicca, as they call her now.'

She told me that her daughter had played Boudicca in a historical re-enactment in the sixties. She was chosen for the part because of her red hair, which was grey now, like her own. We talked about No More Page 3 and she signed the petition, writing on the form, in a shaky hand: *We need more rebellious women.*

My primary school teacher, Mrs Lincoln, used to call my hair rebellious, because it would never stay in place. There were strict rules about having hair tied back for games, and it used to exasperate her. It could be tamed or controlled for a while, with hair bands and Kirby grips, but it would eventually work its way free. I loved the idea of refusing to stay in your place, of showing resistance and bursting free.

I thought of Priya. Yas had helped her to launch My Body Back. Neither of them had a space to work at home, so they'd meet at McDonald's and sit in a booth upstairs, connecting a laptop to the free Wi-Fi.

'We were both skint,' Priya said, 'so we'd just buy a drink and sit there all day, stealing their Wi-Fi. It wasn't the most glamorous place to work, but it was enough.'

Priya and Yas; two young people with no money or professional experience – with no *Wi-Fi* – had successfully changed the curriculum and were revolutionising women's healthcare from a booth upstairs in McDonald's. They saw what wasn't working in schools and hospitals and tried to find a different way. What they'd been offered wasn't enough, and they rebelled against it and, in doing so, changed everything.

So many of us are taught that we are powerless to instigate change, in our own lives and in the world. We are taught that only a privileged few have the authority to make decisions about what is important and how things work. But, every now and then, people like Priya and Yas come along to shake things up. People who are courageous and rebellious enough to insist that they get what they need.

Anything Can Happen

One week before her birthday, Jess told me that she had left Matt. She was renting a small terraced house in Newcastle from a friend of a friend, and Ruby was with her.

She spoke quickly on the phone, and her voice had the kind of breathy, jittery quality you hear when talking to a very cold person, waiting at a bus stop in snow.

'We'd had this weekend of just barely speaking to each other,' she said, 'and when I said it – when I said I was leaving – he didn't threaten me like I thought he would. He was calmer than I expected him to be, and that kind of worried me actually, but . . . well, here I am.'

I couldn't believe she'd done it.

'What can I do?' I asked. 'What do you need?'

'Can you come this weekend,' she said, 'please?'

We quickly made plans. Most of HQ were busy that Saturday, but Rhianne, Evie and Yas were free. We agreed to stay at Jess's new place while her cousin, who lived nearby, would babysit Ruby.

*

I was the last to arrive. Everyone was sitting around the living room, drinking wine, except Yas, who was cradling a cup of herbal tea. Jess was walking around, carrying plates with nowhere to put them down. Music played in the background, and I remembered her saying, 'silence makes me want to scream.'

I was quickly losing confidence in the birthday card I'd bought her. It had seemed funny in the shop, but now it felt ill-judged. She saw it sticking out of my bag, so I handed it over to her with the champagne I'd brought. When she pulled the card from its envelope, Evie laughed and Jess smiled, but with her mouth and not her eyes. The card had printed across the front: 'It's better to have loved and lost than to have to live with that psycho for the rest of your life.'

As she placed it on the mantelpiece with the other cards I thought, *Shit, too soon.*

Jess changed the subject if we asked how she was or what was going on, so we talked about other things, ate fajitas and drank more wine.

'Can we go out now?' Jess said. She'd been pacing around the living room, moving plates before we'd finished the food. 'I think we should go out. I really want to go out.'

The rest of us didn't want to go out. I looked at Rhianne.

'Your birthday, your rules,' she said. 'We'll go wherever you want.' She was such a good friend.

'Let's go to a club!' Jess said and, taking Rhianne's cue, I jumped to my feet with the forced enthusiasm of a children's television presenter.

'Let's get changed then!' she said.

We swapped our hoodies and leggings for dressier things

and left the house. It was raining heavily. Across the street, a cat on a windowsill was crying to be let in and I felt no sympathy. At least the cat could crawl under a hedge and wouldn't have to deal with smoke machines, podiums and being danced at by strangers.

We went to a couple of bars, and Jess made us do karaoke to 'Love Shack', which was surprisingly difficult, because the words didn't seem to fit in the verse. It was at that point that Evie and Yas said they were tired and had had really long days and could they grab the key and go back now?

I tried to tag along with them but Rhianne pulled me back.

'You're coming to the club,' she said. 'Jess wants to go, so we're going.'

Ten minutes later, in the queue outside, I looked at the three of us and realised what an odd group we made. I was wearing a dress that my mum said made me look like a trapeze artist, which I'd taken as a compliment at first, but I was starting to feel self-conscious about it. Jess was wearing skin-tight black jeans, boots and an oversized man's shirt that gave the impression she had spent the night with Jim Morrison and had left his apartment wearing his clothes. Rhianne was sporting an embroidered orange kaftan and looked as if she was about to officiate a handfasting ceremony at Stonehenge.

'We look like we've just got back from very different festivals,' I said.

'God, I wish we were at a festival,' Jess replied and I looked at the queue of drunk people in front of me and thought, *It could be worse, it could always be worse.* At least there were no Portaloos or people with friendship bracelets and drums.

We left our coats in the cloakroom and bought warm cocktails in plastic cups. While Jess danced sensually on her own,
Rhianne and I leaned against a cold metal railing, hating
everything. Jess would shimmy towards us then dance away,
lost in her own world and, roughly every five minutes, a man
would sidle up behind her and try to get involved. She ignored
them all completely until, one by one, they slowly danced away,
as if they'd intended to dance on their own anyway and were
merely grinding past Jess on their way to the toilets. Each time
a new song came on, Rhianne would put her hand up like she
was asking a question in class and say, 'What the fuck is this?'

Despite insisting we go to the club, Rhianne was furious the
entire time. If I tried to talk to her, she'd shout, angrily, 'What?
I can't hear you. No, I can't fucking hear you,' pointing up at
the sky as if the gods of dance music had cursed her life and
ruined her crops.

So I just stood there with my tepid cocktail, looking like I'd
escaped from a circus, while Jess drifted by with her arms in
the air and Rhianne shouted a series of four-letter words at the
ceiling.

When the lights came on at the end of the night, Jess grabbed
us both by the wrist and dragged us towards the cloakroom.
'Come on, quick, let's grab our coats and get to the pizza place
before everybody else.'

We had to jog along wet pavements to keep up with her.

We ordered from a plastic menu filled with pictures of
pizzas with orange cheese, were given a ticket with a number
on it and told to wait on the bench by the door. Jess rested
her head on my shoulder. She suddenly looked exhausted. She

hadn't mentioned Matt all night, but I knew she was thinking about him.

Two drunk women stumbled to the counter and ordered chips and cheese. They had very loud voices.

'I just look so fat in this dress,' one woman said. 'Just a fat mess.'

'No, you don't – you look *fit*,' her friend replied.

'I shouldn't have worn this. It's all wrong.'

'At least you're not wearing *that*,' the friend said. I couldn't tell if she was pointing at Rhianne in her Stonehenge kaftan or me in my trapeze dress.

'Well that's fucking rude,' Rhianne said, and Jess burst out laughing.

'I'm sorry,' she said. 'What a bitch.'

A minute later, the man behind the counter shouted 'Two one seven!' and I went to stand up, but Jess had fallen fast asleep with her head on my shoulder.

'Jess,' I said quietly, 'come on, let's go home.'

She half opened her eyes and said, 'Pizza?'

'It's here.' Rhianne offered her a slice.

She yawned and her eyes watered. 'Thanks for coming, guys. It's been horrible. It's been a horrible week and I needed this.'

And then she fell asleep with her head on the pizza box.

It was a taxing journey back to Kent. I was hungover, and the man sitting next to me on the train left an opened bag of cheese and onion crisps on the little pull-down table, and the smell was deeply distressing. He stretched out on the seat, with his legs open wide enough to birth triplets. I sat with my knees pressed together and my head in my hands, trying not to think of breakfast. Jess had put some vegetarian sausages in the oven and left them there, forgotten, for about an hour. They weren't burnt, just leathery and shrunken: the kind of thing an archaeologist would find in a bog. I'd attempted to eat one out of politeness, but it was no longer food, and I couldn't go through with it.

When I finally arrived back at the flat, I ran a bath and set up my laptop on the bathroom windowsill, all ready to watch *A Room with a View*. I had found a box of fudge in the kitchen cupboard, and was looking forward to wallowing like a hippo while watching Maggie Smith flap around Florence with a handkerchief held up to her face. I was just about to get in when Will called.

'Listen,' he said, and from the tone of his voice I knew immediately that he'd discovered he had a terrible disease. Or had a secret child. Or was in jail. 'I don't know how to say this . . .'

'What is it?' I asked. 'Just tell me.' I sat down, like people do on *Coronation Street* when they get bad news.

'Well, I've just spoken to Mum.'

'Is she OK?'

'Oh yeah, yeah, she's absolutely fine. It's just that . . .'

'What?'

'Well, you know I said she's seeing somebody?'

'Yes.'

'It's just that . . . it's not a big deal or anything. It's . . . well, I found out, I mean, Mum told me that the person she's going out with is . . .'

'Spit it out.'

'Michael Waldon.'

'What?'

'Mum is dating Michael Waldon.'

'Your mum is going out with Michael Waldon?'

'Yes.'

I laughed. 'Don't be daft! It won't be *that* Michael Waldon. I'm sure it's a pretty common name. I mean, it's not like he's called Ebeneezer Pigwitch or anything. There'll be other blokes with that name.'

'Yeah, but it *is* him.'

I waited for him to laugh and say it was a joke, but he didn't say anything at all. There was just silence.

'How?' I asked, after a while. 'How has this happened? How did they even meet?'

'I'm not going to ask my mum about how she met her boyfriend. That would be really weird.'

'So you don't know?'

'Of course I don't know.'

'Can't you just ask her?'

'Why does it matter where they met?'

I made a long moaning sound as I remembered the last conversation I'd had with Will's mother, when we'd had brunch, and I'd spent fifteen minutes slagging off Michael Waldon. Her new boyfriend.

I hung up, grabbed my laptop off the bathroom windowsill and closed the tab open at *A Room with a View*. The evening had changed so dramatically, so quickly, that not even Maggie Smith could make it better. I needed HQ.

Jess: WHAT?

Jess: Sorry, but WHAT???

Rhianne: I don't believe this. It's a joke, right?

Yas: Oh Jo are you serious?

Max: You're fucking KIDDING me?

Max: OMFG I'm horrified and laughing at the same time

Kate: Do you think that perhaps your life isn't real and somebody is writing it for a laugh?

Jess phoned me.

'You know, Max was only saying the other day that Michael Waldon hasn't tweeted us or even mentioned the campaign in months. Maybe Will's mum is a good influence.'

I was quiet for a while, and she said, 'What are you thinking?'

'I was just thinking that anything can happen,' I said. 'Absolutely anything can happen.'

Viva

On the morning of my viva, my dad sent a text, informing me that 6 January was the day of Epiphany. He said he hoped I had one in the exam room.

I thought of the examiners: two women, experts in their field, who were travelling on trains and planes to get to London. One was coming from Germany. I thought of how they had left their homes that morning, eaten breakfast, packed a bag, said goodbye to their families.

I arrived at the Courtauld early, splashed water on my face in the toilets, making my mascara run, and headed upstairs. I stood outside the exam room door and knocked.

'Come in.'

There was no turning back.

The room was so small that the four of us – me, my supervisor and the two examiners – only just fitted in. Our knees touched under the table. There was no small talk, they just dived right in. I was asked question after question for three and a half hours. The examiners would quietly whisper to each other and then open my thesis at a certain page and quote something I'd written back to me. They'd then look up expectantly and

I'd panic and my heart would flutter and then I'd remember to fake it, to act like Max, and I'd make eye contact and find something to say. Over and over, I had to lift myself up, pretend I knew what I was talking about, pretend I had confidence in my own voice. It was hours and hours of make-believe.

Finally, they looked at each other, nodded and asked me to leave the room so they could deliberate. It was like a bad *X Factor* parody with a German Simon Cowell. I could almost hear tense background music as I left the room. I leaned against a radiator in the corridor for fifteen minutes, pulling bits of woodchip off the wall with my fingernail while they talked about me upstairs in the little attic room. I was strangely calm. There was nothing left for me to do.

When they called me back in, there was a moment of unreadable silence, the kind of pause I'd seen on TV in courtroom dramas before the judge gives the verdict. I looked at them all in turn, but their faces gave nothing away.

Then suddenly: 'You've passed, congratulations.'

I made a noise I have never made before or since: the sort of sound a peacock might make after an electric shock. They carried on talking, but I didn't really hear any of it. I was miles away.

'Is that clear?' my supervisor asked. 'You've passed, with minor corrections.' She listed the changes I'd have to make to the thesis before I could be awarded the PhD: replacing a certain word with another, changing a chapter heading, adding a reference or two. It was barely anything. It could be done in a matter of days.

They insisted we go for a drink. I'd never been to the restaurant at Somerset House and didn't feel comfortable sitting at the table with fine linen and heavy cutlery. I just wanted to be somewhere, anywhere, on my own. I needed to process things. It was easier for me to accept bad news than good.

My supervisor asked me how I was feeling.

'I don't know,' I said. 'I feel strange.'

'It's quite common to feel overwhelmed,' she said kindly. 'But you must celebrate your successes. It's very important to celebrate each success.'

My mum and dad celebrated.

'We've got a cake,' my mum said on the phone. 'And some beer and wine.'

'But I can't come to visit until next week.'

'Oh, well, we'll just have it then. Hang on, your dad wants to say something.'

'We're that proud,' he said. 'Can't believe we've got a doctor in the family. Your mother's just opened a bottle of Stella.'

'Cheers!' she shouted in the background.

'She'll be drunk by four and asleep by five,' he said. 'But well done, sweetheart. We knew you'd do it. All the times you said you couldn't do it, we always knew you could.'

Rumours

I spent much of early January wrapped in blankets, eating Jaffa Cakes and catching up on what I'd missed in HQ. Lucy had announced she was pregnant, so a lot of the chat was about cravings, vomiting and babies. I don't really like babies, but I usually pretend otherwise, because a woman who dislikes babies is always considered a psychopath. What I find most uncomfortable is when parents ask if I'd like to hold their baby, which I find as puzzling and bizarre as if they had just walked over to the table, picked up a lamp and said, 'Do you fancy holding this for a bit?' But I loved Lucy and I was happy about the baby because she was happy about it.

It had been a surprise, completely unplanned. She was shocked at first but she had taken time to get her head around the idea, and now she was thrilled. Everyone in HQ made such a fuss. A campaign baby! There were countless offers of tiny clothes and childcare assistance. After a full-on Christmas, Lucy was planning to go to one of her beloved silent retreats in Germany to unwind and relax.

We had plans bubbling away in HQ, but we were moving slowly. We were tired and sluggish. It was January, after all.

Rumours

Lucy was packing for Germany when she got the phone call that kicked us all into gear.

Lucy: Shiiiiiiiiit! Everyone, listen to this

Lucy: Sky News want to do an interview because they think Page 3 is going to go IMMINENTLY and they want to get something in the bag so they can go live with it ASAP when it does!!!

Everyone in HQ typed at once, in caps lock, with exclamation marks.

Lucy: I know, I know! I think it's for real? Sky is Murdoch-owned. They'd know if Page 3 was going, right?

Lucy is typing . . .

Lucy: OH MY GOD – I've just had a call from a journalist who says he's heard *The Sun* have ALREADY dropped Page 3. He says the last ever picture was printed last week.

Lucy: He said 'have a good week . . . I think you might . . .'

Lucy: I fly to sodding Germany in the morning!!!

Lucy: I'm just sitting here freaking out, trying not to cry

We were all saying the same things at the same time. Could it be real? Should we prepare a statement? Who was doing what? How could we take the pressure off Lucy? Were we ready for a media circus?

> Max: Guys, if this is legit, I'm calling an immediate end to Dry January.

> Evie: Look at this, just published on *The Guardian*'s website:

HAVE *THE SUN* AXED PAGE 3?

> Kate: And Twitter has just blown up

> Max: OMG we've just got like 200 notifications all at once

> Me: Where's Jess?

She hadn't been online in a few days, and I didn't want her to miss what was going on. Kate tagged her in a message, I sent a text, but she didn't reply.

> Rhianne: Guys, do you really think this is it, or is Murdoch just messing with us?

> Steve: I wouldn't put it past *The Sun* to be winding us up, to pretend Page 3 is going and

then to relaunch it, to say it was all a joke. It's the kind of thing they'd do.

Kate: But it's Sky – surely their sources are accurate? And now *The Guardian*

Lucy: OH MY LIFE *Newsnight* have just been in touch – they want me to go on the show tonight

Steve: OK even I have to admit it's looking positive

Lucy: I'm too scared to say yes to *Newsnight* and I'm supposed to be flying to Germany in the morning!

Me: Stay here! Cancel Germany

Yas: Totally stay

Max: And say YES to *Newsnight*!!!

Steve: If this is all true, it's the culmination of everything you've fought for. Stay and I'll pay you whatever you spent on the flight, as compensation

Lucy: Shiiiit, so I'm going on *Newsnight*?!

Kate: YES!!!!!

I phoned Jess, but she didn't answer. I phoned Rhianne, Evie, Priya, Will, Assad, my mum. I wanted to say over and over, 'This could be it – Page 3 could be finished.' I shook off the blankets and walked tracks around the carpet with my phone in my hand.

By lunchtime, we'd been contacted by all the major news channels and UK newspapers, requesting interviews. By mid-afternoon, we'd spoken to reporters in America, Germany, Sweden. By early evening, New Zealand, Australia, Japan.

It was dark outside when Jess posted in HQ.

Jess: Guys I can't believe this, is this really happening?

I phoned her again, and this time she answered.

'How are you doing? I've not heard from you in a while.'

'Yeah. OK.' She sounded strained. Her voice was flat.

'What's wrong?'

'Nothing, why?'

'Is everything alright? Ruby's OK?'

'Yeah, fine.'

'Have you heard anything from Matt?'

She was silent.

'Has he been in touch?'

'Yeah, he's here now actually.'

Alarm bells sounded in my head. 'He's there now? In Newcastle? To see Ruby?'

She paused. 'I'm back at the house,' she said. 'In Shropshire. I've moved back in.'

I suddenly felt cold. 'Can he hear you talking to me?'

'Hang on.' I heard her walk to the door and close it. 'It's OK. He's downstairs. I'm in the bedroom.' She sighed. 'I know what you're thinking. I'm an idiot. I know I'm an idiot.'

'You're *not* an idiot. But why didn't you tell me you'd gone back?'

'Because I know how you feel about him. And I made such a big deal out of leaving. I told everybody, and made such a fuss about it.'

'So, you're back together?'

'For now.'

'But you'd done it,' I said. 'You'd done the hard bit – you'd had the conversation and you'd found somewhere to rent, and moved all your stuff out and—'

'That wasn't the hard bit. The hard bit was seeing how devastated Ruby was. How she missed her dad. How confused she was – she just didn't get it, what was happening. And I couldn't afford anything. I couldn't go anywhere, couldn't take Ruby anywhere. The cooker broke and I couldn't afford to get it repaired. I can't live like that. I have nothing of my own. Everything is his. It's all in his name. I can't do it on my own. Not yet anyway. I just can't do it.'

We talked for as long as we could. I told her I understood, and that whatever happened, we'd all be there for her. I was so angry with myself for being so naive, believing that it was that easy; that she'd left for good.

'I'm just taking it a day at a time,' she said. 'That's all I can do.'

I remembered a conversation I'd had with Evie at Jess's birthday.

'Seven times,' she said. 'That's the average, apparently. It takes seven attempts for a woman to leave an abusive relationship for good.'

For some reason, I didn't think this applied to Jess. I'd chosen to believe that it was over, completely, utterly, over.

I heard him shout her name from downstairs. 'I've got to go,' she said, before hanging up.

The only thing to do was to carry on supporting her and loving her, just as Rhianne had suggested a year and a half ago. Carry on, until she was ready to leave for good, no matter how many attempts it took.

It was stated by more and more sources that Page 3 had definitely been dropped, but *The Sun* remained silent, giving no indication either way. Their only response came from their head of PR, Dylan Sharpe, who tweeted that tomorrow Page 3 would be *in the same place it's always been – between page 2 and page 4*.

> Jess: Why can't they just act like adults, just once? If it's for real, why can't they just say, 'after 43 years, we've decided to end Page 3'. Why all the infantile games?

> Max: They'd never allow it to look like a victory for the campaign.

> Jess: God I'm so sick of it. Why can't these men just grow the fuck up?

Rumours

We counted down the hours till *Newsnight*. Evie had suggested that we gather in HQ, so we could be together, if only virtually, to watch it.

'So Lucy will know that we're all there sending her love and cheering her on,' she said.

Page 3 was to be the last item on the show. It was torture waiting for Lucy to come on. We were on tenterhooks. Supporters were live tweeting. My mum and dad were glued to the TV in Rotherham.

Max: HOW THE FUCK ARE WE SUPPOSED TO COPE WITH THE SUSPENSE?

Yas: They've been talking about Milton Keynes for a reeeaaaally long time

Me: Maybe it's on next

Jess: Nope, we've got to sit through Mandelson first

Kate: Mandelson still exists who knew

Max: Christ make it end

And then finally, it was Lucy. I turned up the brightness on my screen. I turned up the volume. I wanted her to be as light and loud as possible.

*

The following morning, the front page of *The Times* read:

THE SUN HAS GOT ITS TOP ON . . .
PAGE 3 COVERS UP AFTER 45 YEARS

Since *The Times* was *The Sun*'s News International sister paper, it felt like an official confirmation.

I was running a campaign workshop in London with Rhianne that morning. I put on my No More Page Three T-shirt and paused in front of the mirror, wondering if this was the last time I'd wear it.

When I followed Rhianne into the workshop venue, we got a standing ovation. I flushed and didn't know what to do with my face or hands. The organiser took a photo of all of us together, with some of us crouched at the front. A woman at the back shouted, 'Stand up – this is no time to crouch!' so I got to my feet, feeling only slightly less powerful and jubilant after getting told off for doing a photo wrong.

While we were at the workshop in the East End, Evie, Yas and Max were at television studios in central London. Max was speaking to Channel 5 news, Yas was being interviewed for Sky and Evie was appearing on breakfast TV. I kept looking at the clock hanging above the door, wondering if they'd finished filming yet. As soon as I was free, I called Evie.

'Oh my god, it was terrifying,' she said. 'I think I did OK, I've no idea, I can't even remember what I said. It's so weird, just sitting really upright on a sofa, pretending to have a casual chat with all these lights and cameras pointing at you.'

It had been the typical debate-style set-up, with Evie and a glamour model. Evie told me that the model, a woman named Nicola, had helped her to calm down before filming.

'I was sitting in the green room and I was almost hyperventilating, I was so nervous. And she came and sat next to me and started giving me all these tips about how to control the nerves and what to do on camera, and I just loved her. She was being really funny and making me laugh, and I felt a thousand times better because she was there. Then filming started and we had to disagree with each other, but we did it in good humour. I really respected her, and I think she respected me too.'

I watched Max on the news. The presenter mentioned a picture of David Beckham shirtless in the paper, and compared it to Page 3. Max said a topless man and a topless woman was not an equal comparison. She said that the male equivalent of Page 3 would probably be a half-dressed model with his testicles hanging out of his pants. The male presenter winced when she said testicles, so she said it a second time.

Yas did more interviews than anyone and spent the whole day travelling around London from studio to studio, recording segments for news channels. A man at Sky News said, off the record, that it was official. 'We were talking about Page 3 in the past tense!' Yas told us.

Girlguiding sent us a congratulatory message, saying, 'We are so, so pleased and proud that we could play a part in the campaign, and that our young members know that when they use their voices, change does come.'

They made a graphic that said: 'I backed the No More Page 3 campaign and my voice made a difference!' Young women were sharing it all over social media. Seeing so many girls say 'my voice made a difference' made my own catch in my throat whenever I spoke about it.

We received thousands of messages from individuals, from the organisations who supported us, the MPs who signed our petition and the football teams we sponsored. We kept having these lovely conversations where we thanked people for all their help and they thanked us back. It felt like the end of a party, when you've been dancing all night and end up in the toilets with your shoes off, telling complete strangers you love their dress and then borrowing their hairbrush.

We toasted each other with wine and beer, and Lucy joined in with lemonade in a champagne flute. We were on such a high that even the trolls didn't dampen our spirits too much.

Kate: A lot of pissed off sexists about today

Me: My favourite type of sexists

There was an unprecedented number of trolls, nastier and more threatening than ever before. We received emails from worried supporters, asking, *Is someone moderating the page? There are threats of violence and porn being posted.*

Kate sent apologies, explaining that we couldn't keep up with the sheer number of trolls.

We couldn't delete the abusive comments fast enough. As soon as one rape threat was deleted, another six would crop up. If a troll was blocked, they would quickly set up a new Facebook page and troll us afresh, hidden behind a different identity. The messages weren't just misogynistic, a huge number were also racist and Islamophobic. Trolls were posting hate messages, blaming the demise of Page 3 on the 'Islamisation' of the UK.

Assad read an article about it on the *Huffington Post*. He had recently been forced to quit Facebook due to a massive increase in racist, Islamophobic content.

'As a British Muslim, I'm taking full credit for the success of the No More Page 3 campaign,' he said, chopping carrots in the kitchen. 'It was all me. I did it single-handedly.'

'You did a great job,' I said, eating the carrot sticks.

'Do you still get hassle from that Michael Waldon dude?' he asked.

Earlier on, Michael Waldon had tweeted:

> Truly fantastic that demise of Page Three is actu-
> ally leading News on @BBCr4today! Wow!

Max had posted the tweet in HQ, saying, 'Fantastic in a good way, Michael???'

'No,' I replied to Assad. 'He keeps his opinions to himself these days.'

'Probably the best place for them,' Assad said.

The following day, the third page of *The Sun* featured a full-size advert for Sainsbury's ready meals.

Evie: So the soft porn has been replaced with a lasagne.

Killjoy

Kate: Lasagne is soft porn to me

The interview requests were still rolling in from around the world, but we were aware that they would soon stop. We would have to face the prospect of slowly winding down the campaign and ending the petition. Of course, we'd always known that when Page 3 ended, the campaign would end too, but the reality of it was just sinking in. We'd spent two years working together, throwing all of our energy and creativity into our activism. My teammates were often the first people I spoke to in the morning and the last I spoke to at night. We had gone through enormous ups and downs together, we'd had adventures and misadventures. We had been part of something so special. I just couldn't picture what life would look like without HQ.

It wasn't just me who was feeling that way. Jess told me that she was queueing in a coffee shop when she suddenly burst into tears.

'*The Sun* was on the counter,' she said. 'And it just hit me that Page 3 wasn't there. That my daughter will never have the experience of sitting in a cafe or on a bus with someone next to her leering at a teenage girl in her pants in the paper. And then I thought of what we've all done together. This thing that we've built. And I just felt so happy that it's over, and also sad that it's over. It was the strangest thing.'

I liked to hear Jess talk about the campaign in that way – the things that we had built and the things that we had done. I hoped the campaign's success would prove to her how much power she had to make change happen.

Labour and Love

That evening, *The Sun* tagged No More Page 3 in a tweet:

> We breast better get on as tomorrow is a new age
> for Page 3. Thank you @NMP3 for our massive
> increase in pre orders!

Attached was a photo of a topless model.

Max: Page 3 is back tomorrow

Max: Fuck fuck fuck

Lucy: I knew they'd do something like this

Lucy: But I still think it's gone

Kate: Do you think it's a one-off gag?

Max: Just to make us look stupid and to show
that they've got the upper hand

Killjoy

Jess: This will backfire on them.

Jess: They'll see that they can't treat people like this any more. There'll be a backlash.

Jess: They think they're just pulling one over on some whining middle-class women. But it's the Girl Guides. It's Rape Crisis. It's thousands of teachers, nurses, workers' unions, universities.

Me: Oh no, the Girl Guides.

I thought of the graphic they were sharing on social media: 'I supported NMP3 and my voice made a difference.' My heart ached for those girls. They believed *The Sun* had listened, had cared.

Lucy: My phone keeps ringing. Getting press calls already

Lucy: I'm not going to answer yet

Kate: OK, we need to work out our position on this. What do we say?

Max: Nothing yet. We've signed off social media for the night. Let's wait until the morning

Yas: And then issue a statement?

Max: Not yet. I think Jess is right. This is going
to backfire on them. So many people are going
to be absolutely furious. They want us to be
mad. They're goading us, waiting for us to
respond. Let's not give them the satisfaction of
knowing how bad we feel about this

Jess: But we've got to say something?

Max: In the morning, let's post 'So it seems the
fight is back on! Anyone fancy coffee, pastries
and a petition share?' Something like that.
Breezy, calm, upbeat.

Kate: We could also thank *The Sun* for all the free
publicity they've given us over the past few days

Lucy: Let's be as encouraging as we can. So
many people are going to feel awful tomorrow.

Me: I feel pretty awful now

Kate: Me too. But we can do this. Come on!
Let's get back to work.

In the morning, I walked to the village shop and stood in
front of the newspaper rack, studying the cover of *The Sun*. In
the top-right-hand corner was a photo of a model winking. It
said: 'We've had a mammary lapse – see page 3.'

Beneath it was the giant headline:

'SLAVE GIRL' BOMBSHELL: MY SEX WITH ANDY AND 8 GIRLS

It was a cover story about Virginia Roberts Giuffre, the survivor of the sex-trafficking ring operated by paedophile Jeffrey Epstein. To the left was a large picture of reality-TV star Sam Faiers in a low-cut dress with the headline:

A FAIER OLD VIEW

The entire cover revolved around men sexualising women's bodies. The Page 3 picture, the cleavage shot, the woman who, at the age of seventeen, was allegedly forced to have sex with rich, privileged men. A 'slave girl' bombshell.

I felt sick.

I turned to page 3.

The lasagne of yesterday was gone and, in its place, a full-on, topless Page 3. The model, Nicole, was winking. Beneath the picture it said:

CLARIFICATIONS AND CORRECTIONS

Further to recent reports in all other media outlets, we would like to clarify that this is Page 3 and this is a picture of Nicole, 22, from Bournemouth.

We would like to apologise on behalf of the print and broadcast journalists who have spent the last two days talking and writing about us.

I closed the paper and slowly walked back to the flat.

Labour and Love

Me: I just saw today's *Sun*.

Jess: It's vile.

Kate: Have you seen Page 3? If we're right and
they did bring it back just as a one-off to put
us in our place, it's bizarrely the best Page 3
I've seen. Decades of models smiling passively
or looking 'sexy' and this is the first picture that
shows so much character and personality in the
model's face. I don't suppose many people are
looking at her face, but you know what I mean.

Evie: Have you seen all the troll action on
Twitter?

Trolls had mocked up Page 3 images of campaign supporters.
They'd made a composite picture of one of the newer members
of HQ, using her profile picture to superimpose her head on
a topless model's body. A troll had written: *Why not whip them
out again for the lads bitch! #FreeTheTits!*

The trolls were jubilant. They thought they had won. They
became more and more vocal, emboldened by *The Sun*'s prank.

Of course, everyone wanted our opinion on the return of
Page 3. The news channels and radio stations all wanted us
back on air. I was tired of it all and didn't want to be a pawn
in any more petty media games. But Evie said, 'It's a chance
for us to give our side of it and to get more publicity for
the campaign.' She went back on breakfast TV, and the trolls

live-tweeted their critique of her performance, calling her an idiot, saying she should have washed her hair, she looked a mess, she was a stupid bitch. Yas and Max went back on air too, and the rest of us spoke to more and more journalists and reporters. It was exhausting.

And then we saw Dylan Sharpe's tweet.

Sharpe, *The Sun*'s head of PR, had tweeted a collage of topless photos to a number of journalists who had written about the demise of Page 3, and to MP Harriet Harman, saying *This one's for (you).*

> Jess: What The Actual FUCK?

> Kate: *The Sun*'s head of PR has sent tit pics to a female MP???

> Evie: Harriet Harman tweeted the other day that she was glad Page 3 was gone, and sent her congratulations 'to Clare Short and the thousands of women who campaigned.' And here's *The Sun*'s response: 'This one's for you' . . . And photos of a topless 22-year-old

> Max: He sent the tweet to Kay Burley too, the Sky News reporter – she's just responded 'I'm sure your mother is incredibly proud of you Dylan. I know I would be.'

Labour and Love

Kate: And to Jess Brammar – the senior
broadcast journalist for *Newsnight*. She replied:
'you're tweeting pictures of topless women to
politicians and journalists. You're a grown man.'

Max: He's just responded to someone on Twitter
who complained, saying 'come on – it's funny,
lighten up!'

Me: How old is Dylan Sharpe?

Steve: 13?

Steve: It's got to be the work of a pubescent
boy.

Jess: His tweet is legitimising the men who
bombard us with porn, ridicule us and tell us to
shut up. If *The Sun*'s head of PR is doing it, it
must be OK.

Kate: There's been a massive spike in online
abuse since *The Sun* tweeted last night. This is
just adding fuel to the fire. It's so irresponsible.

In the past twenty-four hours, our Facebook page had received more than 1.5 million views, but there were so many trolls online that we were forced to temporarily deactivate our account. We received a barrage of porn and threats. We were bombarded with requests for interviews and statements.

Killjoy

By mid-morning, Kate was so tired, she tried to withdraw money from an ATM by shoving her car keys in the card slot. She did this two or three times before she realised what she was doing. We were all worn out, especially Lucy, whose phone wouldn't stop ringing. Before filming a news segment, she started to feel dizzy at the TV studio, and a staff member, who was pregnant herself, gave her a seat and a drink and asked if there was anything she could do. Lucy had rebooked her flight and was due to leave for Germany later that evening. 'I really need to go,' she said. 'I really need some quiet time.'

Articles condemning *The Sun*'s stunt appeared online.

The Independent wrote: 'Page 3 returns: The only organisation that comes out looking stupid here is *The Sun*.' Thousands more signed the petition. We had our biggest day of T-shirt sales ever.

Throughout the afternoon, Max, Kate and Steve would pop up in HQ, posting things that would cheer us up. Steve gave us stats: how many journalists had written positive articles, the number of new followers, the percentage of MPs who had signed the petition.

Max gave us pep talks.

> Max: We can do this. We've done it before, and we can do it again.

> Max: And remember: no matter what happens, we will never be as bad at PR as Dylan Sharpe.

Kate posted supportive messages that had been sent to us, to keep our spirits up. There were hundreds and hundreds of them, from women and men, who had written to tell us they were on our side. She shared fragments of them, one after the next.

Thank you for all the amazing work you're doing under such a barrage of harassment and hate. This is just to send you good vibes for strength and love to continue this incredibly important campaign

This campaign has been inspirational. Please don't be downhearted – this stunt has been designed to suppress you and kill the campaign. I think your work has been incredible. Please don't stop.

I just wanted to say that no matter what else happens, the fact that this campaign exists at all has given literally hundreds of thousands of women a new confidence in their beliefs and the firm knowledge that they're not alone in them. And the effects of that new confidence will be felt in multiple ways for decades. So please don't feel that nothing was achieved by your work.

The NMP3 campaign has achieved great things already. No more will anyone casually pin up a workplace picture of a bare-breasted teenager without it being a HUGE issue. NMP3 has triggered a two-year national conversation about sexism amongst men, boys, sex workers, teenagers, the media in all its forms. That's a huge success, and very courageous. It's not easy raising these issues.

Just to let you know – I have always supported your campaign in a passive sort of way. But the way *The Sun* behaved this week has seriously pissed me off. I'll keep a close eye on your page now, plus repost the petition and any other info you put up. You've got another one for the fight!

Hi, I'm just one person, no one famous or important. I happen to think you're doing an amazing job. I know the amount of abuse you must have received for *The Sun*'s disgusting stunt and I'm just one voice that wants you to know you're doing great. Please don't give up. Keep fighting and all your supporters will keep fighting along with you. Love to you all xxx

Jess: God, I'm a wreck now.

Evie: Any more of these and I will cry for days.

Evie: But don't stop posting them Kate!

Lucy messaged us from the airport.

Labour and Love

Lucy: It's been a hell of a day, and I think we've all done amazingly well. I really think we've done it. I really believe that Page 3 has gone, and today was a final hurrah for *The Sun*.

Lucy: And I keep thinking about this documentary I saw last night. I copied down a quote from it because it really moved me: 'outside of a person's love, the most sacred thing they can give is their labour.'

Lucy: Well, I think we've combined labour with love and we've achieved more than I ever thought possible. And I honestly feel this has been the most incredible experience of my life, and you are all the most remarkable, bravest, funniest, wisest, kindest, cleverest people. I love you all so, so much, I know that we'll somehow always be there for each other.

I thought of Clare Short, telling us that the end result was not the most important thing, but the conversation, the discussion, the debate, the experience itself. She was right.

Max: We have to stick together. You're my family.

Yas: When I first met you all I was 16. So thank you for trusting me – for being the ones who took me to an adult from a teen. We've done

377

something beautiful together, and whatever
happens, nothing can change that.

Jess: I'm eternally grateful to you, Lucy, and to
all of you for entering my life. You've changed
me. I'm a different person because of you.

Kate: Thank you for seeing something in me.
Who knew? I had no idea I was capable of any
of the things I've done over the past couple of
years. Wow. Just wow.

I didn't post anything just then, it felt too much like a goodbye
and I wasn't ready to say goodbye to No More Page 3 or to
HQ.

And, besides, we didn't know for sure that Page 3 wouldn't
be back tomorrow.

We discussed what to do next.

Kate: Let's take a step back, recalibrate, sleep
and watch what happens. If there's no Page 3
for the rest of the week, for the next week and
the week after, then we could think about ending
the petition and drafting an email to supporters?

And so we waited, and we watched.

Labour and Love

Email draft
From: No More Page 3
To: Supporters
12 February 2015

Amazing, extraordinary people, we have been here for two and a half years talking about the need for gender equality in the media and, specifically, for an end to the sexism of Page 3.

Before that, for forty-two years, other women were here, some more prominent than others, but all of them important and all of their experiences valid. From Clare Short, to every single one of the women who wrote to her with their feelings and experiences, from OBJECT and Turn your Back on Page 3 to every incidence of harassment shared on The Everyday Sexism Project. The hundreds of thousands of individuals who have signed our petition have joined the voices of sixty-five organisations and charities and one hundred and fifty-nine MPs. You have been relentless and brave and very, very loud and we thank you all for your incredible commitment to this campaign.

What we have achieved together so far has been extraordinary. The movement has grown and grown, and we have watched with awe as so many found their inner activist and spoke out on this and many other issues.

As most of you will know, some weeks ago, a big media hoo-ha kicked off.

Certain sections of the media seemed to be under the impression (thanks to unknown but apparently strong sources) that Page 3 had been dropped by *The Sun*. We received lots and lots of phone calls and we spoke on television and radio . . . And then, two days later, Page 3 reappeared. The petition gained an extra 25,000 signatures and we sold lots and lots of T-shirts.

That was 22 January 2015. Since then, there have been no further Page 3 pictures in *The Sun*.

Only time will tell whether Page 3 has gone for good and we do not expect an official announcement. But, whatever the circumstances, we hope that this is the first vital step towards gender equality in the media.

There is still a long way to go before we can live in a world where women and men feature in our news for the same reasons: for their achievements, their abilities and the things they do. Until that day arrives, we still have work to do.

We'll still be here, and we hope you will be too.

With love and gratitude,
No More Page 3.

Epilogue

February 2020

I stood on the riverbank, holding a pile of clothes. Jess was next to me, jumping from foot to foot, trying to get up the nerve to run into the water. Kate had gone in first, followed by Evie and Yas, who were flailing their arms around, shrieking at the cold. There was snow on the hills and, even though the sun was at its highest, it was almost freezing and would soon be dark.

When Jess spoke, I could see the clouds of her breath.

'You sure you're not coming in?'

'It's February. In Northumberland. No.'

Jess counted down from five, threw her coat in my direction and ran into the water, screaming, 'Oh my god oh my god OH MY GOD!'

She wanted to prove that she could do it. It was a kind of baptism for her new life.

It was five years, one week and six days since *The Sun* published their last Page 3 picture on 22 January 2015.

It took all the hours, days and weeks of those years for Jess to build up the strength, resolve, money and independence she needed to leave her marriage. She took on work, when he allowed her to, and saved what she could in a secret bank account. She bought bits of furniture here and there; a chest of drawers from a charity shop, a coffee table in a mid-season sale, and stored them away until she needed them. She made new friends, took up running and swimming and got physically stronger.

And then she found a house, a small, two-bed terrace, in a town not far from Newcastle – near enough to her old life to feel secure, and far away enough to start afresh. She was approved for a mortgage, got the keys, and moved in. It had taken five years of planning, saving, building, whispering, walking on eggshells, but now she was free.

'Tell me I'm doing the right thing?' she said over and over.

'You're doing the right thing.'

We were the first visitors to her new house. We turned up with champagne, which we drank from No More Page 3 mugs because she didn't have any wine glasses. Her kettle still had a sticker on the handle and the shelving unit hadn't been put together yet. She was slowly adding bits of herself to the house, with photographs in frames and piles of books on every surface. She said she felt guilty and afraid but, every now and then, there was a spark of excitement in her eyes and she bit her lip, as if the wisest part of her could taste the future.

'Tell me I'm doing the right thing?'

'You're doing the right thing.'

We sat on the floor, eating pizza. Jess caught my eye and whispered, 'You OK?'

It was six weeks since my mum died. It was the first time I'd been out of the house since the funeral. My dad had died just a year before. Cancer, for both of them, sudden and shocking and violent. When I looked at Jess, I saw that we were both walking unsteadily, unsure of our footing, taking tentative steps in a world that didn't feel entirely real or entirely safe.

I'd shared all of it, or most of it, with Jess, as she'd shared all of it, or most of it, with me. The fraught conversations before she left, the careful explaining to Ruby, the long nights when the heaviness settled on her chest and she feared that in saving herself she was hurting her daughter.

I'd told her how, when my dad was dying, my mum had to coach him as he made his last phone calls. 'Go on then, tell them,' she'd say, and he'd tell his sister, his friends, what they meant to him. And then he'd go and lie down in the dark. He'd been taught his whole life to bottle it all up, to never show emotion, so it was hard for him to talk about love.

After my mum was diagnosed, she became angry. She'd lock herself in the bathroom and scream at the top of her voice. 'It's the steroids,' she'd say. 'They make me like that, it's a side effect.'

My No More Page 3 teammates helped me through the most difficult days. I told Laura Bates that the hospice offered tea but no biscuits, so she sent a huge box of gingerbread, cookies, shortbread, jam rings. When I couldn't sleep, Yas sent me bath oils to help me relax. So many parcels arrived that the postman said, 'It must be somebody's birthday!' I didn't correct him, because it was easier to lie about birthdays than to tell the truth about death.

At my dad's funeral, I watched as Jess talked to my relatives, handing around plates of sandwiches and sausage rolls. I watched her moving across the room, making people comfortable, offering drinks, and I thought, *I'll never forget that you did this.*

So much happened over the five years since Page 3 ended. Between us, we married, divorced, had babies, earned degrees, published books, launched new campaigns, changed careers, came out. Max got a big promotion, Lucy wrote books about women and sex, none of which had cupcakes on the cover. Evie went back to university and gained a distinction in her master's degree, Kate switched jobs, boyfriends and houses, Rhianne moved to the country to work on a community farm. Laura Bates wrote more and more books, discussed gender equality at the UN and worked with the British Transport Police to better protect women on buses and trains. Priya started the world's first maternity clinic for survivors of sexual assault. Yas did all kinds of things: campaigning for queer and trans rights, writing books and poetry, travelling and performing a drag act as a Turkish pop star named Tarkan. Yas was also training for an upcoming LGBTQ+ boxing match.

'None of us are afraid of being punched,' Yas told us. 'We've all been hit in the face plenty of times before.'

I moved up North with Will, to a small market town in the Pennines. When I arrived, a local man advised me to buy a 'proper' coat. He said, 'Up here, we have nine months of bad weather, and then winter comes.' I felt the cold, but I loved the place immediately and Will and I built a home together, a place where I felt safe and grounded during the worst days of grief. I started writing every day.

'I'm writing a book about HQ,' I told the team. 'I want to remember all that we did together. And then, when we're old and have forgotten everything, Yas – our best hope for the future – can read it aloud to us.'

Will's mum and Michael Waldon stayed together. I saw him once or twice, and we were civil and polite. We were both focusing on bigger things.

There were huge changes culturally, as well as in our personal lives. After *The Sun* scrapped Page 3, lads' mags began to disappear from newsagent shelves. By the end of 2015, *Loaded*, *Maxim*, *Nuts*, *FHM* and *Zoo* – magazines filled with naked or topless women – all, one by one, dissolved. Things changed in Germany too. Stop Bild Sexism, the No More Page 3 sister campaign launched by Kristina Lunz, was successful. In March 2018, *Bild* said it would 'end an era' by dropping the topless photos, since 'many women find these pictures offensive or degrading, both here in the editorial department and also among our female readers'.

Over here, the *Daily Star* remained stubbornly resolute, at least in the beginning. They issued a statement in 2015, insisting that 'Page 3 is as British as roast beef and Yorkshire pud, fish and chips and seaside postcards. The *Daily Star* is about fun and cheering people up. And that will definitely continue!'

The topless photos did continue for another four years before they were finally scrapped in 2019. The British public have had to find their fun elsewhere ever since.

Of course, issues of representation in the media remain huge, and debates continue over who is seen, what stories are deemed worthy of our attention and how events are framed.

Misogyny, racism, homophobia, transphobia, classism and ableism are still evident in our press. But the end of Page 3 felt symbolic, as if we were closing the door on the insidious sexism of the previous decades and looking ahead to a new way of doing things. We are in a different cultural landscape now, fuelled by Black Lives Matter, Extinction Rebellion, Time's Up, #MeToo. More and more people are talking about prejudice, discrimination and stereotyping. The younger generation is leading the way, dismantling and deconstructing the cultural legacies passed down to them that do not fit within the lives they want to live.

If No More Page 3 taught me anything, it's that we all have more power than we realise, and that we can achieve incredible things when we come together. I learned more during those two and a half years than I learned in a decade at university. And I had the most fun I've had in my entire life.

Back at the riverbank, Jess ran out of the water, shouting over and over, 'I'm so cold I'm so cold OH MY GOD I'M SO COLD!'

She wrapped a towel around her shoulders, grabbed my hand and dragged me towards the car.

'In a few months when it's warmer, we'll come back here and I'm making you get in the water with me. No excuses.'

Epilogue

I couldn't yet imagine warmer days, so I let Jess imagine them for me.

She turned and waved to Yas, Evie and Kate. 'Come on,' she shouted, 'let's go home.'

Acknowledgements

To HQ: you are the most courageous, wonderful people, and you have all enriched my life in so many ways. I would love to thank you individually here, but that would kind of mess up the anonymity thing, so I won't, but I adore you all.

To everyone who supported the campaign, signing the petition, attending protests, wearing T-shirts and writing to your MPs: thank you so much for being part of the movement with us.

Jo Unwin, you are brilliant, hilarious and generous and I am so, so lucky to have you. Milly, Donna and Nisha, thank you for all your help and support.

To my excellent editors, Gill Fitzgerald-Kelly and Francesca Main, I so appreciate all the hard work you have put into this book. A huge thank-you to Emma Harrow, Kish Widyaratna, Paul Baggaley and to everyone at Picador, especially Laura Carr, Gabriela Quattromini, Mary Mount, Emma Bravo and Ami Smithson.

Caroline, thank you so much for reading my draft, and insisting it was good even when it was rubbish. Tony, thanks for setting me challenges around the house whenever I got stressed out – crawling down the stairs head-first like a lizard really does cure writer's block. Ricky and Si, thank you for letting me stay in your gorgeous house despite the biblical disasters that occur whenever I'm there. Thank you to Gary, Abs, Jacob, Izzy and especially to Louby, for all the skating. Assad, you are the best friend ever, ever. Katie, only you would take me to suffragettes' graves at midnight. Spanner, you really will try anything once, and usually two or three times, and I have loved our adventures over the past twenty years. Aisling, thanks for recreating Monty Don videos with me. Katerina, I still think about the time we ran away to France. Sylwia, I want to dance like a salmon with you.

Mum and Dad: sometimes, when you dropped me off at school, you'd sneak chocolate bars into the coat pockets of kids whose parents couldn't afford them, so they'd have a treat at break time. You did it after we'd all filed into class, when the coats were hung up and no one would know. If ever anyone was bullied, you'd tell me to bring them home for tea. You took in any stray animal you found. It would take you hours to go to the shop, because you'd stop and talk to everyone you passed on the way home. You'd say, 'You never know, it could be the only time they speak to anyone all day.' You were so, so kind, and you taught me that what we do, and how we treat one another, matters. I am grateful every day that you were my parents. Thank you, for everything.